# *Rama Speaks*

# *Rama Speaks*

**The Teachings of Rama-
Dr. Frederick Lenz**

By Lawrence Borok

# Table of Contents



Photographs located between chapters 1 & 2; in chapter 5; between chapters 9 & 10; between chapters 13 & 14; between chapters 17 & 18; between Appendix & Endnotes.

# Introduction

I was a student of Dr. Frederick Lenz, PhD (1950-1998), known to his students as Rama, from April, 1982 to April, 1998, and still consider myself to be his student. During that time we practiced Tantric Buddhism, living and working in the world as a way to become more advanced in our spiritual understanding while doing a great deal of meditation and psychic development. While many of the things he taught us can be found in spiritual books, many cannot, and none all in the same place. While there have been a few books written by Rama's students, most of them focus on his life, the experiences of the student writing the book, and the experiences of other students.

This book does not present his biography or my experiences. Instead, I try to present his model of the mind and how to navigate life. In no way do I claim to be presenting everything he taught, nor to anywhere near the depth that he imparted to us. This book is a detailed overview of his teachings. To claim otherwise would be laughable.

The word "Enlightenment" has a very strict definition in Buddhism. It does not mean that you are a saint, or a scholar of a body of religious literature. In Hinduism the term "god realization" is sometimes used to categorize those who have achieved a merging of their consciousness with the Godhead, the undifferentiated pure spirit that creates, sustains, and destroys the Universe. In Buddhism, it's those who are established in salvikalpa samadhi. Throughout history there have been notable yogis, roshis, lamas and other distinguished spiritual teachers acknowledged as being god or self-realized, down to the present day.

Full Enlightenment is different. To Rama, a fully Enlightened being comes from the infinite mind behind that undifferentiated pure spirit. With this perspective, in Hinduism Krishna was Enlightened, as was Shankara and Ramakrishna. In Buddhism, the Buddha was Enlightened, as well as Milarepa, Padmasambhava and Bodhidharma. To Christians, Jesus was Enlightened. So was the Sikh founder, Guru Nanak, as was Lao Tzu, a primary source for all faiths. To Rama, they all came from the same place. He too was from there.

Rama also explained that throughout most of human history, there usually are twelve fully Enlightened beings on this planet at any one time. Most teach a few advanced students and keep a low profile. A few don't teach at all, but simply live among us. Every so often one is more public and explains the Dharma in contemporary terms. So while organized religions each promote the uniqueness of their founder (who never actually began the religion), the point of view which Rama presented, the point of view of Tantric Buddhism, says that it is possible for any human being to become fully Enlightened, and that hundreds, perhaps thousands have.

This is the heart of Tantric and Vajrayana Buddhism. While organized religions emphasize studying scriptures, conducting rituals, and following formal traditions, these two branches of Buddhism focus instead on techniques, meditation being paramount, to experience your complete mind. It further posits that your complete mind actually is the infinite mind of the universe. To become Enlightened therefore means the dissolution of the finite self into that infinite mind.

As human beings we think that the totality of who we are is the combination of our conscious and subconscious. In reality that is only an island in an ocean. Enlightenment is when we become fully aware that we are that ocean.

This perspective is not part of any society. Religions may point to this vast ocean and call it God, but only as something you pray to rather than merge with. The uniqueness of the idea of Enlightenment, its offering of a special kind of hope, is that you have God within you. There is nothing external to kneel before.

However, merely comprehending the concept does not transform your level of consciousness from the ego to the eternal. Instead, through meditation and related practices you start swimming off of your island, a little bit at a time. Gradually you realize that what you thought was your identity is only a small part of your complete mind. Or as the Zen aphorism puts it, our human self is like dust on a mirror, blocking the light.

A subtle aspect of this concept is that you—a human being with a unique identity—do not "attain" Enlightenment. That would be preposterous; the island conquering the ocean. Instead, "becoming Enlightened" means that your island completely dissolves into the ocean. It is a process that is very gradual over many lifetimes. Another way to understand it is that you are gradually experiencing the totality of what you really are. Both of these descriptions, however, leave out how the process works. That's what Rama taught us.

The claim of being "Enlightened" is fraught with suspicion. When Rama explained that he was Enlightened, he never said it in a way to induce obedience or awe. Rather, he explained what Enlightenment was in structural terms. This explanation was completely free of any self-aggrandizement. If anything, Rama preferred to have more privacy, and was very selective about the people he accepted as students, only having a few hundred.

The conundrum about Enlightenment, as stated in Buddhist and Hindu scriptures, is that it is "beyond the mind's ability to grasp." The curious few embark on this journey without fully comprehending that curious fact. Over many years, those who don't give up understand that the "mind" these scriptures refer to is only a layer of our complete mind, but that human beings mistakenly believe that this layer is the totality of who they are. You also see that many of those who claim to want to become Enlightened really are more interested in empowering that one layer, to become a magnified version of who they think they are.

Before meeting Rama, for 10 years I had attended talks and meditations by those who I thought were the most advanced spiritual teachers I could find. They included Buddhists, Hindus, and Sikhs. I read the books of notable "masters," some of whom were considered avatars or Enlightened. I fancied that I could feel a difference, a certain added clarity and serenity. I especially enjoyed reading Zen poetry and stories, and going to Krishnamurti's outdoor talks in Ojai, California.

In the years which followed after being accepted as a student by Rama, I only became more certain that he was Enlightened. During most of that time he held monthly 4-night seminars. Each month when I walked into the meditation hall—usually a small theatre at a college or a ballroom in a hotel—I would quickly feel a different atmosphere, what I can only describe as deeply peaceful and yet very aware simultaneously. Each month I was so happy just to be in the room. Over those 16 years he meditated with us about a thousand times, always filling the room with golden light. After every seminar weekend I'd feel amazingly refreshed, clear and empowered.

Rama referred to his program simply as "self-discovery." He made the vital point that Enlightenment was reachable through methods, and that maximum self-effort was essential. These methods work over time with the student's persistence and introspection. The mind gradually becomes filled with perfect, clear light largely through the practice of meditation, but for the process to work you must also clarify all aspects of your life. In order to succeed, the two must be done together. Full awareness of that perfect, clear light replaces our fixation on being a separate identity.

Beyond this very simplified description it gets complicated, and filling in the blanks is what this book is for. What Rama taught us that I am capable of presenting is described rather directly, usually without comparison to conventional wisdom. Since this book is an overview of his teachings, all of the information presented on the following pages is what he taught us, to the extent of my understanding and ability to communicate.

During our study with him, Rama recorded sets of instructional talks on the topics he was focusing on at the time. There are over 120 individual recorded talks in this collection, as well as several videos. The non-profit foundation which was established after his passing (The Frederick P. Lenz Foundation for American Buddhism), transcribed most of the audio talks into inexpensively-priced books, and made all of the original audio and video recordings available for free. They are described in greater detail in the last chapter and listed in the appendix, with links to the websites. All of his quotations throughout the book are taken from these audio recordings, identifying the name of the set followed by the title of the specific talk.

Finally, there's a world of difference between intellectual comprehension and personally experiencing the truth of something. As he put it, it's like reading a book about how to swim and believing that therefore now you can. Without jumping in the water, you will never learn how to swim. Otherwise, it is beyond the mind's ability to grasp.

# Chapter 1: Welcome to Earth, Again

*"As an Enlightened teacher of Buddhism, I'd like to welcome you to the pathway to Enlightenment. I'd like to encourage you, based upon my own personal experience and the personal experience of countless others, to meditate—to be more positive, to engage in the practice of meditation, to learn how to do this wonderful thing, to make your mind still in a crazy world, where everybody's at war with everybody and certainly with ourselves. I'd like you to learn to be happy and to see things more brightly."*
*(Rama, <u>The Enlightenment Cycle</u>, "The Enlightenment Cycle")*

We are born into this world as a member of the human species. Quickly we identify as a member of a family, and then most of us go about the process of growing into adulthood, immersed in society. We live out our lives and then die.

While this is true, it is also quite incomplete. What is planet Earth for? Why were we born here?

The Earth is what Rama called a "desire plane," a level in a larger structure where the beings that incarnate here are all fixated on this strong impulse. He paired desire with learning how to handle what he called "power," which is more complex than our everyday use of the term. Everyone here is primarily interested in fulfilling their desires, which we believe is done by using power. Eventually some people realize that that's not fulfilling, but as long as you haven't figured it out, you keep coming back.

It is important to clarify what power is. To start, think of it as electricity. It is not good or evil, it just comes out of the wall. It is pure energy, which is omnipresent, making plants grow and enabling us to be creative. Look at what astronomy has shown us of the Universe, all of the different galaxies and stars. Look at what biology has shown us inside the cell. Crucially for our spiritual evolution, it has capabilities that people don't perceive. It maintains our lives in the particular configuration we experience, and can change that configuration for better or worse depending on our behavior and attitude. Power has different characteristics on different levels of mind.

Let's expand the picture to see the larger context. Similar to but slightly different from the classic Buddhist model, Rama said there are Six Worlds, six very different levels, each with their own characteristics. At the top is Nirvana, which is not really a world but the source of all the other levels. Nirvana is the level above what Western Civilization calls God. It is also called the Infinite Mind. The Buddhist and Vedic (original Hindu source) philosophies both state that in reality all beings are merely figments of the Infinite Mind, and it is apparently content to let us remain oblivious to it. It is our choice to become conscious of it. The process to become conscious of it is the pathway to Enlightenment. It is an opportunity that is always available. Very few people here on Earth are interested, because they are so obsessed with desire and power.

Rama's description of the Hindu avatar Sri Krishna provides a view into Nirvana:

*"... Sri Krishna is not from the local area network... he has come from a world that is different because his mind is different. He glows. He doesn't experience the normal round of circumstances inwardly that most people do. He doesn't experience depression. He doesn't really experience elation as human beings would know it. He doesn't experience the kind of grayness and deadness of the human condition. Instead he lives in a perpetual sunrise. He's self-effulgent. The light that he seeks is not external. He doesn't have to turn to the sun for light, or towards another being or towards a God, because he is self-effulgent radiance."*
*(Rama, <u>Tantric Buddhism</u>, "The Bhagavad Gita")*

The level below that is what he called the Unmanifest, or the level of pure spirit. There are no individual beings there. It is the ocean of bliss. We call that God. Cycle after cycle, it creates, sustains and destroys the entire Universe. It lets us play out our lives how we see fit. But each of us, as an individual mind, can experience it. That's what the word "Yoga" means, union with God. Below that level are the heavens described by religions, also called the Higher Astral plane. There is no suffering there. There is only happiness. We feel so good that we forget about our desires.

*"Heaven is the higher astral. There are countless realms and dimensional planes, existences—they go on forever—that are very beautiful, where beings incarnate for a time, where they exist. Sometimes it seems to be timeless, but it does end eventually—which is why we call it structural—and these are the realms of the higher astral.*

*The unmanifest, which is next up, is not heaven. It's beyond heaven. Beyond heaven is pure spirit. Heaven we think of as kind of a cloud, a kingdom, happy experiences, beings singing, laughing, being in ecstasy and meditation. You see it in the Buddhist thangkas—you know, where they're all having a very, very serious party up in the higher astral. Everybody's having a good time. But above that is the unmanifest. You can't put that on a thangka. There's no way to paint it. One can symbolically represent it, but the unmanifest is pure spirit. Yet spirit exists and is perceivable by itself, if nothing else. It knows of its own existence.*

*The world of Enlightenment doesn't know of its own existence. We're beyond both knower and known. There's no conceptual identity whatsoever. Enlightenment is not even conscious of itself—it just is. There's no way to talk about nirvana."*
*(Rama, Tantric Buddhism, "Six Worlds")*

Then there is the desire plane, where beings experience suffering pursuing desires. Each plane has countless worlds in it. He consistently summed up the purpose of living on Earth as a step in a larger evolutionary process:

*"We see power operating constantly in this world because the particular dimensional plane that we're in is a plane of power. The beings who are here, who are incarnate on this planet, the vast majority of them, are at the stage of their evolution where power is the dominant theme. They're learning about power. That's why we live in a world where there are so many wars and so much destruction. Because people are gaining power over others and using that power to destroy anyone or anything that doesn't agree with their point of view. This is an arena of power that we live in."*
*(Rama, Zen Tapes, "Personal Power")*

So there are three planes above this one, increasingly happy, and two more below.

As all religions teach, below this physical world are the hell worlds, also known as the Lower Astral. In Buddhist terms, there are many different hells corresponding to the dominant defilements in a person's mind, and there are many different heavens corresponding to the dominant higher qualities in a person's mind. The reality of death is that after you drop your physical body, your mind gravitates to where it feels most comfortable. It's not necessary for some higher being to judge you. You go to where your mind feels most comfortable. It's pretty automatic, a flow system as Rama called it, going up a level or down a level after death, which in reality is merely dropping your body, the car you've been driving while here. So if you are a mean, nasty person, if those are your strongest mental characteristics, you automatically travel to where that's all there is. Same process for going up.

Below hell is where extremely dark and twisted beings go. Basically you lose your mind and are thrown off the boat of existence.

The scale of these levels is beyond the mind's ability to grasp:

*"And when I say that the higher astral is endless, that the lower astral is endless, that the plane of desire is endless, those that appear to be spatial planes and that the worlds below the lower astral are endless—nirvana, of course, I can't even say it's endless. That's too simplistic. I'm not kidding when I say that, I mean that's the truth. We just grow so used to looking at the stars in the sky and planets and we think that that's what big means. All the far-flung eternities put together doesn't equal a parsec of nirvana, or even one of the higher astral planes."*
*(Rama, <u>Tantric Buddhism</u>, "Six Worlds")*

So in Rama's model there are Six Worlds, three above the desire plane that are ecstatic, blissful, and beyond blissful, all with no suffering whatsoever. The Earth is not in the middle, it is at the top of the unhappy planes. Simply put, that's why there's more suffering here than joy.

Yet even while living here we can do something about our predicament:

*"Happiness is something we know inside our mind when our mind is stretched towards God. When our mind is stretched towards God, we feel*

*free. Needless to say, we are the God that we stretch towards in another form. Here we are, there we are. We're trying to connect. Yet when we're in the world, we must be extremely practical, pragmatic, down-to-earth, funny, loquacious. We must be able to deal with ridicule and scorn, which it always seems that Buddhists receive. But we feel that that doesn't matter. God's laughing at God. I mean, we must seem pretty funny to create so much upheaval—such small groups of people, the Buddhists, seem to upset a lot of people. So we feel that God is laughing at God, and we can take a joke too. We're pretty funny.*

*But we just keep walking. We have somewhere to go, and it's not in this world."*
*(Rama, <u>Tantric Buddhism</u>, "The Mature Monk")*

As human beings, we learn that to achieve or acquire something or someone requires willpower, and that understanding ends up dominating everything we do. Different people utilize many different techniques along a spectrum of passive to aggressive, but throughout our life we approach most everything we do that way. There's the old adage that to a hammer, everything is a nail. To the human mind (not the complete mind), everything is a desire. Our willpower needs energy, which we crudely call power, to try to fulfill that desire. What we miss is that willpower can be used in other ways, to fulfill something else.

Tantric Buddhism teaches that we can utilize power to become Enlightened. Not to conquer Enlightenment, of course, but to increase our internal energy and direct it towards higher levels of mind and grow into them. Without self-effort no spiritual progress occurs. However, while our hammer and nail habit may work at least to get us to look into spiritual growth, as if it were a new hobby, it creates all kinds of blockages if we persist in applying it. As Rama explained, Enlightenment is reached through the "gradual dissolution of the finite self in the white light of eternity."

That scares people because they believe that their limited sense of self as an individual, with a particular history and personality, is the totality of who they are. On top of that, it scares people because the idea that overwhelming happiness involves the dissolution of the finite self is not included as part of any society's value system, much less a subject for study. It's barely mentioned by traditional religions; Hinduism has Karma Yoga, the yoga of selfless giving, Christianity places importance on good works, and both promote unselfish love as ways to relieve you of constant egocentric obsession. Those are steps on the pathway to Enlightenment, but ultimately the only thing that makes you permanently happy is the dissolution of the finite self into the infinite mind. This is the essence of what Rama taught us, what he showed us how to do. He always emphasized that it is done very gradually, in fact over many lifetimes.

In order to get going on the pathway to Enlightenment, obviously we must first start with who we are right now. Let's come back to our everyday lives as they are today. We have all kinds of desires: material, emotional, immediate, long-term. The cornerstone of Buddhism is the recognition that desire is built into physical existence. It is the driving force in human consciousness. A subset of that is fear and wanting to avoid or flee certain situations. Rama called it the "desire/aversion operating system."

Although it seemingly operates on autopilot, everyone knows that they are continually paying attention to different desires all day long. There are strong desires that we set as goals to achieve. An entire lifetime is pretty much defined by this operating system.

You'd think that after a while this would all get a little boring, but apparently not. Even when a desire is fulfilled, often the sense of satisfaction is brief, or turns out to be disappointing. A few moments after achieving the desire the sense of victory begins to fade, which is the second important fact of being alive on Earth: everything is transient. We'll get into transience later, but it is the fact of life that runs this place.

So we suffer if a desire is frustrated, and also when it is fulfilled; it's just a matter of time. The fundamental premise of Buddhism is built on this. The first two of the historical Buddha's (Gautama Shakyamuni, approx. 450 BC) Four Noble Truths is that suffering is intrinsic to being human, and that suffering is caused by attachment to desire. Rama distinguished "attachment to desire" rather than desire alone, as the actual problem. The emphasis is on our attachment to desire, not that desire itself is inherently bad. Desire is a basic fact of life in physical and emotional existence. There's nothing inherently wrong with it. It just comes with the territory. The problem is how we deal with it. The Buddha was making the observation that experiencing suffering results from becoming attached to desires.

Understanding that the human mind, or more accurately the human band of attention within our complete mind, is essentially a desire-chasing machine doesn't seem to lessen its control over us. The complete mind is what in Zen is called the original mind. The original mind isn't an earlier version, it is all-encompassing. Rama simply referred to it as "mind." That's what mind really is.

But in human life on earth, the whole world is dedicated to the pursuit of desires. It takes power to chase a desire, whether it is riches, fame, political domination, romance or simple survival. For the human band of attention, chasing desires is the primary mechanism for us to learn how to gain and use power. But if we're honest about humanity, it's not an appealing picture:

*"Obviously we're not dealing with a very intelligent race of beings if all they can think to do is destroy each other and gain power over each other and manipulate each other at every opportunity, which is what happens most of the time here.... by and large, the human race is in a very basic level of evolution as opposed to other races of beings throughout the cosmos. Some are not as evolved. But this race is not particularly evolved—they're still working on power. That's the dominant operating theme in this world— gaining and using it, usually to oppress others."*
*(Rama, <u>Zen Tapes</u>, "Overcoming Stress")*

So our species isn't so advanced, is it? And yet we think we're so smart, even special in the Universe. But if you accept the premise that there is a divine light within you, then what's going on?

Experiencing power, or what we fantasize it to be, is conjoined with chasing desires to form a two-part whole here on Earth. Power itself is independent from people's efforts at manipulation, domination, and control. It's pure energy. What if we want to get beyond these limited mental states? Remember, desire at its most elemental is just an impulse.

Human beings think that having great material success will make them happier, in other words, will make them freer, but if you're stuck in the basic set of human attitudes, you're in for disappointment. Ask some rich people. While they may have temporarily defeated the material issues of physical life, you'd find that that did not put them into a permanently joyful state of mind. A permanently joyful state of mind is beyond the human band of attention. It is a standard feature of the complete mind.

So how do you reach and then sustain much happier states of mind? Power is needed to reach and sustain higher, happier states of mind. Why not use power to develop the complete mind instead? In his description of the Six Worlds, Rama provided a perspective on our minds that is literally boundless:

*"How you conduct yourself determines what happens. The state of mind you create and live in inside yourself produces these changes in mental states. In a sense, we always want to think of all of these conversations in terms of a spatial realm. That is to say, the higher astral is a place, the earth is a place, the lower astral is a place, the sub-world which goes on forever is a place, spirit is somehow a place and even nirvana is a place. Not really, they're all coexistent inside your own mind.*

*We actually are all those realms. Not we as physical bodies or individual egos, but the deeper we within us is everything. You have to make the metaphysical leap in understanding to see that. You might be able to intellectually appreciate it or not know what I'm talking about. But if you make the metaphysical leap, you will just intuit how we can be these foolish human beings who have trouble sometimes making it through the day or every day, and yet at the same time we can be all of existence, manifest, unmanifest, parinirvana, everything.*

*How we direct our attention determines what we experience or who we even experience, since we are somewhat different in each realm. Yet as we know, there's sort of a spatial world to a certain extent, or at least it appears that way to the senses."*
(Rama, <u>Tantric Buddhism</u>, "Six Worlds")

Looking within this desire realm, we only pay attention to what appears as human existence in physical reality. But we can see that different desires exist within different states of mind. Change your state of mind and your desires change. Elevate your state of mind sufficiently and your attachment to some desires simply falls away. Rather than seek power to fulfill your desires, human or celestial, just let go of that orientation. Easier said than done, and it doesn't happen in a day, or even a lifetime. It is the process Rama called self-discovery. If you take it far enough, you become Enlightenment itself.

As we begin to realize, primarily through meditation but through all manner of life experience, that our mind is much larger than the human band of attention, we experience new and inherently happier states of mind, and each of those states of mind is sustained by different degrees and shadings of power. Self-discovery requires power. It is something to be done. It also requires humility, the essence of self-honesty.

A key point he made is that your understanding of reality is controlled by your level of internal power. As you can imagine, there's a lot to learn, and it takes time. The further you go in self-discovery, the more you realize how vast, even limitless it is. Yes, your spiritual progress is dependent upon the amount of power you have internally. However, progress means that internal power is being used for improving your awareness of higher states of mind; use it to harm others and you drop instantly. Simply put, there's much more to learn and to unlearn than you might initially have thought, which is why it takes more than one incarnation. Appreciating this is another aspect of humility.

*"There are larger views of the world. There's reincarnation, where we wake up a little further and we see that there's a cycle to life, we see what happens before birth and after death, which most people don't know about. There are cosmic cycles where we can, with deeper understanding, view how the whole universe works—well, I don't know about the whole universe, but parts of it. We can gain those understandings. There are understandings of dimensions and how they work, just like there's physical science, understanding matter and energy.*

*But the real undertaking, as I said before, is pretty simple—it's to be free, because those understandings can trap you too. You can get so caught up in learning all about reincarnation, you can get so caught up in learning about structures, fascinating though they may be, that you're not free; you're just studying something else. It's a different textbook, that's all.*

*Freedom then is an inner issue. To find freedom, what you really need is a very quiet life. It's a life in which you really don't interface too much with almost anything. You don't want to define yourself. This may sound nebulous, but it's not, it's exact. But it's exact outside of the world of words."*
(Rama, *Tantric Buddhism*, "Freedom")

Rama described human beings as mental travelers, and reincarnation as a basic fact of life. Our physical bodies are vehicles carrying our minds. Our minds are much more than our brains. At some point the car wears out and can't be repaired. It stops working, and you travel, as he put it, on to your next adventure. Eventually you want to manipulate power again, in order to fulfill some as-yet unsatisfied desires, and back you come to Earth, or to another physical world in this plane.

*"At the time of death, physical death, the aggregates that are your collected self—in other words, all the strands and fibers that join together, that create your personality—dissolve. They go back into a variety of sheathes, they're reabsorbed, they go back where they've come from."*
*(Rama, The Lakshmi Series, "The Tibetan Rebirth Process")*

You have many experiences during each incarnation. Those experiences become aggregated in your mind, and you begin to see life through this conditioning. Over thousands of incarnations we develop tendencies, or patterns of behavior, through which we participate in life. In Buddhism these past life tendencies are called "samskaras." All of them combine to define who you think you are, and thus how you act.

He defined reincarnation as "the evolution of spirit through matter." Your spirit dances with your current embodiment, and at the end of the dance you—your spirit—leaves to learn other lessons in other dimensions. You return for another dance over and over again, experiencing what in Zen are called the ten thousand states of mind. Unless you become interested in what's behind the ten thousand states of mind, you keep reincarnating as an individualized soul forever. Buddhism calls that being on the Wheel of Life. Enlightenment is all about getting off the wheel.

This leads to a more complete understanding of life:

*"Life is forever. Death is only a temporary abridgement, a short pirouette through time and space, where you don't really die. We talk about death as if it is an ending. It is just a state of transition where you will move from one world into another. You will move from the physical planes into the causal planes and from the world of matter into the world of pure energy. Then the essence of your being reincarnates.*

*Your next incarnation is largely determined by this incarnation....your next incarnation is based upon your awareness at the time of death. When you die in this life, whatever your awareness is—awareness meaning not just your mood at the moment you die but the total overall awareness that you have— you might be experiencing pain and confusion—but your overall perceptual field, the structure of your overall perceptual field, will determine your next lifetime. That structure has been determined by the way you've led this life. If you've been very aware, if you've meditated, if you've learned to still your thoughts, if you've become more aware of the inner dimensional planes, then that awareness is yours.*

*You are your awareness. And that awareness, at the time of death, moves forward. The personality structure at the time of death dissolves. You will never be exactly the you you are again. But the essence of your awareness field definitely goes on after death. It goes through death, it goes into non-physical states for a time, and then eventually it's pulled back and it reincarnates."*
*(Rama, <u>Zen Tapes</u>, "Karma")*

He also looked at reincarnation from a future focus. What can you do in this life to be happier and wiser in your future lives? This is a theme woven through everything he taught. The answer is not, as most religions promulgate, earning good karma points by mechanically doing certain traditional things like giving to charity or reciting certain mantras. It depends entirely on your state of mind when you're doing it. If you're doing those things primarily because you believe it will result in a higher (less mental pain) incarnation next time, it won't. If you're doing it with no selfishness, sincerely at that moment to help others, it will. Intent is all important. True selfless giving is rare. It is very liberating.

*"I've lived in worlds where there are three or four suns. We had incredible sunsets, beautiful. But they weren't more beautiful than here, if my mind is more beautiful in each life. Eternity becomes more beautiful as we age, if we age well—and I mean age not just within a lifetime but in a multi-life sequence."*
*(Rama, <u>Tantric Buddhism</u>, "The Best Meditation I Ever Had")*

(Thirty years after he said this, the New York Times published an article about astronomers finding a planet orbiting a group of three stars. Endnote 1)

You can use this lifetime to set up a very positive direction for your future lives. The secret to having increasingly happy future incarnations is to work on having a happier state of mind in this one. So do things that make you happy now! That doesn't mean the intense pursuit of fulfilling human desires, as we discussed earlier. That means taking your mind above the human band of attention.

*"So I believe that the best lifetime hasn't occurred. I don't think the most beautiful sunrise to be seen in the world has been seen on this earth. It isn't that the sunrise will grow more beautiful, it's that we will. And we'll perceive it more completely than any one before."*
*(Rama, <u>Tantric Buddhism</u>, "The Best Meditation I Ever Had")*

One thing to consider is that your next incarnation is limited by your past mental states, unless you make great strides between lifetimes. That period is in fact a tremendous opportunity for spiritual growth; it's much easier to meditate in the higher astral. Otherwise your next life will be overwhelmingly dictated by your samskaras. Your response to various challenges will largely be pre-determined by how you dealt with similar situations in past lives.

Since virtually all human experiences revolve around attachment to desire and the belief that our willpower can attain that desire, as long as we're stuck in that level of consciousness reincarnation ends up being largely a duplication of the same patterns of behavior. The clothes and the language and the buildings may change from lifetime to lifetime, but we're doing the same things over and over again. Our behavior doesn't change because those are the only cards we hold. Unless we develop new patterns that are an improvement over the old ones, improvement meaning that we are happier and wiser, there is no spiritual evolution. The popular belief that everyone eventually becomes Enlightened, or realizes God, is not accurate. Unless you intentionally move out of the desire/aversion operating system, you will stay in those limited states of mind forever. This takes a while to sink in.

*"The path of reincarnation, then, is simply the path of changing awareness. What you are reincarnating into are different states of mind. That which reincarnates is the awareness that perceives each state of mind. That's reincarnation. The whole show is on the inside. And it really doesn't*

*matter that you change bodies from one lifetime to another. That doesn't really change anything. That's just a change in location, not in you. Oh, the memories will fall away from your last lifetime; they're not really necessary in this lifetime. You might remember past lives. For example, let's say that you remember meditating in another lifetime. That's interesting information, and if you're meditating in this lifetime, it's probably true. Because that's what you were doing before, and it carried over into this lifetime. In other words, you're no different in this lifetime than you were in your last lifetime. This lifetime is simply a continuation of your last lifetime, as your last lifetime was a continuation of the prior lifetime.*

*Death doesn't change anything. It just gives you a new location, some new clothes, but you wash out the memories. The physical mind dissolves and doesn't return. But the overriding state of mind that you die in is the state of mind that you are born into. There are other things that we call karmas. They will determine the location, the type of body, how much money, birth into a wealthy family, a poor family, opportunities that will be presented to you throughout life.... the inner aspect of reincarnation, which is the important part, has to do with where you put your mind, and the more expansive the state of mind you enter into, the less suffering there is. Because more expansive states of mind of the ten thousand states of mind are less attached states of mind—they perceive more light. They know about the universe and the way it works. Ultimately they're still bound states. They don't reflect life perfectly, but some mirrors reflect the way things look more accurately, some less accurately....*

*So then, reincarnation is a process of moving from one state of mind to another. Whether you're in a body or out of a body is immaterial, to tell you the truth. Disembodied beings are in a certain state of mind. Embodied beings are in certain states of mind. The disembodied being stays in the same state of mind that it was in when it was embodied, unless it does something to change that while it's out of the body."*
*(Rama, <u>Zen Tapes</u>, "Reincarnation")*

So at all times human beings have the opportunity to improve their state of mind, and that can have a profound effect on how you proceed from one lifetime to the next. This opportunity is maximized through meditation, but is also put into action by everything you do and think.

# Chapter 2: The Basic Paradox

What makes life as a human being so challenging is how difficult it is to see clearly. It is not an exaggeration to say that there is a lot of confusion in our minds, and that the world pretty much is a continual manifestation of people acting out their confusion.

Even people who think they know what they're doing are in mental states filled with assumptions and beliefs that often are badly distorted. Rama likened it to swimming underwater: the visibility is poor and you can't see very far. This is how everybody perceives in human societies. But since everyone is in the pool, we think that our societal agreements about reality are both comprehensive and accurate. Not even close.

What's behind this mass delusion is a basic paradox about how the human mind works. In a news story published on May 22, 2003, Reuters reported that *"Meditation Shown to Light Up Brains of Buddhists,"* and summarized the findings of researchers from three U.S. universities. Neuroscientists from Duke University conducted brain scans of Buddhist monks in Dharamsala, the home of the Dalai Lama in India, and "discovered that certain areas of the brain light up constantly in Buddhists, which indicates positive emotions and good mood. This happens at times even when they are not meditating."

The scans by researchers from the University of Wisconsin Madison "showed activity in the left prefrontal lobes of experienced Buddhist practitioners. The area is linked to positive emotions, self-control and temperament."

A third study, by the University of California San Francisco Medical Center, "suggests that meditation and mindfulness can tame the amygdala, an area of the brain which is the hub of fear memory." They "discovered that experienced Buddhists were less likely to be shocked, flustered, surprised or as angry as other people."

The belief that our minds are fixed in their perceptual capabilities and core attitudes is undercut by this information. These studies show that we have the innate ability to change our vantage point and how we respond to daily experience; in other words, we can choose the state of mind we experience. That is what "free choice" really means.

So the basic paradox of human life is that while the world is constantly reinforcing a set of perceptual norms based on conflicting cultural attitudes, distorted vision and fuzzy thinking, we inherently are built to see clearly and respond accordingly. But for a number of reasons, we keep our minds at a relatively murky level. Using spiritual terminology, there is not enough light in the human mind.

In Chapter One's discussion of willpower, the point was that we primarily use power to chase desires, in the mistaken belief that fulfilling those desires will make us happy. At least this shows that we are seeking happiness. Therefore the task is to not chase after things that prove to be disappointing in providing happiness, but to find the paths where happiness is abundant. The findings of these neuroscientists show that you can use willpower to go into happier states of mind. The truth is that happiness exists in more positive states of mind that are found within yourself. So you can do this instead:

*"We know that what we want lies elsewhere. If we keep reviewing where we've been and who we've been, then that's where we are and who we are. Whereas if we can erase all that and just forget about it and through the principles of self-discovery and occultism hurl our mind, our spirit, our energy and our life force in an outward bound mode, if we can push ourselves further and further into the stillness of eternity, then we've formed lighter identities, new identities, and those identities will fade and we'll erase them again, and so on and so forth.*

*It's an ever-outreaching process whereby the personality structure and what we experience is a lighter, gradated reality. We experience a much more ineffable sense of being. This is the process of occultism; we're erasing ourself because we've been there. We reformat ourself into a much lighter,*

*brighter, happier, deeper, more conscious being…. We're continually reaching towards infinity. Infinity is not out there. We always like to think of it as external. It's not in there. It just is."*
(Rama, <u>Tantric Buddhism</u>, "Freedom")

It should be pointed out that his use of the term "occultism" is devoid of any Halloween-type connotations; as he makes clear, we're reformatting ourselves *"into a much lighter, brighter, happier, deeper, more conscious being."* He used the word in its strict dictionary definition: "occult" is simply something that is not perceivable by the physical senses. That implies being beyond what we perceive as within nature, hence its common association with the word "supernatural." Both Hinduism and Buddhism teach that in order to reach Enlightened mind there are levels of energy beyond what's needed to lead a regular life in society. That's what "supernatural" means here.

Occultism is a term to encompass a collection of techniques to constructively apply those energies for the purpose of spiritual growth. These techniques include meditating on the chakras (confirmed by the Dalai Lama, Endnote 2), which is discussed at length in the chapters on meditation, and the development of intuition, which he termed "seeing," discussed in Chapter 4. Occultism is a one word synonym for a large portion of the traditional tantric pathway to Enlightenment.

*"There's a science to the development of personal power that we call occultism, and it's necessary to have a teacher for two reasons, if not three. One, the teacher empowers you and gives you the energy to get yourself going which is hard to get going on your own. Two, the teacher shows you what to do and what to avoid because there are as many pitfalls as there are—there are actually many more pitfalls than there are correct moves. As you go into the different dimensions and different realities, you can become completely lost. You can do just the opposite. You can go down and not up.*

*And of course, a teacher is there to laugh at you because you have such a high opinion of yourself that you need to be laughed at. You need to sense how small we all are. And to teach you to laugh at life and the world because you have to laugh at all these things—yourself, life, the world, occultism— because it's all so vast and so infinite that the only way you can really deal with it sanely is to laugh at it at times."*
(Rama, <u>Tantric Buddhism</u>, "Peak Experiences")

A key point, however, is that it's not a quick fix. A few meditation sessions won't do it. This is because we are still locked into the socially-conditioned way we live, the desire/aversion operating system. It is not easily transcended, because chunks of it are necessary to deal with everyday events, and the pull of desires has been very deeply ingrained over many lifetimes. It takes a great deal of tenacity to swim against the tide that all humanity accepts as normal.

*"The best way to deal with desire and aversion is to push them away. To cut to the chase, if I may here, we all know what we should be—I believe that—we just don't listen. But we know that we should be terribly humble, completely consistent, and that we should strive to enter the light. There's no reason for that, it just is how it works, just like the fact that we're alive. We know that we should be completely humble, we should stop thinking that we're very marvelous because we're not. We're interesting at best because we're part of life and all of life is interesting. But we're not marvelous. We'll come and we'll go."*
*(Rama, Tantric Buddhism, "Buddhism")*

The incorporation of meditation into your lifestyle, and subsequent development of deeper understandings and perceptions enable you to transform. These deeper understandings and perceptions arise over time, not just in this lifetime but over many lifetimes. Also, the teachings about how to navigate this lifetime are essential to maximize the benefits of meditation while living and working in the world. Without both, in a world like this you won't evolve very much.

Meditation is the most direct way to increase light in the mind. With each meditation you experience happiness directly, and can also increase your internal energy. It's so ironic that so few people are interested.

The Enlightened teacher is showing a way to get out of an unhappy loop—experiencing suffering by chasing desires—that is endless as long as we don't make the effort to get out of it. All we have to do is loosen our grip on this loop which is so embedded in our minds and in society. This is what happens naturally in meditation. Then a variety of skillful techniques in living in society protects this progress. Both will be explained at length throughout the rest of this book, but a key element of true meditation is that it loosens the fixation on desires that grips the mind without us having to forcefully and consciously pry it off.

Through the practice of Tantric Buddhism, the various difficulties that the world throws at us become less threatening because we can see them more clearly. The tantric Enlightened teacher is teaching a refined art, the elevation of our awareness and the resultant changes in how we dance with life. But really the Enlightened teacher is just trying to pull us out of the water we are submerged in.

*"Hopefully the world will eventually have a democratic system everywhere. It is the best system, obviously, because it gives us the most latitude. But the democratic system is still ruled by the people in it, and the people in a democratic system are not necessarily very aware. From the point of view of the person who seeks personal freedom, they're still bound very much by the myths of their culture, by their religious structures, which they don't necessarily understand but have just been handed down to them….*

*A person who seeks to be free wants to blow past all of that because they sense, feel, perhaps remember or project that there is another condition that can be attained—a condition of ecstasy, a condition so far different from what the people of planet Earth experience that it's not even discussible. We're not discussing a minor change in how a person perceives life but such a radical departure that it's as if one were not human. Yet, of course, we're just redefining human. We're saying human can be something more than most people experience it. But it's so different from the normal human psyche that there is no point of comparison."*
*(Rama, <u>Tantric Buddhism</u>, "Freedom")*

The reason we resist so much, even when we are trying hard to evolve, is because we don't realize that we are so stuck in our everyday, conscious mind. Our conscious mind, our ego self, is always in control. It is able to block our perception of anything it feels threatened by. Spiritual growth is its biggest threat because you literally are taking away its dominance.

The paradox is that boundless happiness and joy are simply the normal state, or the "Natural State" of being in the complete mind, as the Indian sage Tilopa called it, while the states of mind human beings inhabit are anything but. The good news is that in reality our mind is the infinite mind. But as human beings in a body in a world of time and space, we also require a mind focused on the physical dimension to get through the day, much less the incarnation. That conscious mind is who we mistakenly think we completely are, when in fact it is only a small but necessary island in a vast ocean of infinite mind. What we call meditation is a process of swimming out past that island a little at a time. What we eventually realize is that the state of mind we experience in a completely immersive meditation is in fact the infinite mind itself. Sometimes it helps to not overthink this:

*"The Buddhist mindset seeks to eliminate the self. That is to say, what we want to experience is life, not self. And when there's less self and more life, we're very content, and when there's more self and less life we're quite unhappy. So we want to experience life, not self.*

*What prevents us from experiencing life is self, but what self is, essentially, is clutter. Self is clutter. Self is just a great deal of clutter, and the clutter in our lives is a reflection of the clutter in our minds. What else could it possibly be?"*
*(Rama, Tantric Buddhism, "A Clean Room")*

Rather than renounce the world and try to suppress the conscious mind, which many monastic traditions are based on, Tantric Buddhism is a set of methods to remain in the world and go far beyond it at the same time. Our conscious mind must be fully engaged and kept very neat in order to successfully live in the world, but we must put it aside in order to experience our complete mind. Doing both is the process of balanced spiritual growth. In Tantric Buddhism as Rama taught it, you can and must do both together.

# Chapter 3:  Three Bodies, Not One

While being alive on Earth means that we have a physical body, yoga and a few other spiritual traditions define additional layers. It is generally agreed that in addition to our physical body, we have a subtle physical body, also called the aura or the astral body, which surrounds the physical body, and a causal body, which is at our core.

Before going further into this model, it is worthwhile to put into perspective the terminology building that all religions engage in. Rama explained that,

*"The thing that is important to understand in this study of consciousness is that you really can't explain anything verbally. You can only allude to, point in a general direction of. But all the systems that try to present different worlds, planes of being, dimensions, different bodies, chakras, energy centers—all of these systems ultimately fail if you try to make them work or make them all-inclusive—because they're all symbolic representations of something that lies beyond the world of thought and description or analysis. They're meant to point a direction and they shouldn't be taken literally."*
*(Rama, Zen Tapes, "Reincarnation")*

With that important caveat, let's try to understand the three bodies that we have. The physical body, the subtle physical body, and the causal body comprise the human being. You constantly receive information from all three bodies. However, the personality you craft and identify with so completely isn't capable of fully receiving all of that input. In the complete mind there are layers, and some of the layers beyond the human band of attention hear the subtle and causal bodies loud and clear. The problem with a lot of confusion, indecision, and bad choices is that your personality, also known as your ego self, is in total control, and often won't listen to those other levels of awareness. At this point, having the ego self listen to the subtle body and the causal body would make a huge improvement in your quality of life.

The physical body is the car we drive on planet Earth. It requires constant nutrition, fuel on which to run. From birth it grows and develops into its genetically-driven final form, though modified by the social, economic and environmental conditions it exists in. We can do things to strengthen or weaken its muscles and immune system. We have five physically-based perceptual systems for visual, auditory, tactile, smell and taste sensations, through which we perceive our physical surroundings.

Rama half-jokingly said that the only time you notice your health is when you're sick. It's tougher to meditate if you're not feeling well. Some spiritual traditions, such as certain forms of Hinduism, see the physical body as a hindrance to spiritual progress, something to be denied. In the mistaken belief that it is the source of desires, and that desires must be crushed, they practice severe asceticism and austerities. Sometimes a temporary purity is achieved from such practices, but that soon passes. The body is not the source of desire, it is your human band of attention that is pursuing desires, some of which may include physicality, but many are entirely mental. Desires are what fill your fantasy life.

Other spiritual traditions venerate the physical body, referring to it as a temple. But worshipping the body doesn't expand your consciousness either. It's best to simply accept it as the vehicle for your mind. It is much more accurate to see yourself as a mental traveler, whether in a body or not. The mind is much more than most philosophies recognize, and the body far more complex.

We are very familiar with the physical body, its organ systems, skeleton, and muscles. We have a good idea about its nutritional needs, immune system, how it grows and ages. We've practically mastered how to optimize its strength and reflexes. Tremendous scientific research has explored it at the DNA and cellular levels. Unfortunately, science cannot yet measure the glow of your aura. But thousands of years of Yoga certainly accepts it.

The subtle physical body, also known as the aura or the astral body, is a body of many thin filaments that surround the physical body.

*"The subtle body surrounds and protects the physical body….The aura changes color from time to time, depending upon the intensity of the kundalini energy that is passing through it….The subtle physical body is a body of light. It is a much truer body, it is closer to what we are really like than our physical bodies are."*
*(Rama, <u>The Lakshmi Series</u>, "The Subtle Physical Body")*

It is not in the average human visible light spectrum, but that doesn't mean it doesn't exist. Consider the proven fact that dogs can hear sounds above the range of human hearing; just because the human eyes have difficulty seeing it doesn't mean that it cannot exist. The subtle body holds energy, and changes color depending on our state of mind and the energies we are dealing with. When we interact with people, whether in person or just thinking about someone, the non-physical (beyond our five physical senses) aspects of the interaction are going on through the aura. The aura is processing the energies of that interaction. Not only does the aura experience the strength and force of those energies, but the emotions and the state of mind of the other person or persons.

A key function of the subtle physical body is to act as a shield in our human interactions. Rama succinctly explained that the aura is a kind of immune system, keeping things out. A healthy subtle physical body is filled with bright, shiny energy, but it is constantly dealing with energies, whether emotions or thoughts, projected by other people. Those people do not need to be in your physical presence to affect you. Whenever someone thinks of you, however many thousands of miles away they may be, that thought touches your aura.

It is important to understand health in terms of the relationship between your aura and your physical body. The health of your physical body is much more dependent upon your subtle physical body than people realize. Rama went as far as to say that most disease is the result of damage to the subtle body first, which then manifests in the physical body. Your aura is like a big, glowing shield protecting your body. People throw all kinds of energies around constantly, some positive but many negative. Think angry thoughts about someone, and the abrasive energy in those thoughts shoots out and hits that person. Their conscious mind may not register it, but their aura is affected. Take enough hits and eventually you can develop serious chronic diseases.

The subtle physical body is also affected by the surrounding environment. Every place has its own unique energy, both in quantity and quality. Some areas are bona fide power places; when you're there you inexplicably feel better and calmer. Others, just the opposite. It's your aura that's experiencing the unique characteristics of the energy of the place. That then filters into your conscious mind, for example when you feel that where you are feels nice or creepy. Your causal body, filled with behavioral patterns from past lives, may suggest a certain way to handle that.

What your personality needs to do is listen to them. That's not anything like Enlightened mind, but it is what "holistic" really means. That's a necessary step towards entering the pathway to Enlightenment.

So how do you optimize the dynamics between your three bodies? First of all, if you can keep your subtle physical body strong and healthy, your physical body will be much better able to resist illness and disease. The way you do that is through daily washing with water, exercise, and meditation.

Water neutralizes negative energy and washes much of it away. Taking a shower more than once a day is very effective. You know how you usually feel "clean" after a shower? That has more to do with your aura being cleared than just the soap on your skin.

*"...it's very important to take showers or baths two or three times a day, if you're practicing mysticism, because water is a terrific neutralizer. During the day we pick up all kinds of different energies that come through the ether and through other human beings, and if you take a shower two or three times a day it cleanses you, not only physically but psychically. It neutralizes any bad energy that you pick up."*
*(Rama, The Lakshmi Series, "The Yoga of Mysticism and Power")*

Negative energy also accumulates overnight while dreaming during sleep, depending on where you go in dreaming. So a shower every morning clears away those overnight experiences. Take a shower before your morning meditation, it'll make a big difference! Negative energies accumulate each day from our interactions with people. They can be especially damaging if we are around people all the time who are in unhappy, confused states of mind, or who direct their negativity at us, or if we persistently think of people who don't like us regardless of whether they're in our physical presence. The hostility of others is like sandpaper on our subtle physical body.

Regular, vigorous exercise is essential for keeping your physical body fully capable of supporting your spiritual practice. One of the key things Rama emphasized was that advanced meditative practice requires more energy and physical fitness than what normally is sufficient. The image of the "soft" spiritual person was inaccurate. It wasn't that you needed to be a professional body builder, but that the body is taxed when entering into higher dimensions. If you were out of shape it was unlikely that you could reach those heights or stay in them for very long.

Rama enjoyed distance running. He recommended jogging a few miles several times a week, if not daily. Going for a run after work flushes out the negative energies that accumulate in your subtle body, as well as being an excellent overall conditioning exercise. Breaking a sweat and maintaining a strenuous enough pace to elevate your heart rate for 20-30 minutes was an important part of the support system that he taught us.

The primary reason why after jogging a few miles you feel so great afterwards is because it totally flushes your aura. Your mind becomes clear. If you meditate daily, it makes a crucial difference to work out regularly. Of course then taking a shower and afterwards you might even feel a kind of refreshing glow within you, which actually is who you really are. That's a lot closer to your natural state.

While the showering and cardio exercise directly benefit your physical body, they do the same for your subtle body. A huge benefit of that fully cleared aura is then meditation fills it with wonderful energy. The result is that a fully refreshed and charged aura automatically repels any bad energy. Quite simply, the bulk of the negative energies that come your way each day bounce off.

Without that aura kept clean with water and cardio exercise and filled with light from meditation, your day is going be a lot rougher, which is probably the way many days have gone for you. The quality of your daily life is dependent upon how much negative energy is absorbed by your aura. With a weak subtle body, more bad energy gets through. That's why people feel tired by the end of the workday, especially in jobs that involve lots of contact with people. That's why you want to maximize how much bounces off instead.

So to summarize, the health of the subtle body is critical for the health of the physical body. The subtle body is bombarded by the thoughts and energies projected by people every day. For most people, that fills the subtle body with a kind of sludge; if you do not flush it out, it'll eventually make you sick, not to mention the unhappy states of mind you'll constantly feel.

The subtle physical body has other capabilities beyond keeping your physical body safe and healthy. Not only does it protect both the physical body and mind, it also is connected to higher planes of consciousness. While we like to think of them as physically above the human plane, in truth they are inside of our own minds. As mentioned before, our conscious mind is merely one plane of consciousness in our complete mind. We have others, both higher and lower. We've spent enough time in lower, unhappy ones, obviously. Of course the higher ones are more aware, beautiful and joyous states of mind. The question is how to reach them.

Structurally, some of these higher planes, better understood as levels of attention in our mind, are accessed in the subtle physical body through what in Sanskrit are called chakras, or energy centers. This is done largely through chakra-focusing meditation techniques. Chakras are places in the subtle physical body where its filaments form a vortex. There are 7 main chakras, large ones parallel to the spine, and then many small ones throughout the aura, for example in the hands and feet. There is a subtle body equivalent to your spine, a tube called the shushumna, which has two smaller tubes, the ida and pingala, on each side.

The 7 main chakras start at the base of the spine and go up to the top of the head. The one at the base of the spine is known as the root chakra. It is a pool of powerful energy, called kundalini, symbolized in Yoga as a coiled serpent. The next chakra is a few inches higher, and is the sexual energy center. Above that is the navel center chakra, just a little below your belly button. The fourth chakra, often referred to as the heart chakra, is located in the center of the chest. The fifth chakra is at the base of the throat, and the sixth chakra, called the Third Eye or the agni chakra, is between the eyebrows and a little above. Finally, the seventh chakra, known as the Crown Chakra, or the thousand-petalled lotus of light, is at the top of the head. The basic idea is to let the kundalini energy, the coiled serpent uncoil up the shushumna. In so doing you enter higher levels of awareness.

Kundalini energy is central to human life, and the evolution of consciousness is dependent upon its motions. There is a great deal of misinformation and abuse of its special capabilities. Some groups teach ways to force the kundalini energy to rise up through the top of the head, which if you are not prepared for it can be harmful. Instead, it is best to let the kundalini rise on its own terms. This happens naturally as the result of becoming very still in meditation.

Rama explained it this way:

*"Normally, kundalini is always flowing through all your chakras, through your subtle physical body, what we call your astral body. Kundalini is the blood of the astral. And it's doing everything it needs to, but it doesn't need to flow much more than it is, unless there's reason, unless there's demand, unless there's activity. So in human life, unless there's something very major that happens of an emotional nature, there's very rarely an elevation in, kind of, the serotonin level of kundalini. It doesn't change much. But when you seek to enter into other states of consciousness, that requires more energy, and so the kundalini flows."*
*(Rama, <u>Tantric Buddhism</u>, "Focus and Meditation")*

As is readily observable, most people spend their whole lives in the first and second chakra, consumed by desires for power and sex, and hardly ever go any higher. If you have ever felt very centered and grounded, at those moments you were in the third (navel) chakra. When you feel very emotionally balanced, or filled with a sincere, selfless love, you're in the fourth. If you've ever felt especially artistic or creative, you've touched the fifth. If you've had any psychic experiences, such as knowing what someone is thinking or feeling a kind of transcendence or a deep wisdom, it's coming through the sixth chakra, the Third Eye. The seventh, or crown chakra, is separate from the shushumna that connects the other six. It has its own kind of emergence after the others have been mostly developed. You may feel a tingling sensation or unfolding on top of your head during a totally still, prolonged meditation, or when meditating with a very advanced spiritual teacher, and even then that will rarely occur until you're more advanced in meditation.

Now if your mind perceives other levels besides what is experienced through the senses, then you might wonder how it does that. It does that through the chakras. Each chakra is connected to other levels of attention, in other words, not to the physical senses, or even normal emotional or intellectual levels of consciousness.

*"The planes of consciousness are correlated to what we call the chakras, which are located along the shushumna. There are six of them. Then there's one other chakra of the primary chakras, which is not directly connected to the other six, that is located approximately at the very top of the head or an inch or two above it in the astral body, that's the seventh.*

*Each of these chakras really are dimensions. We think of them as objects, but they're not really. They're dimensional access points whereby we can enter into different levels of mind, and that happens automatically. It's kind of like the mercury in the thermometer rises as it gets hotter. As that mercury goes up, it hits little plateaus and when we hit those plateaus, everything shifts. We pop into a different dimension where we perceive ourselves, the universe and mind completely differently. When we get to the top one, if we do, we're in very high planes of attention. And the higher we go, the less physical things are, the less time and space exists."*
(Rama, <u>Tantric Buddhism</u>, "Focus and Meditation")

Focusing on one of them with full concentration for an uninterrupted period of time brings you into an increasingly deep meditative state. In a deep meditative state, focusing on a chakra for 15 or 20 minutes or more, you become immersed in that higher state of mind. One of Rama's key phrases was that "What you focus on, you become." Many sides of this concept will be discussed throughout the rest of the book, but its most constructive application is in meditation. Quite simply, that is what is occurring during meditation. When you meditate on a chakra, during that time you actually become the higher plane of consciousness associated with that chakra. That's how you can evolve rapidly, over and over again in this single lifetime, rather than waiting until death.

The better the quality of the meditation, i.e. less and less thinking during the meditation, the more light and power fills you. You literally are experiencing more of what you really are, rather than just the artificial, transient personality.

That's why you'll feel elevated or energized after a good meditation, good simply meaning keeping the mind still. That light is the most powerful force to clear out negative energies. The deepest cleaning of all is through meditation. That's also why it's especially important not to think of anyone during meditation; you only want to feel your innermost purity.

So doing all three, daily showering, regular cardio exercise, and daily chakra meditation, will keep your subtle physical body clean, clear, energized, and full of the highest light. Just these three things get you well on your way toward being happy regardless of external circumstances. Since unhappiness is rooted more in your attachments and aversions than anything else, you need a constant supply of the clearest energy to let go of them. These three steps establish the best possible foundation for accomplishing that, the result of which is a deep and abiding freedom.

The causal body is where the samskaras, the behavioral patterns built up over past lives, are stored. Those patterns themselves are aggregates of patterns, and in each incarnation some of them are dominant. So your identity, who you think you are in this lifetime, is a subset of all the samskaras. You can cycle through them forever. As they define you, so they hold you in a rigid mold, yet that mold has many different, competing aspects.

These include deeper life lessons that you've learned from your past lives; you draw on them when you have a sudden insight, or try to feel what the right thing to do is in a situation. Your intuition draws on it. The limitations you think you've got, built up over your past lives, are also all there; you draw on them more than you'd like. Fortunately, you don't need to deconstruct them, but rather spend more time filling your mind with light. That gradually refines and dissolves them.

*"What we're seeking to do is become transparent. Sort of a transparent window on reality. But that takes time to do. We're starting with a very solid, objectified view of ourselves and existence. To change that around, it's necessary to gradually loosen up the glue that binds the self together.*

*....the theory of personality transmutation is that the self... is an aggregate, it's a series of formations that has a karma to it. It's going around in a circle. There's a pattern to it, just like the DNA causes a growth structure pattern....*

*The self, too, has some kind of—it's like a DNA. We call it the causal body. There's a part of us that has a coding, and that coding follows a progression just as the growth of the body does. The progression of the self is implicit in its own structures. But normally those structures only change at the time of death."*

*(Rama, Tantric Buddhism, "The Nexus of All Pathways")*


So the causal body contains all of the conditioning you've had from all the experiences from all of your past lives. It's what makes "you" you, and it contains the blueprint for how this lifetime will unfold.

In society it might be called your fate, or destiny. But those are very loaded words, which society uses to ascribe some supernatural force that controls your life. That is another fantasy that people indulge in. It would be more accurate to call it the box that all of your past lives have stuck you in. Unless you do something in this lifetime to transcend those patterns, your life will not be much different than your prior lives. Your "fate" via your samskaras is to keep repeating the same choices over and over in every lifetime. Only the scenery has changed. You're still on the same stage, basically acting out the same part, over and over again.

Rama made a joke about this, saying that people spend their entire lives in a closet, even spending that lifetime only facing one wall. From one lifetime to the next they may turn and face another wall, but that's about it. Once in a while, someone might turn and face another wall within a lifetime, and believe that they've accomplished great self-improvement. From lifetime to lifetime, only the clothes hanging in the closet change. Self-discovery is getting out of that closet, and seeing that you're in a mansion.

*"There is something that controls perception, or your inner evolution—which is the causal structure. The causal structure determines the rate and method of evolution, the level of intelligence, your awareness of the universe….You go on forever, but just as the wave whips across the ocean and changes shape a little bit from time to time, so do you. There are laws or forces that govern those changes, and those are manifested by the causal body, just in the same way that your body grows in an orderly fashion, matures in an orderly fashion and decays in an orderly fashion. So the causal body is the determining factor in the changes that occur within your structure or growth rate."*

*(Rama, Zen Tapes, "Reincarnation")*

Our complete mind, the original mind, is not just our brain and physical body where our thinking and sense perception occurs. That's the definition of being sentient. The sentient mind is nowhere near complete. Our complete mind is the sentient section plus the levels which feel the aura and know the causal body. The dimensions connected to the subtle body at the seven main chakras are far more expansive, happy, and powerful than the sentient mind is capable of perceiving. To know the causal body is to know the history of how you've become who you are.

Understanding that you have three bodies, not one, enables you to put into an enlarged, more accurate perspective what your life as a human being is affected by. This understanding is substantiated with new skills and perceptual capabilities to successfully deal with how the world presses in on you each and every day. These skills unlock the higher, happier levels of your mind.

# Chapter 4: Understanding that You're Psychic

*"Believe in yourself, always. You have no idea what you're capable of. You haven't tried. Try. You'll be surprised, very pleasantly."*
*(Rama, <u>Tantric Buddhism</u>, "Possibilities")*

Connotations for the word "psychic" all revolve around the belief that very few people have this capability, and that it is strange and mysterious. Rama explained that the opposite was true, that in fact everyone is psychic, and even though the social environment poses big obstacles to developing it, we use truncated versions of this capability all the time.

*"Each human being has an aura. An aura is the energy body that surrounds your physical body. Your body of energy gives off impressions like radio waves—short wave, long wave—and you feel those impressions. You feel the thoughts and feelings of others, particularly people you are in close contact with, either physically or emotionally. You're very open to them. But you also feel the vibrations of the people in your neighborhood, at your school, where you work, where you drive your car, your town, your state, your country and your planet. Most particularly you feel the vibrations in a radius of about 100 miles from where your physical body is.*

*Everyone is psychic. People just don't know that. They think so much; they worry so much. They're so caught up in unhappy emotions. They're not still enough. They're not wise and silent enough to see that 90 percent of what they think and feel is alien to them. Ninety percent of what they think and feel, 90 percent of what you think and feel, are not your own thoughts and emotions. They're somebody else's, a lot of other people's.*

*...The billions of people on this overcrowded planet put out so much energy and so much of it is unhappy, that it makes everybody's minds active.*

*Everybody is thinking all the time, stressed out, can't slow down, can't feel what lies beyond this dimension. Normally it's very easy to do that. If you don't believe me, take a walk in the woods. Find a nice wooded path that not too many people have been on, where there are not a lot of impressions. Take a walk. Take a hike. You will notice that your mind, if you monitor it, becomes very quiet. You don't think much."*
*(Rama, The Enlightenment Cycle, "Meditation")*

So you are psychic, but the reason you're largely unaware of that is because the noise level from a huge human population drowns it out. Our minds are significantly larger and more expansive than is commonly believed.

Even with billions of noisy minds around us, there are some people who can see probable futures or into past lives, can communicate with people who have died or read people's minds. They developed it over multiple past lives. It is very likely that you have experienced fragments of such moments more than once in your life. These psychic abilities are skills which can be developed, and are a byproduct of meditative practice. The key point is that across a wide range of situations, sometimes you can understand things better by skipping the step of thinking when processing perception. That's being psychic.

As introduced in the preceding chapter, the belief that our physical body-based senses are the only perceptual tools we have is the first thing to see through. It's obvious to us that our minds are dominated by thoughts and emotions. Thoughts and emotions come from a lot of sources other than the five senses, such as memories and hopes. But if 90% of the thoughts going through our minds are not originating within us, then at a minimum you're tolerating a certain amount of constant mental confusion. In this thought-obsessed world you can't be sure who you are.

We must distinguish between which are our own thoughts, and which we mistakenly believe are our own but are coming in from other people. To deal with this problem, obviously you begin by paying attention to what's going through your mind. Each thought must be observed. That's the essence of mindfulness practice. Be still and watch the clouds moving across the sky. Observe the thoughts and feelings going through your mind and distinguish which are your own. This is something most people don't do. Now it is a survival skill for your mental health.

The bigger picture is that your mind is constantly processing many different thoughts and feelings, whether originating in you or not. You want to not be so overloaded. There should be a level of mental serenity you constantly reside in. That's your center. It actually is already there inside your mind, a lake for you to jump into. One reason to meditate is that it puts you in that lake every time.

There is a branch of Yoga which addresses this problem and several related ones. It is Jnana Yoga, the Yoga of Discrimination. While it was developed as a spiritual practice for reaching advanced states of consciousness, its principles are very applicable to the modern mental swamp. The basic concept behind jnana yoga is that, regardless of the source, most thoughts are illusions, fantasies that we weave around desires, or fantasies about who we are, both of which are transitory. By stilling the mind completely, the jnana yoga practitioner is able to distinguish these passing illusions from the highest levels of consciousness, which are not transient. As you pluck out each illusion, eventually nothing is left except the unchanging ultimate reality.

While jnana yoga has the loftiest of objectives, its methodology can be applied to the many thoughts and emotions crossing your mind each day. The task is to determine whether each thought is yours or not. Of course first you must become more aware of what's going through your mind. That's why mindfulness is essential, not only for spiritual growth but for sanity.

Here's how Rama applied it to all the thoughts and emotions we have:

*"But meanwhile, back in the relative world, if you discriminate, if you use the power of discrimination, then you will see that there is a hidden truth in all things and that you can perceive that truth. Just as all things are not good for us—it's not good for us to eat arsenic, all things are not meant for human beings, while it is good, perhaps, to eat a salad—so all experiences are not good for us. We have to discriminate and determine which experiences are good for us.*

*So if you practice a little jnana yoga in your daily life, it will help you tremendously in this sense. You can learn that which is right and useful and*

*that which should be avoided at your current stage of evolution. The way to do this is very easy, absolutely easy. All you have to do is ask yourself one question and if you ask yourself this question whenever you're trying to decide what to do, you'll always do exactly what is right. You'll discriminate and cut your way through illusion and you'll always do that which is right. The question is very, very simple. The question is, 'Where is truth? Is there truth in what I am doing now?' That's all you have to ask yourself."*
*(Rama, The Lakshmi Series, "The Yoga of Discrimination")*

To do this requires that you learn to still your mind, so that you become familiar with a baseline level of having very few, if any thoughts. That's meditation. The essence of meditation is stilling the mind. When the mind is still, there are no thoughts going through it. Your mind has become a sky with no clouds.

What other survival skills might you utilize that you haven't discovered yet? As you grow into the wonderful opportunity of accelerating your spiritual growth, naturally you're interested in finding out if there's anything in the world that might be of assistance. Shouldn't there be helpful energies here on Earth for spiritual growth? It may not be apparent to humanity generally, but some of the best are the energies behind the changing of the seasons, the solstices and equinoxes.

Rama explained that utilizing the solstices and equinoxes is an important psychic skill that should be developed and applied every year. It is a multi-step process which starts with having a well-ordered and uncluttered life:

*"What a good occultist does, is they hook themselves to the summer solstice. It's a very powerful time. It's a feeling. You know it's coming internally because your mind is quiet, because you meditate and your life is not filled with a lot of things that distract you, because you're centered and you have your goals set forward and that's what you put your time and energy into. Because you've eliminated anything unnecessary from your life and your mind isn't cluttered, you can feel things that other people don't feel. You can feel the power of the solstice....*

*Consequently, if you're aware of these energies, you can hook onto them and utilize them to pull you or push you to different places, either physically or in terms of outer world accomplishments, or just in terms of shifting mental states—flipping from one plane of consciousness to another, flipping from one self to another, things like that.*

*... And the way you do it is—as we do everything in occultism and Buddhism, advanced Buddhism—the way we do it is with a feeling. You have to feel the solstice."*
(Rama, <u>Tantric Buddhism</u>, "Solstices and Equinoxes")

He then went on to teach us how to connect with it:

*"It's sort of like when you see something in your peripheral vision, see it out of the corner of your eye, you just sort of notice something. That's how an occultist feels energies, as a rule.*

*Now, we don't really want to look directly into the sun. If you look at the sun long enough you go blind. If you look at anything powerful directly for too long, you tend not to see it. Power masks itself. When you look into power for too long, it almost overcomes you; it kind of enchants you and you don't really see it carefully. Sometimes when you look directly at a thing you can't see it very well. When you look at it out of the corner of your eye, you see it better because you're not distracted by its appearance. In other words, what we want to look at is not the way the thing looks, but the way it is. Appearances are oft times deceptive. Very often the appearance of something has nothing to do with its reality.*

*So when you look into the solstice, when you look into that energy field, you might not see it. You may become so caught up with the feelings, the intensity, that you won't see where it's going and how you can hook yourself to it. What a good occultist does is feel; you feel the solstice. You know it's very powerful, and so you just—it's like having a program operating in the background—you just put a part of your second attention, part of your inner self there. There's no way to explain these things, as I'm sure you know. You do this for every solstice and every equinox."*
(Rama, <u>Tantric Buddhism</u>, "Solstices and Equinoxes")

While for some people this may sound too intangible, it's not:

*"Let's say that you wanted to make a career jump. The average person would just go out and try to get a job, get their resume together, submit it, try and get any information they can. An occultist doesn't go about things*

*that way. We use internal energies to accomplish what we do. That's what occultism means—it means hidden, the other side of things. Hidden not in the sense that somebody's trying to hide it from you, but what is not apparent to the senses. You can't see it with the physical eyes, feel it with the hands, taste it, touch it or smell it. But it's there. It's more real, perhaps, than anything else.*

*An occultist who is trying to make a big change in their life would build that change around the energies of the next solstice or the next equinox. They'd hook themselves to it. We have a very powerful solstice coming up (1990), which is why I particularly draw your attention to it. At this time it's very easy for an occultist to make a major shift of any kind they choose because so much power is going to be available from the solstice. Not the day of the solstice.*

*The day of the solstice is just totality. It's a very interesting and powerful time, of course, but as you get closer to it, if you just think of it as a four-point ratio—we've gone through an equinox and you've hit the totality of the equinox on the 21st of March or September, but then you will stay in the field of the equinox for about another month as you leave it, you're still really in it. We define it as a singular day but it isn't just a day, it's a time period.*

*But then about a month out, you start to pick up the radiance of the coming solstice, which is about two months down the road. And then, of course, about halfway through that next month you're right in between, which is a midpoint....*

*So around the middle, you shift. In other words, it's as if we launch a spacecraft and we're trying to get from one planet to another—we aim it at the gravitational pull of a planet. Even though we're not going to stop at that planet, we pick up its gravitational pull and it will accelerate the spacecraft. Then when we get close to that planet, instead of smashing into it, we fire our rockets, bounce around it, escape its gravitational field and push past it....*

*Except that in the case of a solstice or during the equinox, it doesn't trap you. It pulls you to it and then it pushes you away."*
*(Rama, <u>Tantric Buddhism</u>, "Solstices and Equinoxes")*

As he said at the beginning of this discussion, taking advantage of the solstices and equinoxes is predicated upon being able to feel them. Since there are so many people on Earth, it makes it much more difficult to feel these energies. You have to work a lot harder now to perceive it:

*"Occultism is really a science whereby we are able to accomplish incredible things, things that other people can't imagine, because we're dealing with forces and powers that they're not aware of—we train our bodies and our minds and our spirits to be aware of these powers. We do this by continually cleansing ourselves. We purify ourselves endlessly so that we become empty, so that we're not filled with ego, we're not filled with vanity, we're not filled with a lot of stupid desires. And we do this by meditating, leading very deliberate lives. By doing that, we become conscious of these forces and powers. And it's much more difficult now to do this than it used to be because the population is so great. There's so much human aura on this particular planet with 5.3 billion people that it's very hard to feel these things. Human aura is just like a kind of gray smog that covers over things.*

*In the time of ancient Egypt, it was a lot easier to feel things. You could feel the solstice coming much more strongly. Now, you have to be very, very sensitized. The power is there, it's just as strong, but there's so much interference, there's so much gray sludge from the overcrowded earth that it interferes with your ability. An occultist today has to train themselves to a much higher degree than an occultist did even a hundred years ago.*

*That's why we call this a dark age. It's a dark age in the sense that there are so many people on earth who are so unattuned that they create such a level of white noise, in a sense, that it drowns out things that we'd like to see....*

*So occultists depend upon, for their very existence as occultists, the internal powers and energies of the universe. We train ourselves; we go through a long training process and purification process, whereby we become highly sensitized. Then we have to guard that sensitivity because once you're sensitized, you can also pick up a lot of junk. In other words, we have to become so much more sensitive now because the earth is so polluted, but that pollution poses a tremendous danger to someone who's sensitive. It's always been that way. An occultist, in other words—once as an occultist you sensitize yourself, you now have to guard that sensitivity. Sensitivity is a two-way street like everything, and the sensitivity will enable you to do amazing things but can also be incredibly painful if you don't guard it properly."*
(Rama, <u>Tantric Buddhism</u>, "Solstices and Equinoxes")

The most important psychic capability for successfully guarding that sensitivity is what Rama defined as "Seeing." He spoke of it often and in many contexts. It was a skill that naturally emerged from meditation, but had to be developed and then implemented. He made it clear that seeing was an essential skill for a spiritual seeker in today's overcrowded world.

*"Seeing is the ability to tell what really is. There are many different forms of seeing. Some forms of seeing involve apprehending that which is occurring in the world. Other forms of seeing are more esoteric, and they involve the perception of perception itself. Without seeing, it's very difficult to practice self-discovery. You're quite blind. Most people of course, think of seeing as the thing we do with our eyesight. We're using the word 'seeing' not in that sense at all, but as a metaphor, almost a mixed metaphor, for knowing. Perhaps 'knowing' is a better word. It's a little bit of both."*

*(Rama, Insights: Talks on the Nature of Existence, "Modular Mysticism: Seeing")*

Growing into your innate psychic ability begins with greatly strengthening your intuition. In the beginning, seeing can be equated to intuition. In practical terms, that intuition extends to many choices you make in your life. You subsequently may apply rationality and analytical thought to verify what you intuitively see as the right decision, but the vast majority of the time, you can just trust your intuition. As a first step, you need to trust the impressions you get of people, rather than what they project.

*"Seeing is the art of detachment. In order to see, you have to be able to push away any and all descriptions of existence and move into a different modality, a different plane of understanding, of awareness, which we call intuition or knowledge."*

*(Rama, Insights: Talks on the Nature of Existence, "Modular Mysticism: Seeing")*

In a world like this, being aware of being manipulated or drained before it's too late is a necessary skill for navigating your life. We are aware of other people's thoughts and emotions through their physical or verbal expression, but also through our awareness on a mental level. They may be smiling on the outside but frowning on the inside. It's not that hard to sense what someone else is thinking or feeling, at least some of the time.

*"You're going to develop a… second level of attention. This is intuition. With intuition we 'know' things. We can know what something looks like without having to look at it physically. Actually, we can 'see' what it looks like completely. We can feel something without having to go through an emotional process. Intuition is shorthand; it's a faster method of apprehending the true nature of something. We're going to learn to develop a field of attention called intuition, the second field of attention, to a very fine and exacting point. To do this, though, it's also necessary to bring order into the primary level of attention, the island of the first attention."*
*(Rama, <u>The Lakshmi Series</u>, "The Yoga of Mysticism and Power")*

So the awareness of thoughts and emotions, either in ourselves or in others, is not always dependent upon the physical, human senses of seeing, hearing, touching, tasting, or smelling. The fundamental level of being psychic is trusting your intuition, but you must remove a lot of mental clutter for it to operate effectively.

Everyone presents themselves to others. We make ourselves appear to be more relaxed, feel in control, or any one of a dozen other images to project. These behaviors all come out of what we believe is the primacy of social reality, which is an artificial construct combining how the world was described to us when we were children coupled with being immersed in society ever since. This artificial construct plus patterns from many past lives create our idea of the world and our place in it. The first step in seeing is freeing ourselves from this very limited definition of reality that we are trapped in. This is the closet we must break out of.

*"Seeing is an ancient process and there are definite means to go about seeing. There are definite ways. It's not accidental at all. It's something that you work at every day and every night. Otherwise you won't learn to see…. Seeing is initially more of a process of tearing down something—we're trying to tear down this silly description of reality that we have, the way of seeing that we now have. We developed a habit, and the habit is very strong. So we're going to try and break through that habit, even if only for a moment, and then gradually we'll be able to break through it a little bit more and a little bit more. And we can't be too hasty, or too abrupt. Because if we are, if we tear down the description too quickly and we don't have anything to replace it, we'll feel lost. And we'll feel so awful that we'll feel that nothing else exists beyond our description of existence, and it's so painful without it that we'll cling to it all the more.*

*That's why it's very, very important not to hurry the process of self-discovery. Because if you hurry it, you alienate yourself from the process itself. You need to develop a sense of gentleness and grace. You shouldn't force yourself. Because while forcing yourself may give you some kind of immediate result, the result probably won't last because your being will rebel. It's better to be gradual but to continue and then gradually, of course, you'll see that it's not so gradual."*

*(Rama, <u>Insights: Talks on the Nature of Existence</u>, "Modular Mysticism: Seeing")*

You reduce the clutter in your mind by relaxing your grip on your attachments and aversions. As this occurs, your intuition will naturally arise. You will begin to discern when people are being deceptive, and also when they are being forthright. That's how seeing works in the affairs of people. Here's an example that Rama gave of an experience he had:

*"So a fellow came up to me, and he's had many spiritual experiences, what we call spiritual experiences. He told me about times he had been up on top of mountains when he had seen and experienced other realities and different things. When he said this, of course, I—since I can see, I can see inside whether something's true or not—I saw that everything he told me was the truth. He also told me he'd spent some time in some different mental institutions, which was also obvious when one looked at him. One can see— you can see these things."*

*(Rama, <u>Insights: Talks on the Nature of Existence</u>, "Modular Mysticism: The Sorcerer's Explanation")*

Fortunately, seeing is a skill that can be learned. Rama presented a technique for developing seeing:

*"Psychic development, of course, is the study of how you gain energy, gain power, gain awareness, gain knowledge, and move towards a condition-less condition that is neither above, below, within or without, called Enlightenment. Seeing is an integral part of doing all that. It's a skill that has to be developed, just like driving a car is a skill that you learn. Driving a car isn't essentially hard once you know how, is it? You take it for granted. But the first time you ever got in a car, it might have been a little complex. Flying an airplane isn't necessarily much harder, you have some more things to calculate. Seeing is similar to both, because there's a sense of movement in*

*seeing. Seeing is not a passive experience, necessarily. It has a certain volition, a movement to it. It has a sense of going someplace; that's why I compare it to driving or flying, or even walking.*

*Seeing means that there's a sense of destination, a sense of where you are now. We're taking points within an infinite universe and creating a mindset of a type, a kind of a geography, star map, points of reference.*

*In order to see you have to have points of reference. What are the points of reference for seeing? Well, the ultimate point of reference is the level of your own attention or consciousness. In other words, seeing is, to a certain degree, based upon comparison. How do you know that your seeing today is more accurate than your seeing yesterday? In a relative world, where everything changes all the time, it's hard to know. You can wake up today, and not feel as well as you did a month ago, but not realize that, because consciousness is fluid, your awareness changes all the time, and there isn't necessarily a sense of how much it changes.*

*… A little humility takes you a long way in seeing. Consciousness, as I said, changes, it moves, but it tends to forget where it was. You may remember where you were yesterday physically or the people you saw, but can you exactly define the state of mind you were in five years ago? How do you know that the state of mind that you're in now is vaster? Well, you need a comparison point.*

*In navigation, or when you're driving your car, OK, but let's think of navigation, you're out there on the big ocean, and you can't see any land. How do you know which way to go? Well naturally, you have to get a point of reference. A North Star, and you know where South, East, and West are. The Sun, setting in the West or rising in the East. Something like that. You need points of reference in seeing, too.*

*The points of reference in seeing are a little different, though. They're not physical locations. The inner navigation is rather accomplished by a sense of association with awareness. By that I mean that you have to be able to gauge what level your awareness is. Now let's not assign levels; some people like to think of awareness in levels, in other words they want to make a list of the different levels of consciousness and stuff like that. I think that's an interesting practice but it's just another idea….*

*But you can tell, without having to name it, when your awareness is shifting. So what you need to do is, Step One, in learning to see, find yourself a few places of power. These are places where you will store and recollect shifts in your awareness. You'll map the ever-changing you.*

*Now a place of power, in my opinion a good one, usually has no people around it or as few as possible. In other words, it's some land that still has some energy in it. It's not necessary to go thousands of miles to the top of a mountain in Tibet or way down to central Mexico to a little hill someplace. There are places of power everywhere, in every community. It could be a park, and there's a little quiet spot in that park that just feels good to you.*

*It's good to pick something that they're not going to build on, so it'll be there for a while. It's good to pick a spot in a nature conservancy or a park.... Find yourself a nice little park or nature area or a nature trail, but hopefully something that's again owned by the state or federal government or in some kind of private reserve, that's going to be there, and go there. Have a couple. And just go there and sit for a while. And look at your life and look at the world.*

*And look at your awareness. Notice how you feel when you're there. What your awareness is like. Step outside of yourself for a moment and look. Are you happy, is your life going well? Are you unhappy, what are your goals? Just sort of think about your life for half an hour, walk around, look at the trees, look at the grass, look at the snow, and then go on with your life.*

*Forget about it. Then you should try and come back to that place about every six months, every three months, every month, every year, every two years, it depends. And only in that place will you really be able to tell whether you're seeing more or less clearly. Whether your awareness is actually evolving or devolving.*

*Because when you're out in the world among people you can't tell, because everyone is psychic, much more than human beings realize. Everybody is busy thinking almost everybody else's thoughts all the time, just no one knows that because hardly anyone sees.*

*But when you go to that little nature area, for you it's special. It's a special place for you, and you create a kind of a field of power. For the short time that you're there, you're walking or sitting, or whatever. For that short time, you're creating a field of power there. It's your spot. Other people may come and go there, that won't affect it being your spot. But it's definitely your spot because you staked it out. And when you go there you'll see your awareness. You'll see how much luminosity you have.*

*You can be drained by others. They can act on you and drain your energy. You can be drained by the thoughts of others that enter you. You can be drained by your conditioning. There are so many things. And you can be drained so far that you don't realize that you're being drained. It's happened to me at times. I think it happens to literally everyone on the path to knowledge.*

*So the only way you can tell, the easiest way, is to go to your spot and see how you feel. And you will remember how you felt there before. See what I'm getting at?*

*Normally you can't tell, because you're so in the flux, you're so in change. But it's like going to Nirvana for a brief vacation. You're stepping outside the circle of your life and you're examining your awareness. It's like taking your pulse, going to the doctor and having a regular checkup. No one can do it for you, only you can do it."*

*(Rama, Psychic Development, "Seeing")*

# Chapter 5: Meditation, Part One: Focus

*"We're going to take perception into itself, into the perceiver, and see that what's there is perfect, qualityless, endless radiant light, which is a way of talking about something. It's not really just qualityless light; those are human abstractions. But it's nirvana; perfect perfection, beyond comprehension—ecstasy."*
*(Rama, <u>Tantric Buddhism</u>, "Focus and Meditation")*

Rama stressed that meditation was, is, and always will be the pathway to Enlightenment. Not any hidden knowledge of some special secret, but deep and ultimately perfect meditation. As mentioned earlier, one way to summarize the lack of spiritual awareness in people is that there is a lack of light in the mind. Rama defined light as awareness itself, like shining a light on something. The way the human mind is constantly thinking blocks our more perceptive faculties. This constant thinking not only blocks our awareness of the full scope of what we're perceiving, it blocks the light. Meditation lets it through.

The deeper levels of mind are intrinsically happy. Happiness is already inside your mind. Thought and sense perceptions keep us on the level of physicality, where transience and suffering dominate. Meditation simply means to stop thinking and paying attention to the world. If you can do that for even five minutes, as Rama put it, you'll experience a very deep light, a beautiful, perfect light.

Three chapters of this book are devoted to meditation. It is the core of everything he taught. Every topic he discussed, from psychic development to career success to samadhi and the superconscious states, came back to meditation as the foundation and underlying solution.

He taught us meditation in stages, one building upon the next. As we improved, he explained it more deeply. So rather than mesh the understanding of meditation that he brought us to with the introductory and intermediate levels that we passed through, I will try to present it in the sequence that he taught it to us. It is a beautiful progression.

*"The practice of meditation is emptying the mind. When the mind is empty, completely empty, it's perfect meditation. It's really that simple....What we're doing is stopping thought. But really, before that, we're learning to control thought. And really, before that, we're learning just to sit down and focus on something."*
*(Rama, Tantric Buddhism, "Focus and Meditation")*

Learning to meditate is not shrouded in mystery; today there are many books and videos on the subject explaining, demonstrating, or guiding people through it. However, as the above quote demonstrates, it is more complex than what is popularly offered in today's progressive culture. Practically all of those books and videos only teach rudimentary mindfulness, learning how to watch thoughts pass through your mind without hopping onboard each one. Often these popular sources emphasize the stress-reduction features of meditation. Remaining still while thoughts or emotions pass through your mind reduces anxiety simply because it is our entanglement with highly charged thoughts and feelings that generates the anxiety in the first place. But anxiety-reduction is merely a nice by-product of meditation. Nor is meditation a mindfulness exercise. In fact, mindfulness is something to practice the rest of the time between meditations.

It is best to learn meditation in stages because it is comprised of certain mental skills that people have largely not been taught in school or anywhere else. If these mental skills are not strengthened first, you will give up on meditation, regardless of your initial aspiration. So this first of three chapters on meditation presents the meditation technique that Rama had us do for the first few years.

The basic problem is that our human minds are constantly looking for sensory information, whether external or internal. As it touches those stimuli, it weaves thoughts about them. As it thinks, it is constantly oscillating between attraction and aversion. That is a stressful process.

Meditation is putting your grasping human mind aside for a while and experiencing stillness. Your education in meditation begins with learning that this mental stillness actually is full of very pure energy and has great depth. A metaphor he applied to it was that rather than be fixated on the choppy waves at the surface of the ocean, go below the surface where the water is much more still. Instead of seeing meditation as some insurmountable mountain to climb, which is how the ego sees it, see it as developing the ability to change your perception, to experience many levels of perception in addition to what is ordinary for human beings. Rama took this even further to condense the definition of Buddhism as the development of this ability, as the one characteristic that differentiates Buddhism from other religions. If you meditate you're a Buddhist, he said.

Meditation requires the mental skill of one-pointed concentration. That means the ability to focus totally on a single thing for a prolonged period of time. There is no meditation without it, even though during a meditation you will not rely on it the entire time.

The best way to understand this is an analogy he used in teaching meditation: think of yourself as an astronaut in a space capsule atop a rocket. The rocket must produce a great deal of power in order to get free of the Earth's gravity. Once past the gravity, then it can coast.

One-pointed concentration is that rocket. Without it, as many people who have done a little meditation know, you sit there flitting from thought to thought, not meditating at all.

So the first level of meditation is the strengthening of your mind's concentration muscles:

*"What I suggest a person do for their practice is to focus on something with their eyes open for half the meditation, and for the second half of the meditation to focus on something with their eyes closed. The length of time depends upon how long a person has been meditating. If a person wants to start meditating, I recommend that they meditate for fifteen minutes a day, once a day. After they've been meditating perhaps for a few weeks, then I would suggest that they double the time and go to half an hour. After several months, I would suggest that they increase the time to 45 minutes and then, that they stay at 45 minutes for a while, until they've been meditating about a year, every day consistently. After a year, if a person chooses to, they can*

*increase the time, perhaps to an hour—maybe for another six months or a year. Then maybe after two years, go up to an hour and a half, ninety minutes."*

*(Rama, <u>Tantric Buddhism</u>, "Focus and Meditation")*

Rama gave us what is known as the Sri Yantra to focus on with the eyes open. It is a traditional Hindu geometric design of nine overlapping triangles surrounded by rings of lotus petals, with a dot in the center. In Hinduism it symbolizes the multi-leveled universe and the balance between male and female. The technique is simple: focus on that dot in the center. Here is the Sri Yantra that we used:

*"When we meditate, then, what we're doing is not just simply concentrating. We're raising the kundalini through focus, through concentration. There's a metaphysical astral process that's taking place. What I would recommend is, if you're meditating for half an hour, sit down with the eyes open, look at your little power rock or flower or candle flame or anything—yantra, geometrical design. Focus on one point and hold your attention there. The mind will waver, you'll think a million thoughts, but each time you do, bring your mind back to the point of concentration, seeing it visually. If one were blind, one can simply focus on a feeling."*

*(Rama, <u>Tantric Buddhism</u>, "Focus and Meditation")*

After the eyes-open visual portion, then for the second half of each meditation Rama had us focus on one of three chakras with our eyes closed. It became a cycle of three meditations over three days. For the second half of the first day's meditation, focus on the navel chakra. For the second half of the second day's meditation, focus on the heart chakra. For the second half of the third day's meditation, focus on the third eye chakra. Then start the cycle again, with the eyes-closed section of the daily meditation again on the navel chakra, then the heart chakra on the second day, and finally the third eye on the third day.

Meditation, at any stage of development, should be intense but never stressful. As you sustain the one-pointed focus, you will find that the mind will begin to feel calm. As your concentration improves, you'll find that the initial effort produces a kind of mental relaxation. You've escaped the Earth's gravity.

*"Naturally in the beginning, if you're undisciplined, which everyone is mentally when they start meditation, you'll think a million thoughts, a lot of images will come through your mind. But if you focus on the object and you keep focusing, gradually the thoughts will become quieter and quieter, gradually the images will disappear from the mind. What's happening is, through the power of focus, as you look at something and concentrate on it, the kundalini energy which is situated in the base of the spine, in the astral, begins its long journey up through what we call the shushumna, which is an astral nerve tube that goes from the bottom of the spine up to between the eyebrows and a little bit above, which is the agni chakra. And as that energy begins to radiate and rise, it causes the mind to become quiet, and the further that energy goes up, the higher we go into different planes of consciousness."*

*(Rama, <u>Tantric Buddhism</u>, "Focus and Meditation")*

Even if you were not interested in meditation, focusing on this yantra would greatly improve your ability to concentrate and think clearly. Another aspect of yantra meditation is that you are strengthening your willpower. In a world as noisy and crowded as Earth is today, just sitting down and meditating on a regular basis takes a significant amount of willpower. Willpower is a necessity on the path to Enlightenment. Training the mind to stay still requires willpower, but you are using your will only to keep focusing one-pointedly, not to battle your thoughts. If you battle your thoughts, you've lost before you've begun. It also requires balance, even love. Try loving the yantra or the chakra some time. Remember, this is all about self-discovery.

Devote your willpower to being totally absorbed in the yantra and then the chakra, and ignore everything else. Focus completely on the dot in the center of the yantra completely. You may see the yantra glow, or perhaps begin to expand or pulsate. That's the energy of it, which you see as you rise above body consciousness. But don't get distracted by visual phenomena, regardless of how interesting it might be. Just keep concentrating on that dot.

*"By disciplining and training the mind to focus on one thing, we gain control of our perception; we learn to grab it and put it someplace we want it to be rather than just in any sense that happens to be operating, or in any thought that happens to be passing through, or in any feeling that just happens to be going through us—who knows why, or even if we do know why.*

*We're learning to take our perception and place it in one place. By focusing on something, we do that. And be not discouraged. Everyone goes through the process you're going through. Takes a while to do it. Takes a number of years to learn to hold the mind perfectly in one place. But each day we do it a little better, and in the doing of it we're releasing energy that is taking our mind into higher, diffuse planes of attention in which we're seeing life more as it really is. And if we do that every day, there is an add-up process. It's kind of like—as we release more kundalini, we use a little bit of it but we also save it; we store it; it resides in our awareness field. So that as we meditate, it isn't just that we go up and come back down, we come down a little bit less each time.*

*'Come down' isn't really the right phrase because that implies we're getting high; high implies that it's an abnormal state and low is the regular state. The opposite is true. Our current perception is very cloudy and all screwed up and as our perception increases through meditation, we're seeing life more correctly. The higher our perception, the more kundalini that's active and being properly focused, the more correct our perception is."*
*(Rama, <u>Tantric Buddhism</u>, "Focus and Meditation")*

There are several basic time-and-space components to meditation, in other words when and where to meditate. While this may not seem critical, Rama explained how they made a big difference.

Always try to meditate in the morning or whenever your day begins (after a shower is helpful). Don't eat before meditating, that just makes you feel heavy and more blood is used digesting than can freely circulate. A little coffee or tea is OK if you really must, but caffeine stimulates thinking, which obviously is counterproductive. Water is better. Meditating before you have breakfast or engage the world in any way makes a big difference. Don't watch or read the news before the morning meditation, or anything else that cranks up your thinking. If the mind hasn't yet engaged with anything happening in the world, the mind is already in a relatively quiet state from sleeping. This makes it much easier to still the mind—there's much less going on inside of it. You want to optimize the situation, and thus maximize the potential benefit.

The morning meditation is essential because it charges up your batteries to go out into the world. It makes all the difference between having an easy time getting through the day or instead experiencing what the Buddha called "the nightmare of the day." Meditation fills your aura with light and power. That influx of light and power turns your aura into a very strong shield that literally blocks negative thoughts and energy from getting through. All that bad energy bounces off of an aura filled with energy from the morning meditation. In other words, the amount of suffering you experience each day is directly dependent upon whether you meditate in the morning or not.

Try not to skip days, or else you won't derive much benefit from this technique. You're building up important mental muscles. Consistency is the secret to its long-term success.

Where you meditate is also very important. Pick a quiet, private spot in your home where you can meditate regularly without people walking through it or otherwise interrupting you. It should not be a spot that, once you're done, resumes another role for you or anyone else living with you. It's great if you have a small empty room you can devote to meditation; a place in your bedroom is also good. It should be a spot that feels right. You will be storing power there.

Sit up straight, either on a cushion on the floor or in a chair, so that the energy naturally flows up the spine. If you are sitting on a cushion on the floor, sitting in the half-lotus position takes a lot of the pressure off of your back muscles. If you can sit in a full lotus, you'll find that the back stays straight with practically no pressure on you back muscles, but the full lotus requires training in yoga and is not something you just twist into, or else you'll probably hurt your knees, ankles, or hips. Don't meditate lying down; the body goes into sleep mode too much.

Here's Rama sitting in the half-lotus:

During the meditation, don't start analyzing or judging it! Quite literally what's going on is beyond your conscious mind's direct comprehension. Keep in mind that as soon as you start analyzing your meditation, then of course you're no longer meditating, but thinking instead. Just keep focusing on the yantra or the chakra. If thoughts pop into your head, disregard them and return to paying full attention to the yantra or the chakra. That can be more difficult than it sounds. It takes willpower to do this, but the effort always pays off. Afterwards, you'll feel better every time.

Don't analyze or judge the meditation afterwards, either. Instead, notice how you feel about half an hour after you've finished. If you've really concentrated for most of the time, if not completely, then you should enjoy a kind of quiet, internal strength and your mind will be clearer.

The only bad meditation is the one you skip. Remember, your ego mind cannot really perceive the other levels of mind you are experiencing. Perhaps your third eye will start to activate, or you'll feel some energy in your heart. You might feel energy tingling in some part of your body, or begin to see light. Don't divert your attention to these phenomena, as fascinating as they may be. Or you might notice nothing. It doesn't matter at all. Just keep going, relax, but keep that strong focus; then you'll go even deeper.

Don't be concerned if it is more difficult to focus on one of the chakras compared to the others. That naturally evens out over time. Often the navel center is the most difficult for beginners, since it is your power center.

During this first phase of learning to meditate, the practice of focusing on the yantra dramatically strengthens your mind; it's like going to the gym and lifting weights. As your mind gets stronger at focusing, you'll appreciate the benefits of this new-found strength in many other parts of your life, obviously at work or school.

After a while you might tend to take it for granted, and during your meditation not focus as strongly or for as long. Sometimes after initial progress has been made in this art, practitioners shift into cruise control. Instead, you should be so encouraged by the progress that you meditate longer, that you get even better at it. Don't kick back and let your mind wander during meditation. Absolutely do not start thinking about people and events. Warning! Doing this trashes your meditation!

*"Normally your aura is like an immune system. It keeps things out. But in meditation, that immune system is removed, consciously. We want it removed. Because not only does it block out things that are negative, it also blocks out things that are positive....Then, at the end of meditation, the protective aura will be even stronger because we're energized, and it will block out everything negative. We've filled ourselves up with so much light, that we're set....*

*Now when a lot of people meditate, what they do is, the whole time they're there, they're thinking about other people, sometimes even psychically talking to them, telepathically. This is a terrible mistake.... Because during the period of meditation, when you drop that auric immune system shield, if you focus on another person, if you feel different people, you take in their energy in your body completely. You completely absorb their energy, and you experience a kind of a psychic overload. All their thoughts, their desires, their impressions, their restlessness, their unhappiness, their confusions—all enter you. So if you were to think of ten or 15 people in a row for a few moments even each during meditation, you're in such a psychic state, it's so powerful, that each of those person's minds will enter your mind and you'll just be completely gummed up psychically....*

*You're going to end the period of meditation in a much lower state, lower vibratory state, than when you started.... The way to avoid this is to have things to focus on during meditation."*
*(Rama, <u>The Enlightenment Cycle</u>, "Intermediate Meditation")*

The only thing to do is to keep the mind still. If thoughts appear, let them go by like clouds passing across the sky. Easier said than done, but that's all you have to do. Keep focusing on the yantra and then on the chakra.

So to summarize, meditation is keeping the mind still without any thinking of any kind. When the mind is completely still for more than a few minutes, you automatically relax and tension flows away. Really meditating—actually having thought stop for prolonged periods of time—is difficult because we have trained our minds to do the opposite for most of our lives. In Western civilization this is ingrained—"I think therefore I am." So taking up a practice in which thought is stopped as a way to inner peace is something that society inherently opposes. In other words, you need extra tenacity to overcome that social pressure and conditioning just to get started.

Rama had to spend years explaining this opposition to us from different angles, as we became more aware of the different sides of ourselves, in particular how we internalized so much of it. There are a lot of things you must do with your life in order to optimize meditation. In short, you must tighten up all aspects of your life, which if left sloppy both drain the energy gained during meditation and limit the depths you can reach.

That's why it's important to practice mindfulness the rest of the day. Mindfulness means observing the thoughts that go through your mind. In particular, when any kind of negative thought comes into your mind, simply let it pass. Don't dwell on it. Move your mind to more positive or constructive things. With chakra meditation, you're storing great amounts of bright, clear energy that circulates throughout your whole being. That energy combats stress. Don't waste it on negative thoughts that are very draining. Practice mindfulness, turn it into a game. It is critical to your meditation progress. It is what prolongs and sustains the increased awareness and energy attained in the meditation.

Don't expect any sudden miracles from meditation, but you should begin to notice a difference after a few weeks, though more realistically after a few months. After a year there should be substantial improvement in your energy level, mental calmness and clarity. The mind will come to enjoy the silence and will naturally enter into it. Things are happening at a much deeper level than the conscious mind, and the energy and serenity inherent in the practice accumulates over many years. It may seem like nothing is happening—or that great things are happening—but your willpower to sit down and try is the real success. That effort carries over into every part of your life. This meditation/mindfulness lifestyle helps every aspect of your life.

The underlying assumption behind meditation is that the mind is incredibly vast. In Tibetan Buddhism, they add that the mind is like a diamond.

They use this image in two interlocking ways, first that the mind actually is indestructible like a diamond, and second, we can polish our minds to a diamond-like clarity to let the Original Mind, the mind of the universe that is behind all of our individual minds shine through. Our growing experience of it, most directly through meditation, is the pathway to Enlightenment.

*"The following is the truth. Within silence all things are contained. What appears to our eyes to be life is but a thin curtain, a gauze penumbra, which stultifies our vision, which prevents us from seeing the truth. The truth is that life is eternal, that eternity is life. What we call life is an acknowledgement of a succession of births of awareness. Time does not really exist as we know it, rather, it's a transfiguration of a concept in which mortality or mutability is conditioned. The mind is empty.*

*Nothing really is as it appears to be. The essence of timelessness is the center of things—to reach the center of things, that place which is not geographically located anywhere or perhaps is everywhere and yet is timeless, which we call nirvana. Nirvana is limitless awareness, without a field, without a knower. It is a body of light; the sense that we are not physical or mental; that we do not really have a history or a place that we're going to; that all of the universes are but phantoms, mirages, and while they have their own essence, their own pantomime—like the dumb shows, the pantomimes in the 18$^{th}$ century in England and in the mystery plays—they pass, forgotten.*

*Nothing is as it appears to be. We open our eyes, we look at life, the world, the seasons, the earth, the peoples. Everything seems to be solid; everything seems to have its own eternality. Or we see that it's mutable, that everything changes and transforms; everything goes through the cycle of birth, growth, maturation, decay and death. But all this is an illusion. Everything we see is an illusion. Even our perceptions of truth are illusory, illusory in the sense that they're not complete.*

*When we silence the mind in meditation, when there's no thought, no image, no pictures, no memories, no desires, no sense of a self that is in any way participating in an experiential ongoing life, we reach a plateau of awareness that is beyond creation, transformation and destruction. It's beyond birth and death. That awareness is within all things. It is all things."*

*(Rama, <u>Insights: Talks on the Nature of Existence</u>, "Modular Mysticism: Tibetan Yoga and the Secret Doctrine")*

# Chapter 6:  A Systems Analysis of Your Energy Flow

*"The sum total of your personal power, your awareness, is what causes everything to happen. You can gain awareness, and to an extent you can lose it, just like a battery can gain a charge or lose a charge."*
(Rama, <u>Psychic Development</u>, "Seeing")

As stated in the Introduction, this book presents an overview of what Rama taught us, but more specifically, his model of the mind and how to navigate life in this world. These two topics were integrated in many discussions he had with us. Everything depends upon your amount of internal power. The quality and level of your perception is dependent upon your energy level. The state of mind you're in and how you handle different situations is dependent upon your energy level. Who you even are at any one time is dependent upon your energy level. How you advance your consciousness is dependent upon your energy level. So if your main interest is to strongly advance your spiritual evolution, the essential task is learning how to increase your internal energy and minimize its loss.

Think of your physical existence, your life in this world, as a trampoline for spiritual growth. The more taut the trampoline, the higher you can bounce. That is also about the most concise definition of Tantric Buddhism.

So how do you turn this human life of yours into a trampoline? You begin by conducting a systems analysis of your energy flow. This means ascertaining the things in your life that increase your energy, and the things that decrease it. In other words, identifying the positive and negative energies that flow into you, and the positive and negative energies that flow out of you. Answering these questions, and of course then acting on them, will facilitate a great improvement in how you navigate through the rest of your life, and how far your meditation will progress.

*"So it's necessary, then, to do systems analysis of your life—to look at where you gain power, where you lose power, and to do the things that empower you and avoid the things that drain you….*

*So what the mystic does, is they set up their life as a field of power. In other words, you can draw power from everything in your life, and that power will roll into your being. It will increase your own power and it will also trigger a reaction. And that reaction will be the release of the power within yourself, just as when we split an atom—the tremendous power and energy released—matter converts into energy. So we split the atom, the nucleus of our own being where all our power from all our lives is stored. But in order to do that, everything has to be set up in a proper way. Otherwise, it won't work or the results will be catastrophic.*

*So it's necessary to groom our life, to bring it into order, to examine each thing in our life and ask ourselves if it's bringing power and force and energy into our life or if it's draining it. So it's necessary to look at each relationship we have, at our career, where we live, at our habits and routines, at our thought patterns. Each item has to be carefully gone through and constantly improved and checked and rechecked. The question you have to ask yourself, the most basic question is, is your life taking power from you? Or is it adding power to you? You need an honest answer. Are you stronger each day?*

*When I say stronger, I don't simply mean your physical body, but is your awareness stronger? And remember, the way we measure awareness is by how long you can stop thought."*
(Rama, <u>On the Road with Rama</u>, "Power")

Where to begin the systems analysis of your energy flow? The main underlying problem is that human beings are consumed with manipulating each other, in order to gain a degree of control if not domination. Virtually everybody does it. And while it frequently ends up manifesting in physical reality, the bulk of it takes place psychically.

Some people see manipulation as a way not just to control others, but as a way to steal their energy. Either through attraction, making you want them, or through aversion, making you fear them. Anyone who you think you need, or anyone you're afraid of, has successfully manipulated you. The truth is that you don't need anyone else for you to succeed in life. In reality, you are deathless, you live in one form or another forever, so there's nothing to be afraid of.

While this last point may seem idealistic, it is absolute fact. Even though we are not conscious of it, and society presents the opposite of this except when eulogizing the dead, it is a very liberating bit of knowledge. Rama mentioned this many times in the middle of all sorts of discussions. He took it for granted, and it informed everything he did.

For someone primarily interested in self-discovery, managing and increasing your energy is a basic life task. On this overcrowded planet it's very important to see clearly. People may hold on to some romantic or religious belief that they believe explains Life, but it fails them when they're in a confrontation or things go wrong. Instead, accept that you live in a world full of many unhappy people whose behavior is very erratic and unpredictable. In such an environment the most important skill you need is to see clearly—and quickly. Seeing! In a world like this, being aware of being manipulated and drained before it's too late is a crucial tool for dealing with all the people you will interact with. Rama called it psychic self-defense.

But since you probably haven't been practicing psychic self-defense thus far, it's very likely that you've accrued a substantial amount of unnecessary baggage. You want to clear away everything that's slowing you down. There are three main areas to address. The first third of the systems analysis of your energy flow is recognizing the people, past and present, whom you are losing energy to. The second third is identifying what you do that drains you or is harmful to others, both of which lower your state of mind. Lastly, you need to recognize what increases your energy, what brings positive energy into you.

*"If you want to become Enlightened, you've got to get all the bullshit out of your life. You have to clear up your mind completely. You have to unhook from anything that's impure and focus only on things that are completely pure and perfect all the time. And we do it a little at the beginning and then more and then more, and then eventually it consumes us. Literally. Until there's no self, there's only light."*
*(Rama, Tantric Buddhism, "Buddhist Enlightenment")*

It should be noted that he did not define purity as being celibate or a vegetarian or any other do's or don'ts. He considered those types of definitions as avoiding the real issue. Purity is entirely a question of your immediate state of mind, which has nothing to do with any dogma. Impurity is a nasty attitude. It is fooling yourself as well as others. Purity is the measure of the clarity of your mind. It is the lack of illusions within your mind.

So let's begin the systems analysis of your energy flow with that first third, the people, past and present, who have decreased your energy. Rama had a method for cutting through a wide range of mental confusion that he applied to different aspects of our life. This method was particularly relevant to the fact that we're more psychic than we think. In fact it utilized our psychic perception, and as a result also furthered its development.

The method was to make a list. In analyzing your energy system, you want to begin with what decreases it. He used the analogy of a drafty cabin during a snowstorm. First you get a fire going. That's meditation. Then you start plugging the leaks. In making a list of what was and may still be draining, you are bringing up to your conscious mind all manner of disturbing emotional interactions you've probably buried. That negative personal history both clouds your awareness and drains your energy. So make a list of all the people who have ever harmed you, been mean to you, or who you were or are afraid of. Go back into your childhood as far as you can. Take your time, you probably won't finish the list in one sitting.

At first there will be people whose names you can't remember. Just make a note about them and move on. Return to the list over a few days, fill in a few more names, remember a few more events. At the oddest moments you'll suddenly remember that bully's name from the 4th grade.

Everyone on the list has an energy line into you, an astral cord connected to your navel chakra. These lines are very real, however dusty from disuse they may be. When you're about to score a big success, someone will feel the rise in your power and try to siphon some of it off or knock you off balance. Now go through the list, one person at a time. Focus on that person with complete calm. Stay centered. Get to the point where you feel completely detached towards them. Don't rush. Get to the point where you absolutely don't care whether they live or die. Take as long as you need.

Then cross them off the list. It's a good idea to meditate before starting this elimination process, since meditation will increase your internal power and you will see more clearly. Do a few at a time, and take a break. When you start to feel tired, stop, and resume the next day. Have a bite to eat, perhaps something sweet. A little sugar actually offsets negative energy.

When you've finished the whole process, notice how you feel over the next few days. You have dropped your attachment to each of them. With this clean slate, it'll be easier to notice if anyone tries to reconnect. If they do, your complete disinterest is key.

You don't need to physically confront anyone, or get on the phone and yell at them. Going through this method using your psychic strength is not only all that's needed, it finishes everything for you. Why get into a confrontation with someone which will alert them to your insight and likely prompt them to throw more hostility at you, which hits your subtle body like acid. Instead, just eliminate them from your memory, or from your life, or if that's not entirely possible, establish considerable distance psychologically from them.

One theory that people interested in spiritual growth need to disabuse themselves of is the belief that you're supposed to deal with hostile people with loving kindness. Almost always the other person you are showing love to in the face of their hate simply sees it as weakness and harms you even more. It is your strong inner stillness that makes the difference, your firm inner strength that they feel which makes them back off.

Rama was very clear that there are no fixed rules, and that your actions are entirely dependent upon the situation and the individual involved. As he once said, on a specific day, in a specific situation, with a specific person, turning the other cheek is the correct action. On another day, in the same situation, with the same person, a roundhouse kick to the head is the correct action. Your only responsibility is to see Dharma, to see what is correct at that moment, and any belief about what's the right or wrong thing to do only gets in the way of clear seeing.

In this systems analysis, the real problem you're confronting is attraction and aversion. People play on your desires and fears. Are they able to do that because your mind has become habituated to those desires and fears? That makes us very predictable, thus easy to manipulate. Let's take a psychic experience many people have had. Ever unexpectedly think of someone for no reason, and then the phone rings and it's that person? That's an example of psychic vision. Work on your seeing and you'll know the phone is about to ring because first, out of nowhere you started thinking about that person.

What's occurred took place on another of those many bands of attention that comprise your complete mind. First, you had a connection with the person who called, such as a family member or close friend. That person was thinking strongly about calling you. You probably felt that person thinking about you but didn't bring that into your conscious mind. Then the phone rang.

Variations on this theme happen all the time. There's a certain part of your mind that is constantly aware of this going on, with all the people who you have a connection with. As mentioned earlier, that connection is an astral cord between your navel chakra and theirs. It can also be the result of recent impressions on your subtle body that you haven't cleared away. But the stronger ones actually are that astral cord between your navel chakra and theirs. They yank on it and you notice them, or you yank on it and they notice you.

In ordinary human reality, this is going on all the time. It's entirely psychic. Many families spend a great deal of their lives engaged in this behavior. The same thing takes place at work or school. All of these people are pushing out their desires and fears, their very limited concept of human life, and your mind has been soaking them up your whole life.

A subtle but important point to understand about attraction and aversion, which will be discussed more fully later in the book, is that they are opposite sides of the same coin. As this example demonstrates, it doesn't matter whether you desire or fear the person who has a line into you, the end result is the same. Taken a step further, the big problem is your attachment to them, much more than their attachment to you. Attachment is the biggest issue which blocks spiritual growth. It's a deeper problem than you might think.

*"Now the big attachments in self-discovery have nothing to do with attachments to cars or people or love relationships. Those are the basics. And if you're still working on those, I suggest you work through them quickly because there are larger and more exciting challenges ahead of you. The big*

*challenges, the big attachments, are states of being, are states of awareness. Universes. The big attachment is not to someone else or something else, but it's to ourselves. To the way we see life, to what we believe we are—our understandings, our ideas. And these are the best, the most fun, the most exciting attachments to destroy or to slay. You use discrimination, meaning you can see beyond the surface to eternity. Then you rid yourself of all attachments and then you're free."*
*(Rama, The Lakshmi Series, "Inaccessibility and Attachment")*

So in an adversarial world like ours, in which psychic warfare is a basic fact of life, how can you minimize the damage on an ongoing basis, if you want to evolve spiritually and grow into higher, happier states of mind? The answer is what Rama termed "inaccessibility." He devoted substantial time teaching us its many variations.

Inaccessibility has many sides. It does not mean becoming a hermit, though it does include living in less densely populated areas. It is a crucial technique for navigating life.

In contrast with some contemporary views which encourage being very open about your personal history and feelings, Rama taught that you had to be extremely careful about sharing such matters. In truth, most people aren't even interested, instead being consumed with themselves. But when you open yourself that way, some people see it as an opportunity to get a line in. They will play the part of being your friend, of caring about you. They will exploit it. Instead, make them earn your trust first.

*"To be sharp, to be clear, to be focused, not showing all your cards, not letting anyone really know who you are or what you're like—there's a wisdom to this. Why should anyone know? It's personal. It's private, who you are. Also, if you define yourself, then you're defined. People have a fixed impression of you. They hold you in their mind a certain way, and that actually makes it difficult to change.*

*It's very wise to be inaccessible—not to hide, but simply not to be too personal. So keep the deepest feelings of your heart to yourself. They tend to stay more pure if you do. There is wisdom to that."*
*(Rama, The Enlightenment Cycle, "Wisdom")*

From a spiritual growth standpoint, you don't know yourself that well, at least not across the breadth and depth of your complete mind. You don't know why you are alive on this earth, and who you've been in past lives. You barely know what you want to accomplish in this one. Most of the time, your mind is like a flag waving in the wind, as the Tibetans put it.

So if most people have strong manipulative tendencies, you should be careful about who you open up to. Instead of eventually adding them to the list you just finished processing, you want not to put them on it in the first place.

Inaccessibility means, first of all, understanding that your privacy is important to you. That should be obvious. Friendship should be earned, not given away. Your life should grow in self-reliance, not in dependencies, whether emotional or material. Most significant, opening yourself to others really boils down to sharing your personal history. Is that history who you really are today? All you're doing is reinforcing and staying in a past that holds you back.

Instead, share the present moment with the people you are around. It sounds cliché, but be here now. Whatever the situation may be with other people at the time, just be fully present. Most importantly, that means being fully aware. It's not about you or any of them, it's the moment that you're all sharing. As you'll come to realize, that's all there is. The past has vanished, the future hasn't happened. There is only the present, all the time. So just stay centered and try to be as aware in the present as you can.

The reason for becoming more inaccessible is that spiritual development takes more energy than leading a typically normal human life. In this age, it is mostly due to the sheer scale of the negativity in such an overpopulated world filled with people of very limited awareness. The result is that it simply takes more effort to meditate regularly and practice mindfulness. But self-discovery has always required more energy and effort.

Another inaccessibility technique is blending in rather than standing out. That doesn't mean being meek or overly deferential, not at all. But it does mean not being an egomaniac constantly calling attention to yourself. Don't dress to be conspicuous, don't dominate every conversation. Try walking across a crowded room so that no one notices you.

Do these things and see if you aren't more free. You're free of all those people with lines into you. The result is that you're more balanced, more centered, and more relaxed.

*"You must be very careful in the world. The world is filled with violence. The way spiritual people escape violence is to perceive it before it comes and avoiding it. That's what God has given us. God has given the highly evolved people not necessarily physical strength—sometimes we have that—but God has given the spiritually evolved people two great gifts to survive. One is the ability to see and sense danger and problems before they occur through our intuition and to avoid them, and also to be very pleasant when we are in a difficult situation. The other is when we get in that difficult situation, God has given us complete unattachment, so we can do whatever is necessary, without any feelings of remorse, without getting caught up in our emotions....*

*Inaccessibility and overcoming attachments give you a very beautiful life. As you meditate and go deeper within the self, you find that there's radiant happiness everywhere. There's a kind of fulfillment far beyond the muck that most people call love and happiness. But you have to live yourself at that higher level, you have to burn through your different selves until you come to the purified being that you really are, and this is the process of self-discovery. So try to apply these principles in your life. If you do, I think that you'll be very, very pleased with the results."*
*(Rama, The Lakshmi Series, "Inaccessibility and Attachment")*

The final third of the systems analysis of your energy flow is developing ways that increase your energy. You need more energy in order to elevate your awareness and keep it there. Life in this era is so abrasive that it literally wears you down, so getting that rocket through the atmosphere requires even more energy.

Self-control is an essential skill to avoid dropping into lower states of mind. Anger, hate, fear are powerful emotions which drain your energy level. You don't have to be sweet all the time, you have to be more dispassionate as the world swirls around you. Everything is transient here, so let go of more messy moments. By applying self-control in your daily life, it facilitates self-discovery. For example, its application in your career directly supports your spiritual growth:

*"Self-control is completely necessary for increasing and raising your attention level. One of the places you practice that is at work. You work many, many hours. It's the major activity of your life. Obviously, you can lose a lot of energy or gain a lot of energy from it. When you put your full attention into it and you do a good job, not just for the paycheck but because it's part of your impeccability, then you'll find it'll heighten you. Oh, we all become physically tired from working, but if we work with the right intent, we're inspired. Our mind goes higher. Our level is more expansive."*
*(Rama, <u>Zen Tapes</u>, "Managing and Increasing Your Energy")*

The next thing to understand is that meditation is the single most powerful thing you can do to increase your energy, and then sustain that more empowered level:

*"So the trick in life, of course, is keeping your personal power level as high as possible, and that's what meditation does."*
*(Rama, <u>Tantric Buddhism</u>, "Professional Meditation")*

He also recommended a very flexible approach to deal with certain situations which utilized several unexpected things in order better get through them. During the first few years of our study, Rama advocated a vegetarian diet. A vegetarian diet cleans out a lot of toxins in the physical body. But later, as we grew into the tantric path and became more involved in the world, he presented the concept of the strategic use of different foods, including meat, depending on the energy requirements of the situation.

He didn't suggest eating meat all the time, although he thought that having more protein in this era was necessary and a strict vegetarian diet was lacking in that regard. Eating fish occasionally was a good idea, and he pointed out that the human mind was not really affected by the consciousness of fish, since it was so fundamentally different from ours, that they lived in such a different environment.

He said that in certain situations eating red meat would be helpful. This was for two reasons: red meat was a complete protein and that our bodies were well-adapted to eating it and extracting all of the energy possible from it, and it had the interesting psychic effect of creating a sense of detachment in a situation. He also recommended that ground meat minimized the pickup of the animal's consciousness into our minds.

So have a burger before going into an important meeting. It works.

Another way to increase energy is by helping others. However, in order for it to increase your energy, helping others must be done with a level of honesty and, as much as possible, selfless giving. Helping others but having a hidden agenda will backfire, because your intent is corrupt, in other words, your state of mind is impure.

*"When we give energy, we gain energy. Now this is different than having someone manipulate you, take your energy, you know, that sort of thing. We're not talking about that. We're talking about energy that's freely given....*

*Whenever you take the time to inspire someone, to aid them in their inner search, you'll find energy will come back to you—unless, of course, you're ego tripping or you're trying to manipulate them or make them feel that you're powerful and wonderful. Then it's better not to. It's better to keep to yourself. You'll create very painful karmic situations for yourself. You'll lose energy.*

*The inner laws on this subject are very strict. They were written a long time ago. They're not about to change. You also have to be careful that in giving energy, you do not allow yourself to be excessively drained or used. There can be a sort of a depressive person whom you always try and inspire, and they never change, they just feed on the energy and pull you down in the process. That's not what I mean. That's pouring water through a sieve. None of that collects. It all goes out.*

*The alternative, of course, is to inspire people very selectively with sincerity and with respect. We have the opportunity to do this constantly. You want to increase your energy? Tremendously? Then want, inside your heart, to inspire others. You don't have to get up on a stage and teach. Just want that, and you will find life will occasionally cause you to encounter someone whom you can inspire. And it will lift you tremendously—one of the best ways to increase your energy. Meditate. Inspire others. Spend time by yourself. Spend time away from people. Manage your career properly. Work at something that's constructive, that doesn't injure others, and put your full attention into it."*

*(Rama, <u>Zen Tapes</u>, "Managing and Increasing Your Energy")*

As someone who wants to make substantial progress in your spiritual evolution, it is crucial that you understand the necessity of clearing away everything that is draining. Otherwise you can wax philosophic about self-discovery endlessly, but not do very much of it. You'll be the one missing out, and no one else will care.

Conducting a systems analysis of your energy flow, and thus learning how to manage and increase your energy, is a prime example of learning by doing. Talking about it, thinking about it, won't improve the situation whatsoever. However, if you jump in and do it with your full life force, the result will turn your life into a trampoline.

# Chapter 7: Your Current Mental State is Your Karma

How have you arrived at your current state of mind? We're not talking about momentary shifts as different experiences occur during the day, but your overall state of mind, who you are, with all of your psychological traits arrayed before you. Rama explained that karma is the sum total of all of the experiences you've ever had throughout all of your lifetimes. That's the real definition of karma; all of those experiences, including every moment in this incarnation, rolled forward into right now, to create the "I" we are at this moment.

The common idea of karma is that if you do something to someone, it will bounce back to you in this lifetime, and that a prominent event that occurs in this lifetime is reciprocity from an event in a past life. That's not how it works:

*"Just because you do something or create an action of some type, it does not mean that an action of the same type or nature will be returned to you. That is absolutely not the case….*

*When you cause something to happen, whether it's physically or you simply think a thought or feel an emotion, it causes a shift in your attention field, in your awareness. Shifts in your awareness ultimately will result in a pattern shift in your life. So Bob, who previously was your easy-going guy, will now be in a very different mental state because he just killed somebody for profit. This will cause Bob's attention field to drop. When Bob's attention field drops, he will now be on a new pattern in life. Certain things that might have come to him, won't come to him. Certain things that wouldn't, would.*

*Bob, for example, now will become a different kind of person as his mental state shifts, because we only are our mental state. And as he becomes that different kind of person or personality, he will make choices that he wouldn't have made. He will associate with people he wouldn't have associated with. In other words, a new future will open up to Bob, and in Bob's case, the future will not be as bright."*
*(Rama, <u>Zen Tapes</u>, "Karma")*

So rather than a simple physical reciprocity function for our actions, karma answers a deeper question, which is how did you become who you are now? You are your current level of awareness and consciousness. That's who you identify as. This is the end result of all of your experiences in this and past lives. This overall state of mind is what you're living through every day. If you are interested in Enlightenment, it's impossible to attain until you have broken free of that aggregated experience. The Zen aphorism that our mind is a mirror, but there's dust on it that's blocking the light, applies. Most of the dust is all of that aggregated experience that we are attached to.

For now though, rather than dwell on the past, take this definition of karma from the present into the next moment. In that next moment you have the opportunity to immediately change your karma. Karma is an ongoing, dynamic process. It is completely modifiable right now. If we increase our awareness, our karma—our current state of mind—improves.

But at this moment, since your karma is your current identity, and your identity is the accumulation of everything you've learned from experiences in this and past lives, that can be quite a mountain. The choices you make in this life are overwhelmingly dictated by that mountain. Normally you'd be trapped, living out the rest of your life in pretty much the same state of mind you're now in. That's without practicing meditation and other self-discovery techniques. With them, a tremendous mental freedom not only becomes possible, it becomes your new normal.

That mountain of personal history and reinforced patterns is why you have the desires and aversions you have today, why you are so attached to certain attitudes and not others. Think of them as different trails that run across its slopes.

Self-discovery posits that that mountain is blocking the infinite light of eternity from your perception. We are so used to walking and hiking those trails that we don't even notice that the mountain is actually something that we created. The good news is that we don't have to tear it down, boulder by boulder. We just have to release our perceptual lock on it. This is done by becoming unattached to the desires and aversions that comprise it.

Since karma is changeable now, changing our state of mind in a positive, happier, constructive direction is essentially all that's required to let go of the mountain. With each meditation or selfless act some of it is washed away.

*"There are selfish actions and there are selfless actions. Selfless actions create a higher karma, which brings you into a higher state of mind. When you're in a higher state of mind, you will see things that you never saw before. So for example, you gave money to the United Fund or to your local spiritual cause or whatever it is that turns you on. When you did this—and you could have just kept the money for yourself, or maybe you put in a few extra hours at work so that you could do that—when you did this, you did something noble. This will cause a release of energy. It causes a vibratory shift. It means you're moving into a different plateau of consciousness. Just like there are different roads that lead different places, so there are different levels of awareness that lead different places and we shift in and out of them. These are the ten thousand states of mind that we study in Zen.*

*When you give—let's say you gave to United Fund or your local spiritual cause—when you give, what happens is you go onto a certain highway. That action of giving is in a certain vibratory level, meaning giving exists in a certain plane of consciousness. It's a highway we call giving. To give means you got on that highway. That highway will have a certain view. Let's say that highway runs way up to the top of the mountain. From the top of the mountain, you can see things that you couldn't see on another highway, which was called selfishness.*

*Selfishness is a state of mind. It is a plateau of attention, and it has a certain view. All states of mind have certain views. So in the case of selfishness, now you're on a lower highway and the view is obstructed—you can't see very well, so you might have an accident. On the higher plateau, on the higher highway, you'll suddenly see a career opportunity. You will meet somebody you wouldn't have met. You will attract people who are more selfless. Opportunities will open to you because you can see them. That's what karma really is. Do you follow?*

*Karma means that through your thoughts and feelings and actions, you are generating a state of mind. That state of mind has a view. That view will cause things to happen to you or not happen to you. So the real active force behind action and interaction is state of mind. There is a point, in other words, to noble thoughts and noble actions. It's not simply a moral fantasy....*

*When you meditate and practice zazen, when you stop your thought, when you focus, you're creating karmas. You're shifting your state of mind to a higher vibratory level which will give you a much more expansive view. When you allow desire, anger and frustration to dominate you, you're losing power, your airplane is falling to a lower altitude. If it falls too low, it will crash."*
*(Rama, <u>Zen Tapes</u>, "Karma")*

He also pointed out that good karma doesn't prevent you from living in a war-torn country, but it does sustain you through such terrible times. Your physical situation may be very difficult but your attitude will be good. You'll be better able to handle it.

Another way to think of all of that aggregated experience is to think of each lifetime as a jigsaw puzzle, the kind with many odd-shaped pieces that, when completed, displays a coherent picture. As Rama put it, given your well-established karmic pattern, you're just going to keep putting the puzzle together pretty much the same way in every lifetime. Think about it for a moment: lifetime after lifetime, you've only got the same pieces to work with, i.e. all those past life experiences which have clumped into samskaras, the aggregates that have created the identity you are today.

This is the trap of selfhood. In computer programming terminology, it's an endless loop. Looking at human life from this perspective, the identity we have developed over many incarnations is a bug rather than a feature. It's blocking us from experiencing our complete mind.

*"There are endless realities. William Blake wrote a poem called 'The Mental Traveler,' and that's really kind of what we are. We are a mind that travels. We travel through perception. And we just perceive ourselves in variant forms and variant conditions forever—unless the perceiver can awaken to that fact, realize that everything that they're seeing is a self-reflection. Therefore, it's sort of like an endless jigsaw puzzle that you can put*

*together in endless ways but it always comes out the same way, because you're the one who puts it together and you can only put it together in the way that you know, and there's a limited number of ways that you know.*

*You will put this puzzle together in every lifetime. But you can only put it together in the way that you know. And the way that you know a thousand lives from now won't be intrinsically different. It may have a slightly different order, coloration. This puzzle, in other words, the grooves in the puzzle, you make them what they are; you fit them together. And eventually you create a picture of yourself. Your life is a reflection of your perception of yourself. Everything you do is predicated upon that.*

*.... What people do is they just create a world out of their self-reflection. Then they wonder why they're not happy.... In other words, what keeps us going is the belief that tomorrow will be different, but suppose it won't be? Well, it won't be. No life will be different; eternity isn't different if it's always just a self-reflection. Death does not end self-reflection, it just changes it in an incremental way. But in the next life, the aggregate of the self reassembles and we are pretty much who we were.*

*So metaphysics is the study of how to shift the self. How to get outside of the self-reflection and to just gaze with awe and wonder at the countless universes, the countless celestial radiances of mind, of life, of Enlightenment, nirvana, or God—whatever you want to call it. Power."*
*(Rama, <u>Tantric Buddhism</u>, "Metaphysics")*

Unless you do something to loosen the grip those samskaras have on who you think you are, with each lifetime people can become more stuck in a constricted identity. "Old souls" are not necessarily wise, though those who do seek wisdom over many incarnations can become more open-minded and aware. By practicing meditation you are creating opportunities for freeing your mind of its conditioned limitations. You are using power to free yourself of entrenched desires, attachments, and fears. You are changing your karma.

Also, the fascination people have with who they were in past lives becomes unnecessary, even irrelevant. All those past lives, all those experiences, have rolled forward to create who you are in this life. Knowing the specifics about a single past life, in light of the many thousands you've had, isn't going to make some neurosis disappear. Often our psychological problems are more the result of our childhood and the imprinting we received in this life. Seeing how your current mind works with increasing clarity is what unravels the mess. The search for past life knowledge is no different than any other desire you become attached to.

On a positive note, certain past life aggregates can produce a focus in this life, such as artistic, athletic or scientific abilities. If you've worked on the same thing for many past lives, that may be why you're so interested in it this time. But as Rama pointed out, that latent expertise rarely emerges effortlessly. It might take years of extra effort in something you're very interested in before your "natural" talent emerges into professional mastery.

The secret to having increasingly happy future incarnations is to work on having a happier state of mind in this one. So do things that make you happy now! That doesn't mean the intense pursuit of fulfilling human desires, as discussed earlier. That means learning what your mind is like above the human band of attention.

To unwind your karma you need to shift your current state of mind. There's a way to do that, by recognizing the state of mind you're in and then your level within it:

*"What you can do is determine the state of mind you are in, and the state of mind you are in is heaven or hell. All heavens and hells are within the mind, within your mind. Heaven is a state of awareness. Hell is a state of awareness. There are lots of states in between that are mixtures of both—ten thousand of them, ten thousand states of mind.*

*… All karmas, however, originate in the mind because of mental activity. The types of thoughts that you think create a state of mind. The reason you think the thoughts that you do results from your level of energy or power.... In other words, you can only conceive of what lies beyond the state of mind you're in from the point of view of the state of mind you're in. However, within any state of mind there is a gradation, since all states of mind are basically structurally the same. That gradation will run, we could say, from darkness to light. So, for example, you're in a really confused state of mind. But even in that confusion, there will be a higher and lower end to it....*

*Anyone has the ability, if they choose to—and this is the freedom of perception—to move to the higher end of the state of mind that they're in. From that higher end of the state of mind, they can generate another state of*

*mind, which is successively higher. So by generating good karma, even within the limited state of mind, you can move to the next state of mind, and so on and so forth, up the ascending ladder to the higher states of mind. Or you can move downward by dwelling in the lower states of mind."*
*(Rama, Zen Tapes, "Karma")*

Since your karma is your current state of mind, mindfulness, monitoring the thoughts going through your mind, is a necessary first step. Add a systems analysis of your energy flow, and you have an up-to-the-minute status report of your karma.

Meditation has a special role in modifying karma. When you are truly meditating, i.e. minimal if actually no thought in the mind, you are temporarily liberated from your karma. Rama explained that meditation carries you beyond your karma. While you are meditating you are free of the mountain of all your aggregated experiences. The more still your mind, the more you are in a timeless, unbound moment. You are being filled with clear, totally positive energy that automatically propels you into better states of mind.

By clearing your mind through meditation you enjoy much more beauty and happiness, which by definition is being in the best possible state of mind, i.e. the best karma. Karma is the elemental force that keeps the Wheel of Life turning. Through meditation you are in charge of how it spins for you.

*"While you in your next lifetime will go off to this world or another world—dependent upon your karmas, the actions you performed and the states of mind you've been in will lead to your next rebirth—the Enlightened person isn't bound by anything like that. They are fluid light inside. Oh, you are too, but it's deeper inside you. It hasn't come out yet. A little bit, maybe.*

*Enlightenment puts an end to suffering. Enlightenment is self-knowledge. Most Enlightened people can do what you would call miracles. They know how to use energy on different levels."*
*(Rama, Zen Tapes, "Enlightenment")*

# Chapter 8:  The Biggest Obstacle is Personal History

So far we've covered a sequence of subjects that when taken together give you a good idea of Rama's deeper and broader definition of who and what we are. We started in Chapter 1 with knowing where you are currently located (the desire plane), and the primary process through which you've developed (reincarnation). Chapter 2 presented the fundamental paradox of how most people choose to remain in confused states of mind while a few others go in much happier directions. This provided a redefinition of "free will" and the opportunity which self-discovery offers. Next was his redefinition, in Chapter 3, of our "body" as in fact comprised of three distinct layers, and how they are interdependent. Chapter 4 expanded who you are by discussing your innate psychic capabilities, and how to develop them, particularly seeing.

This led to Chapter 5's detailed explanation of the first meditation method he taught us, implementing one-pointed focusing and concentration which are the cornerstone of all self-discovery techniques. Entering into wonderful states of mind through meditation not only elevates your consciousness, it dramatically increases your internal power level. It becomes very important to learn how to maintain these improvements, which Chapter 6 presented in the systems analysis terms he employed. To round things out, Chapter 7 delved into what karma really is and how it works, thus giving you useful information about the process which has shaped each of us into who we are today and carries us into the future.

So now you have a more accurate picture of who and what you are, and your current place in the universe. Let's finish this phase of understanding ourselves by taking a deeper look at how our identity is developed. The sense of self is what each of us depends on psychologically. That sense of self comes out of our personal history.

*"When the sun sets, beautiful though it may be, billions of stars appear. The ego is but one sun. When that sun sets, there are endless suns, endless horizons beyond it. The sun and the earth are interesting for a while but once we've seen them, it's fun to move on and see what other wonders creation affords us."*
*(Rama, Tantric Buddhism, "Tantric Buddhism")*

Rama compared the challenge of self-discovery to a hot air balloon held down by lots of sand bags. If you want to rise up into the sky, you've got to cut off those sand bags. Those sandbags are your attachments and aversions. The heaviest ones are your personal history, which are filled with the attachments and aversions most important to you, primarily from this lifetime. They may originate from your samskaras, but you are making them even more entrenched.

Keep in mind that all those attachments and aversions are choices you made. This is a desire plane, don't forget. The problem is that everyone takes the entire desire/aversion environment for granted. We naturally assume that this environment is the only option, that it is what life is all about. Instead, what self-discovery assumes is that living within the desire/aversion environment is optional. This is the core of Buddhism. Buddhism claims that it's your choice, and presents an orientation and techniques to make the transition to independence.

*"Nothing burns or hurts you like desire. It destroys everything beautiful in your life."*
*(Rama, Tantric Buddhism, "Buddhism")*

If you look at yourself, you see that most of your personality is dedicated to pursuing desires, and what you like and dislike gives your personality its distinctive character. Getting into a vicious circle of repressing and denying your desires doesn't free you from them. You're still completely attached to those desires, only from the opposite direction. You don't have to fight them, you have to be independent from them. The problem isn't the desire or aversion itself, it is your attachment to it.

It takes a lot of willpower to drop those attachments. The good news is that you're already getting that extra willpower from your daily meditation. Your daily meditation is also increasing your clarity. What if you really saw through this big game and developed some detachment from it? What would your personality be then?

To begin with, it would be more fluid. You would be more interested in being more aware of what's going on than passing judgement all the time. You'd be trying to see more clearly rather than imposing yourself upon every situation.

Before outlining the steps towards freeing yourself from your attachments and aversions, let's look at a particular aspect of childhood that has a disproportionately large impact. It's how the adults who were around you when you were a little child imprinted you. This imprinting is the foundation of the personality edifice in each incarnation.

Imprinting is not some sinister plot, it simply is a basic construct of all human societies:

*"When you were born, you were free. Your attention field, your awareness is not yet formed. Your attention field is the sum total of your experiences from other lives, yes, but yet, it is not conditioned. It is not fully manifested as a seed. Within the seed is the tree….*

*So, when you were born, you were a seed. You were the seed of your past experiences and actions in other theatres of existence, in other worlds, in other lives. Those lives are gone, for all intents and purposes…. The child may not outwardly evidence any of those traits or characteristics yet, but one who sees looks through the physical and temporal and can tell you the potential of a child….*

*Conditioning comes from parents and the adults or others around the child…. The conditions, though, are not so much the geographical areas but the people, the luminous beings who surround the child. Each person has an attention field. Their attention field is the sum total of their awareness and their imprinting. There is normally, in the life of each child, a dominant male and dominant female…. In other words, the male or female that the child has the most exposure to in the first four to six years of its life, particularly the first four, is the primary imprinter of the child. The imprinter of the child will condition the child.*

*Now, a child could have many, many imprinters in those first years. And of course, one is imprinted also in the following years, but the most serious imprinting occurs in those first years….*

*A child is imprinted not by simply teaching, not by saying, 'Johnny, this is a good action, and this is a bad action.' Of course that's an obvious imprinting. But attention is like soft, soft clay, a child's attention field. And the attention fields of adults, in particular, are stratified. They're like hard clay, and they have different shapes, if you could see them inwardly.*

*So imagine that we have a young child, and the body is made of clay. It's very soft. Let's say we take one male and one female, and let's say that the male's shape is square and the female's shape is round. And let's say… we push them on each side of the child's attention field. And let's say that we push the round field of the woman on the left side of the child and the square field on the right side of the child. And we push them in, and push them and push them, and we let them hold there until the clay of the child hardens. Then we back them off, and now the child is imprinted.*

*In other words, nothing has to be said, nothing has to be explained. Just by being around the awareness field of the male or female imprinter, the child is imprinted. The child will also gain imprints, obviously, from others, and in later life—teachers, lovers, husbands, wives. We continue to imprint throughout our lives, but the critical imprinting, the deepest imprinting, occurs in the first four years."*

*(Rama, <u>On the Road with Rama</u>, "Power")*

That's how your personality was formed. Yet while this came from outside of you, it is what you believe to be intrinsic to yourself. As Rama also explained, it might be in conflict in some significant ways with who you developed into over many past lives, despite possibly choosing your parents during the rebirth process. The key point is that this imprinting, such an integral part of human society, does two critical things. Since your parents (or whoever the primary imprinters were) likely believed it, the assumption that the pursuit of desires is the primary activity in life becomes deeply entrenched in your psyche. The other is that many of your deeply held attitudes aren't really yours at all.

*"If your parents were strong in one way and weak in another, you will be strong in the same way and weak in the same way. Even though you may detest the weakness that you saw in them, you will find that you will do exactly the same things in the same situation because they imprinted you. Not by choice. That is to say, they didn't want to give you a weak imprint. They might have wanted the opposite, but they couldn't help themselves. Perhaps they were imprinted in the same way."*
*(Rama, <u>On the Road with Rama</u>, "Power")*

As someone interested in self-discovery, you can see how limiting this is to your growth. The goal is transcendent mental clarity, which means being free of all of the attitudes and behaviors that run on autopilot in your mind. Personal history is like a wall blocking your liberation. As another old Buddhist aphorism puts it, recognition is liberation.

But rather than rail against the whole imprinting process and blaming it for most of your problems in life, it's healthy to understand its value:

*"In mysticism, the first course of action is to do away with the imprinting. We have to take all the imprinting that's occurred to us in this life and wash it. We have to make ourselves soft again and push it all aside. Then, we need to be re-imprinted, but in a different way. Imprinting is important. Without it, we don't survive. The child needs to be imprinted. It seeks it, as a matter of fact. It's essential. The child seeks to be imprinted because it has to have a way of dealing with the world, and those who imprint it obviously have managed to survive in this world. Imprinting is critical....*

*So the mystic, one who studies the ways of power, seeks to end the imprinting process because in imprinting we lose power, we lose attention. We're formatted to do certain things. But obviously the people who imprinted us are not completely happy and they're not completely powerful. If you lived in a world of completely powerful Enlightened beings, then obviously you would have a clean imprint. But we don't. We live in a world filled with poverty, suffering, war and unhappiness and transitory joy. So naturally we receive that imprint, and we have to fight our whole life against that imprinting.*

*But we need a new imprinting. We need the imprinting of Enlightenment, of freedom. And that comes through our association with a higher being. So classically what occurs, is one meets a teacher—one who has knowledge. And that being will teach you how to overcome your old imprinting by changing your way of life and by teaching you the ways of power—how to store it, collect it, amplify it, how to stop losing it. By bringing enough power into your life, you will gradually erase or actually overcome your imprinting.*

*… You will go beyond the teacher's imprint…. In the last stages, you will overcome it. But it won't be something that will hold you back. It will fall away naturally if it was a correct imprint….*

*So it's necessary then to do a systems analysis of your life—to look at where you gain power, where you lose power, and to do the things that empower you and avoid the things that drain you. And then it's necessary to seek out one who can re-imprint you."*
*(Rama, <u>On the Road with Rama</u>, "Power")*

One very important thing to understand about what Rama is explaining here is his use of the word "power." He is specifically referring to the energy gained through meditation or similar activities, and has nothing to with what people do out in the world to try and gain control over others. His definition of power is the energy present in higher states of awareness, in liberating and joyous fields of attention.

Personal history is all the imprinting and all of the experiences you've had in this incarnation. As much as the samskaras from past lives determine who you are in a deeper sense, your personal history in this one looms even larger because you are so aware of it and you identify with it so completely. To you, your personal history has shaped you into the unique individual you've become. It's your biggest attachment, by far.

While that's inevitable as a human being, if you've been meditating and have reached some degree of inner stillness, you've learned that that stillness is also who you are. You've repeatedly experienced a deeper identity independent of your current life experience. And you've found that it feels great, with an inherent level of serenity so different from the tumult of your life in the world. In this world it's mandatory to push your personality forward much of the time.

*"What are you still carrying? Are you still carrying everyone who's insulted you, injured you or in some way defamed you or bothered you or hurt you,*

*attacked you or interfered with you? That's a lot of weight. I'd let it go, personally, and just move on and forget. Whether you forgive or not doesn't matter. Forgiveness is a silly word. Forget is the correct word. Be in the moment. Don't even notice. Personal power means that you can <u>not</u> notice things. You see them in your peripheral vision but they're not worth focusing on because you only get caught up in them, and to get caught up in them distracts you from someplace you want to be—eternal awareness of light.*

*The only issue is, how long will it take you to wake up? As long as you choose; it's completely within your control. The more deeply you meditate, the more quietly you work, the less excuses you make, the more you simplify your life, the less you expect to be happy here, and the more you move your mind into the upward radiances of the ten thousand lights of Enlightenment, the ten thousand radiances of Enlightenment, that's when you'll be happy. All this work is simply to gain the mental control to put the mind in alignment with the ten thousand radiances of Enlightenment and experience them in various gradations forever. That's our only purpose. All of this is only to do that."*

*(Rama, <u>Tantric Buddhism</u>, "The Mature Monk")*

So the question becomes, who are you without all that personal history? What happens to your sense of self? What happens to your identity? How do you keep making the transition to less bound versions of self? The answer is the Caretaker Personality paradigm.

Rama presented the Caretaker Personality as the replacement for personal history. Like most everything he taught us, we were not supposed to impulsively jump into it, but begin by applying it in certain situations at certain times, and then as we understood and experienced its psychological and spiritual benefits, gradually utilize it more fully. It may seem like an unusual idea, but not really. Most people already adjust or shift their personality, in limited degrees, depending on the demands of different situations.

With a caretaker personality we intentionally forget about whom we normally see ourselves as. We may become like an innocent child or a courageous warrior. We're temporarily letting go of our attachments and aversions and adopting a role that is not fixated on protecting who we think we are.

*"The reason you think is not just habitual, it's not just a habit. It's because you're being pushed and pulled by attachments. Only when they are gone will your mind know peace and will you be able to stop thought. Teaching a person to stop thought does not simply involve practice. I know many people who have practiced meditation diligently for 30 or 40 years who can't go into samadhi. That is because they have not let go of their attachments. They have not gone through the training necessary in self-discovery to let go of everything that one must let go of. Only then will thought stop completely. Only after you've overcome jealousy, fear, anxiety, hatred—all of these things, at least for a time, can be set aside—only then will thought stop, along of course, with using the will to stop thought."*

*(Rama, <u>Insights: Talks on the Nature of Existence</u>, "Modular Mysticism: The Sorcerer's Explanation")*

For self-discovery, the usefulness of adopting caretaker personalities is two-fold: first, what we're doing is freeing ourselves from the trap of self-reflection, and second, if the ego gets too possessive, progress in self-discovery stops.

Naturally your self-reflection changes as you progress in your self-discovery. That's endemic to meditation; by pulling higher light into your mind you are modifying your self-reflection every time you meditate. If you've meditated well, you are a different, more aware person every time, even though you probably won't be conscious of it. Your self-reflection is a normal human function in the mind that is running constantly in the background. It's your identity. But your meditation and other self-discovery work makes it outdated.

The basic reason for self-discovery is that you want to greatly improve your level of awareness. However, as you increase your level of awareness, it's very likely that you're coming into conflict with your imprinting as well as samskaras.

At some point you might experience inner conflict over this growing dichotomy. You might retreat back into your less aware self. In reality, that's your ego feeling threatened. The ego is a formidable edifice constructed of your imprinting and accumulated experiences in this incarnation, resting on a foundation of deeply entrenched past life patterns. It is your personality in all its glory; it's who you think you are.

A big part of the challenge of self-discovery, even just taking up meditation, is dealing with your ego. It is necessary, over time, for your ego to let go of its dominance of your identity, because it blocks your self-discovery. In the <u>Bhagavad Gita</u>, one of Hinduism's oldest and most important texts, Sri Krishna points out that out of the millions of people who aspire to become Enlightened, only a handful don't give up. This is why.

The ego is completely vested in your current human personality. That normally results in becoming more rigid, more self-righteous. If you can permit yourself to use personality in a more fluid way, you can minimize the blockage. Instead, re-envision personality as a big garage full of different cars that you have a choice of driving. Select the vehicle that best suits the current weather and road conditions.

Rama discussed several prototype caretaker personalities for us to adopt in different situations. Not only would these enable us to deal much more effectively with difficult situations, they would loosen the grip of our entrenched personal history on our growth. As mentioned earlier, the ones he thought were most beneficial were an innocent child, and a courageous warrior.

It's important to understand that each of these were appropriate only for certain circumstances. The caretaker personality of an innocent child is definitely not for dealing with conflict; it would be utilized when alone in nature, or comparably safe situation. The caretaker personality of the courageous warrior has obvious applications in confrontations, but must be attuned to a sense of inner strength and self-sacrifice. There were a few others, but he recommended trying those only after many years of meditation. They include the inquisitive student, which would be an efficient way to handle certain professional or social situations, and the sage, although this is not to be used until you know you're not faking it.

*"The caretaker personality of the child is innocence. Just think of the idyllic, if you will, qualities of the child—excitement, love, trust, humility, purity, joy. I'm speaking of a very young child, a very good child, about age four—the child who looks with wonder and awe at all of the world, who sees magic in everything, who is not preoccupied with her or himself, who becomes absorbed totally in the moment....*

*You can use this caretaker personality—in other words you can enter into this mode of consciousness, you can choose to do so—when you're with friends whom you can trust; who love you and whom you love; when you're with yourself; when there's no one else around; in other words, when it's safe.*

*… But when you deal with the world more directly, I suggest the caretaker personality of the warrior. The warrior is calm and efficient. The warrior uses discipline. The warrior is happy. The weapon of the warrior is laughter. The warrior learns to be impeccable, to use her or his life as a way of attaining liberation….*

*The warrior never feels sorry for him or herself. If the warrior has to be upset, the warrior does so alone, and when the warrior goes out with others the warrior smiles. The warrior doesn't have time for self-indulgence, for self-pity…. The warrior has true humility, if the warrior is a spiritual warrior, and the courage and cunning to succeed in even the most difficult of situations. If you adopt this caretaker personality when you're in the world, then you'll find it very easy to effectively deal with the world."*
*(Rama, <u>The Lakshmi Series</u>, "The Caretaker Personality")*

Going even further, he presented a special caretaker personality meditation that came directly out of your psychic development:

*"As you meditate and practice your gazing exercises, you'll become more and more psychic, and you'll be able to see beyond the surface, within people. And you'll start to understand on deeper levels how they work. Examine their personality structures. In other words, everybody's evolved one if not more caretaker personalities already. There are nothing but caretaker personalities. There is no real personality. And once you realize that, it's easy to change from one personality form to another. It's fun.*

*So begin to look at the caretaker personality structures. In other words, don't view a person as just a person. They are just a caretaker personality that they've woven in this lifetime or has been woven for them that they wear. They may have several, and inside there's something else entirely. It's just a cover.*

*So look at them and see if there's anything you like in them. And if there is, add it to yours. If there's something that you don't like in others you probably don't like it in yourself, and delete it. Be an architect of your own being. Design a new you. It's fun.*

*And probe even deeper beyond the caretaker personality into that absolute reality within. That is your essence and your substance, from which all things come forth and to which all things return. That's what we really are. The luminous totality, nirvana. Meditate on that and you will be free.*

*There is a particular meditation technique that will help you do all of this, and I'd like to describe it to you. It's pretty simple and if you practice it once in a while, I think it'll help.*

*When you're sitting down to meditate, relax, sit-up nice and straight, in a chair or on the floor, any way that you're comfortable. The back should be straight. And start your meditation.*

*Then I'd like you to close your eyes, and visualize the sky filled with stars. Now this is a little astral travel. Imagine that you're going to leave your body and go right up into the stars. And as you go through the stars you're going to change. Your earthly personality is going to fall away. And now your etheric self will be there, your subtle physical self, your astral self.*

*Now you're going to go above the stars into other dimensions, and you're going to go through them really quickly, one after another. They're all going to be different colors, and you're going to kind of zip through them, and just feel yourself going through them. Needless to say this is not actually a visualization, you're actually doing it.*

*And as you go through each one, more and more of the self that you've been is going to fall away. And your being will get clearer and clearer. As you go through these dimensional planes, the parts of you that are from them will go back to them.*

*Finally you'll get above all the dimensional planes and you'll enter into a flux, a kind of a golden, luminous light. It doesn't really move, nor is it still. There's no direction, no dimension, and you're going to go right into that. It's like going right into the heart of the sun. And merge with that, be that.*

*Feel yourself in that, get lost in it. Study it, be it. Stop your thoughts, be still. Just hold yourself in it with your whole psyche and all your power as long as you can. And then gradually feel you're coming back down after a couple of minutes or a few seconds, as long as you can be in that totality. Just imagine it.*

*Come back to those dimensional planes, and as you do, you're going to come back shiny and clear. As you pass through each color and each dimensional plane you're going to take on new qualities, new hope, new belief, new power. Finally, down through the stars and onto the Earth. A strong, new, radiant self. The right self will come back with you, the right caretaker personality.*

*Don't worry about what it is, it'll just be from then. Visualize that, practice that. It really works. Spend about ten minutes on it, fifteen minutes each time you do it. Five minutes going up maybe, five minutes there, five coming down. Or whatever, you don't have to time it. Maybe just a minute or two to start with, then increase the time. Eventually it'll become timelessness. Good luck, have fun."*

*(Rama, <u>Psychic Development</u>, "The Caretaker Personality")*

Now you have a fuller picture of your mind and how to open some of its doors. The rest of the book builds upon this foundation as the next stages of the self-discovery process unfold.

# Chapter 9:  Transience and the Tibetan Rebirth Process

What if you were perpetually happy? What if the feeling you experienced during some wonderful moment never ended?

The simple fact that that's not the case here on Earth tells you a lot. In Buddhist, Hindu, and Taoist literature, they all position sentient life as lacking an unchanging, never-ending state of happiness in physical reality. They give it a name—the samsara—the always changing reality. This is in contrast with the highest, purest level of consciousness—nirvana—which actually is beyond consciousness itself. On some of the Wheel of Life Tibetan thangkas, Rama pointed out that there's a Buddha in an upper corner pointing away from the Wheel. In other words, skip the experiences on the Wheel of Life and go directly to nirvana. Much better, as he succinctly put it.

We take for granted that everything dies here. We don't really think about it. We mourn the loss of a loved one, or are saddened by a fatal plane crash or some other disaster. And then go on about our business.

It's obvious that for all living things on Earth, life is temporary. Everything that is born, dies. But that's a subset; transience applies to all experiences. Transience not only is apparent in the fact that every living thing will cease living at some point, but each and every experience we have is transient. Each experience arises, occurs, and then disappears, just like we do.

So all experiences have a beginning and an end. From the fact that each day lasts for 24 hours, to eating dinner, what we call Reality is dominated by transience.

*"Nothing works here in the transient. Everything changes, everything shifts. If you bother to study the nature of reality, if you wake up for a moment and look around at life, you will observe that nothing here lasts, nothing works out. There are no happy endings. There are happy moments. But everything culminates in death; all accomplishments are washed away by death or by the next moment."*
*(Rama, Tantric Buddhism, "Buddhist Yoga")*

People generally don't consider this at all. Instead, they spend most of their lives believing that by pursuing the acquisition of material things they will reach a permanently idyllic happiness. That's not how life works. What is recorded History but the proof of the transience of all human endeavor?

We want to hold onto something and never lose it, but that's not the nature of sentient existence. Everything we become attached to changes and sooner or later we no longer have it. We suffer from the loss. As the Buddha pointed out, in this world of transience all attachments lead to suffering.

Looking into it more deeply, transience is half of a perceptual paradox:

*"Buddhism is essentially the establishment of one's mind in that which is ineffable. Ineffable meaning it does not appear to be solid, but actually is much more solid than that which appears to be solid, which is actually much more ineffable. The world that we say is solid, knock on wood, is transient. Nothing here lasts. The wood doesn't last; the whole planet won't last forever. But on the other hand, that which is ineffable, which is the world of light—meaning it's hard to see at first, can't perceive it through the senses— that lasts forever; it's always been and will always be. And its very nature is happiness, ecstasy. So if we take our time and, rather than building up some huge fortune which then is swept away, we take our time and instead invest in stocks that are infinite, as opposed to finite, then we get to enjoy them forever."*
*(Rama, Tantric Buddhism, "Buddhism")*

Rather than seeing transience as a depressing fact of life everyone must grapple with their entire life, Rama suggested looking at it from the perspective of being immortal, as a mind in this current physical body that wants to reach the essence of what they really are. In other words, take advantage of this situation for spiritual progress (which is what Tantric Buddhism is all about):

*"When we meditate we stop our thought. When your thought stops, the mind is perfect. There is no transience. No thought, no transience. That's what is eternal—when there is no thought, no sense of self and no impressions. That's eternity—what you feel, that reality that you are. That's eternal. That's beyond transience. That's what we really are, of course. Yet, surprise—we get to have two bodies, a transient body and an eternal body. We forget about the eternal body when we're really caught up in the transient body, and things appear very frightening from the transient body's point of view because it knows it's going to die, it knows it's going to dissolve and it's afraid of that. But if we switch to the eternal body, if we bring up and wake up our eternal awareness, then there's nothing very frightening about being transient because we realize it's only a part of us that is transient.*

*... We can't really say that we are the transient part. I mean for a short time, sure. For a little while I'm a body, I'm a mind, I'm a personality, I'm a fear, I'm a desire, I'm an anguish, I'm a love, I'm a hate, I'm a dispassion. Whatever it is that we're experiencing at any given moment, well, that's who we are for a short time, as short as a moment or as short as a lifetime. But that's not really who we are. I mean we can't really just be who we are for a moment. That's more like a place we pass through; it's a location.*

*We're travelers, we're mental travelers. We're a mind in time and space. When we drive through an area, we don't say that we're the area. We're the one who drives through. So I don't really think we can say that we are who we experience at any given moment in any given lifetime, because we're just driving through. We're driving through moments. We're driving through bodies, through selves. It helps to know this. The only way you can know it, really, is to meditate. When you meditate you stop thought. When there's no thought, that's eternity. That's the eternal part.*

*To conceptually know this is just another moment that you're driving through. You're driving through the moment when you knew this. Then you'll forget it, and then you'll experience the fear, the obsessions of a transient moment, mistaking it for reality. Whereas when you know that you're driving through, you're just passing through as the song says, then it doesn't matter so much. It matters for a moment, just like driving through any place matters for the moment that you're there. You're there. But the confusion of self is that we mistake ourselves for where we are. We are not the body. We're not the personality. We're eternity, which is passing through all this, all these wonderful forms that we see that we call life. We're the formless. The formless."*

*(Rama, <u>Tantric Buddhism</u>, "Transience")*

So how do we become more conscious of being the eternal part rather than the transient part? Tantric Buddhism's answer is to apply the fact of being transient to your current identity. The way to leverage transience in order to accelerate your progress on the pathway to Enlightenment is to go through many lifetimes in a single lifetime. That's the alternative to living out each incarnation as the same person you were born as, with the same samskaras and a single imprinting you stay within until you die.

You can repurpose the rules of sentient existence to your self-discovery advantage. That, in fact, is a key element of Tantric Buddhism, always trying to utilize the existing conditions to advance your spiritual growth, rather than just suffer through whatever worldly experience you find yourself in. So take the all-encompassing fact of transience and apply it to your desire for Enlightenment. If every experience arises, exists, and then disappears, why wait for physical death to undergo an uplifting transformation? Rather than wait until death to transform once, why not do it many times within a single human incarnation?

The term "each new self" is often used in books about meditation and spiritual growth, and it's usually applied in a casual way. But it is a core concept that is implemented over and over again in Tantric Buddhism. It is the hallmark of self-discovery. So the way to capitalize on transience to accelerate your spiritual progress is what Rama called the Tibetan Rebirth Process:

*"The Tibetan rebirth process involves the choosing of a caretaker personality. Now as you know, the personality in most cases is formed early in life—the initial experiences that we have with our parents, particularly in the teaching of language, language being a set of loaded dice. Our experiences in the world with friends, family, and so on, and the propensities of the soul and karmas cause us to create a personality, a sense of self. 'I am an individual. I am special.'....*

*Most people are stuck with the same personality all their lives. In the process of self-discovery, it's not only possible but necessary to dissolve your personality. The idea is that through a series of, let's say, a thousand lifetimes, you will go through a thousand personality structures. Each personality structure would be slightly more advanced than the preceding personality structure. Each would be more fluid... the soul progresses. It grows spiritually as it moves toward Enlightenment.*

*The secret teachings of the oral traditions suggest that it's possible to take the thousand lifetimes it would have taken to become conscious of consciousness, and to compress it into one lifetime. With the aid of the benign forces and God and an Enlightened teacher, and with proper motivation and proper evolution, you can do that. Therefore, what you will do is create a series of personalities. This is where it gets fun....*

*As we go within the self, we discover that all the voices of our past lives are still there. They still exist. As we peel ourselves, which is a process very much like peeling an onion—it's often compared to that—we discover that there are many selves within the self.... And you will find, as you progress, that these selves will begin to come out....*

*So the selves come out, and we see that we're not one self. It's fascinating. Jung was moving a little bit in this direction in his research with his archetypes, although he just scratched the surface. We are many, many selves. We're not just a finite being. These selves don't necessarily speak in words; it's not like channeling or bringing some force through you. But they are you. You just become more conscious that you're much more complex than you realized. It's necessary then, to design new personalities as you progress.*

*What makes this possible is the kundalini."*
*(Rama, Insights: Talks on the Nature of Existence, "Modular Mysticism: Tibetan Yoga and the Secret Doctrine")*

From a self-discovery standpoint, a major structural problem with the normal round of birth, death, and rebirth is that with each new physical incarnation, you are imprinted and are socialized into the family, culture and country where you are born. That takes up the first 20 years, and then you begin again to wash away all that conditioning in order to go further in your multi-life self-discovery process. So if you can go through multiple selves in a single lifetime, you don't have to go through as many of those 20 year socialization periods, and the years after that to transcend it all.

As much as desire dominates humanity, fear does too. Much of the time people individually as well as entire societies collectively use fear as a primary motivator. Although in reality death is only a doorway, it is the ultimate fear people have. The Tibetan rebirth process goes straight into the center of that fear and shatters it. You're afraid of dying at the end of this one lifetime? Then let's do it many times in this one lifetime! Let's use the fact of transience in this world as a vehicle for rapid spiritual growth.

This is the real opportunity presented at the time of death. However, our capability to take advantage of this opportunity is greatly diminished by our attachments, by all of the personal history we keep holding on to:

*"At the time of death, at the moment of death and shortly thereafter, there is a moment when you are set face to face with the clear light of reality. In other words you will see, shortly after your death, this incredible light and this light is so bright in its appearance that it frightens most persons. When you see this light, while initially you may be attracted to it, suddenly you'll be seized with fear and you'll try to run away from that light. If you had been able to accept and embrace that light without running towards it or away from it, in other words, if you could be neither attracted nor repulsed by that light, then you would pass on to spiritual liberation.*

*It's kind of like asking you to keep your composure in the middle of a nuclear test, when you're at ground zero, and as you watch your being being atomized and vaporized to just be calm, relaxed and happy. If you still have any fears at that time, they will come out. At the moment of death when you're set face to face with the clear light of reality, with the essence of existence, if you still have any attachments to this world, people, desires, they will all come out. All these things will arise. They will all stand before you and it's necessary for you to be neither attracted nor repulsed by any of them. If you are, which most people are, you will then drop to a lower level."*
*(Rama, The Lakshmi Series, "The Tibetan Rebirth Process")*

The Tibetan rebirth process is only possible if you have made the conceptual leap to see it as something quite feasible. You only see it as feasible by spending enough time in complete stillness during meditation. If you really do see through the desires and attachments that have defined you, when you let go of them and feel free in a deep sense, then the Tibetan rebirth process becomes a natural thing to do. You don't have to be talked into it.

Rama made it clear that normally you must be meditating at an advanced level in order to be able to engage in the Tibetan rebirth process. You would have to be going into salvikalpa samadhi, which means keeping the mind perfectly still to the point where you enter what in Chapter 1 was called the "unmanifest" level, the level above heaven. But before you get to that stage, first you need to get very good at mindfulness, let go of attachments and desires with conviction, and learn to be inaccessible. Then you are ready to restructure your life in more serious ways, which is facilitated by the Enlightened teacher. When you're ready, the Enlightened teacher carefully lets you experience some of the dissolution process sooner.

*"It is necessary to learn to dissolve your old self, that's the first step. To dissolve your old self you must first want to. You have to sense the need for a higher rebirth. You're willing to let your old personality wash away in the clear light of eternity. You don't have to choose a new self. You see the trick of the reentry process, that is to say—let's say you can meditate very, very well and go into salvikalpa samadhi. If you go into samadhi, at that time your old self will actually dissolve. Samadhi, that type of meditation, is such a powerful state of existence, your old self dissolves; it's gone. Now getting rid of your old self is the easy part, in my estimation....*

*So you sit down and you meditate and let's say you go into salvikalpa samadhi. You're absorbed in eternity. Bam! The old self goes away and you don't exist for a while. It's exactly the same as death. In other words, what I'm saying is that you can die in this lifetime without your body having to die and experience everything you would experience at death. I do that hundreds of times a day now. The tricky part is not that, but that suddenly there'll be a new self born. It will be you. Oh, your memories and everything will still be swimming around, you're not going to lose all that. I mean you're not going to walk out into the world unable to function or anything, but the actual structure, the weave of your energies that hold you together, that make you what you are, will be loosened for a while in samadhi. Then they will reform. The trick is to let them reform by themselves. The mistake that most people make when they have a high spiritual experience is they are attracted back to their old lifestyle, their old habits and their old ways....*

*Now, you do not actually have to wait until you can individually go into samadhi to do this. That's the advantage of an Enlightened teacher. The reason that they say you should have an Enlightened teacher is, of course, not just because the teacher can point things out, but the teacher has a power. When you meditate with an Enlightened person, even though you are not capable of going into samadhi yourself, if you're a good meditator and if you've taken the teacher's advice and swept the island of your being and put yourself together and made yourself lucid and pliable and eager and inspired and happy and balanced, when you've gone through the basic years of self-discovery and not just walked through them but done well with them, then when you meditate with a teacher, if you have a self-realized teacher, the teacher's meditation can be so powerful that it actually dissolves your self. Then for a period of about a week—it depends how powerful the teacher is, but usually for about a week maximum—the glue that holds together your personal form will become loose and then it is possible for you to reenter.*

*So, instead of taking another hundred incarnations of spiritual practice to be able to go into samadhi by yourself, if you can be accepted by and work with an Enlightened teacher, and if you're really gung ho, the teacher can give you that experience in this life. The advantage to having that experience in this life is not just that the experience of samadhi is enjoyable, but it allows you to make that big step, and the teacher doesn't do that with you once but again and again and again. The teacher can just lift up the curtain of immortality so you can peek under and get a view, but then you have to put yourself back together.*

*Now the way you reenter, which is the tricky part, is by not trying. If you try too hard to rebuild yourself it won't work because any image you can project or think of will be limited. So rather than following an image you project, let God work through you, to select for you. Rather, in other words, than having to do, you just have to stay out of the way. The river knows exactly how to flow. Your job is simply, during that period of time, to neither be attracted nor repulsed by any ideas, not to seek your old ways nor shun them, but just to allow eternity to reorder your being....*

*So the way to a successful rebirth, then, is by not doing, not trying, which doesn't mean that you're not active in the world and at your job and working. It means internally, not what you're doing physically. Physically, we drive our cars and go places and so on, but while that show is going on there's an inner show going on. Your mind is talking, thoughts and emotions are passing through you and the trick is not to hook on to any of them while you're in this very fragile intermediate state, and just not be afraid of the light."*
*(Rama, <u>The Lakshmi Series</u>, "The Tibetan Rebirth Process")*

# Chapter 10:  Meditation, Part Two: Merge

*"Intermediate meditation is about experiencing the happiness that's inside your mind."*
*(Rama, The Enlightenment Cycle, "Intermediate Meditation")*

After the recognition that suffering is intrinsic to human existence, and that it is caused by attachment to desire, the third of Buddha's Four Noble Truths states that there is a way out of suffering. Rama modified the fourth, traditionally termed the Eightfold Path, to be meditation, since meditation is the foundation upon which all aspects of the Eightfold Path are fully actualized. In addition, Rama's view of Buddhism redefined it not as a religion but in more universal terms: if you meditated, you were a Buddhist. The word "buddha" simply means "Enlightened mind," which anyone of any religion could be interested in. Meditation is the essential method for reaching the awareness of Enlightened mind within you.

In the first meditation method, a daily session is split between focusing on an external object with the eyes open and focusing internally on a chakra with the eyes closed. The goal is the development of your mind's ability to concentrate one-pointedly, without which it is impossible to sustain a period unbroken by thought. Using the Sri Yantra as the visual focus object has the added advantage of illustrating a calming geometric balance as well as its access to higher, peaceful dimensions. The focus on each chakra raises the kundalini from the base of the spine up to that location in the subtle body, which immediately moves your awareness from the ego, from an individualized identity, into an area of your higher mind. You are leaving the island of your worldly life and swimming out into the ocean of eternity. That's not an exaggeration.

*"When you meditate, always try and be hopeful. It's very important. It's necessary to realize the infinite possibilities that life offers you at any moment. Most people are engaged in a limited dharma. They are traversing in a given lifetime through a sequence of possible events, but the events are not too widely chartered in the sense that the possible variations within that sequence are limited. Meditation offers us the prospect of changing that. The suggestion is that instead of staying with the destiny that you have now, that you've incurred through previous karmas, actions in this life and other lives— family, social position, economic or religious background, racial background—it's possible to transcend all of that and within the structure of a lifetime to be born again many times."*

*(Rama, Insights: Talks on the Nature of Existence, "Modular Mysticism: Tibetan Yoga and the Secret Doctrine")*

In this second meditation method, you are using your strengthened focusing ability to go further into the upper reaches of your mind. You focus on those same three chakras, only now within a single meditation session, and without the yantra. You keep the eyes closed the entire time, focusing on each chakra in the same sequence, each for about 20 minutes for an hour-long meditation. You begin at the navel chakra, go next to the heart chakra, and finish at the third eye, while listening to music composed for this sequence.

In this method you are meditating twice a day, in the morning and in the evening, or optionally later at night. As explained in Chapter 5, meditating in the morning before you engage with the world is critically important. In doing so you clear your mind and empower it by connecting to higher dimensions within you. That also fills your aura with light, which serves as a shield protecting you from any problematical energies encountered during the day. For the evening meditation, meditating at sunset is always good; that's when there's a transition between day and night. Rama called it "the crack between the worlds." Optionally, meditating late at night can be very strong because it's quieter then. It's easier simply because as people go to bed, there are far fewer human thoughts in the psychic environment. Also, at night an entirely different set of dimensions become more accessible than those readily available in the morning.

It'll be different every time, but the important thing is to focus equally on each of the three chakras so that they are in balance. You may gravitate towards a particular chakra, but that's only a superficial and temporary preference and is not important. The goal is to merge equally with each one. All of the higher dimensions accessed in a proper meditation are wonderful; think of them as facets of the same diamond.

As long as the mind is noisy you can't feel the deeper, serene, and empowering energies which are, in fact, part of your mind. The chakras are access points to very high, powerful and clear dimensions in our mind. In some literature these are referred to as the causal dimensions, those closest to nirvana. By focusing on the chakras with music also connected to those dimensions we're going much deeper into the meditative state.

As Rama carefully explained, meditation does not build a "substratum modification" of our ego mind and its conditioned perceptual system and intellect, but instead provides the entrance into higher states of mind and awareness that are beyond the socially engineered limits of human consciousness.

As in the yantra concentration meditation method, sit up straight, either on the floor or in a chair, so that the energy naturally flows up the spine. As also mentioned before, don't meditate lying down; the body's enjoyment of resting takes over. By now your meditation room or place in your bedroom should have a nice reservoir of good energy. Now in this second stage of meditation, we're adding an evening meditation to the morning one. Now you are meditating before and after your mind has engaged with the world.

The addition of some very specific music that Rama composed with the band Zazen, three of his students who were accomplished musicians, makes it easier and more transformational.

*"What I have done is create two albums—there are others, but these two in particular…. 'Enlightenment' and 'Canyons of Light' are like having a private Enlightened teacher. I have infused each of the albums with the light of Enlightenment and with a tremendous amount of kundalini. The composition of the work actually came out of 30 different dimensions. Each song is actually—I can't explain how it is done, but let's just say that it's hooked up to a certain dimensional access point. So when you listen to the songs, the level is actually there of a particular universe, a very high plane, and it will lift you up, if you can just listen to it, into these higher dimensions,*

*the same way it would if you were meditating with me or with another Enlightened teacher.*

*So when you put on the tape or the disc, essentially you're sitting down with an Enlightened teacher and meditating with them. They're holding a plane for four minutes and you experience it as you focus on a chakra and you shift to another and another. Gradually, the kundalini rises from the base of the spine to the third eye, opening up the chakras, in the morning and of course in the evening.*

*After you meditate, after you finish the session, always bow….We just like to offer our meditation to the universe. And sit still for a couple of minutes. Relax. Never judge or analyze a meditation. Just do it. Focus as hard as you can on the chakras while you meditate."*
*(Rama, <u>The Enlightenment Cycle</u>, "Meditation")*

The reason for adding this music was to solve the problem of making substantial progress in meditation in such an overcrowded and mentally noisy world, where it's much more difficult to find and then remain in higher states:

*"It is kind of tricky to meditate in this age, in short, and I've figured out a way to do it, to make it easy for you. It's to meditate to music…. There's one for morning meditation and one for evening meditation. There are 15 songs on each album. They're about four minutes each. And each album is designed to provide a morning or an evening meditation. The 'Enlightenment' tape is for morning meditation. 'Canyons of Light' is for evening meditation….*

*Each of the 15 songs has been composed around a dimension, and they're in ascending order. The morning tape offers you an experience of 15 different higher dimensions of light that provide the energy, the insight, and the power to go out and have a wonderful day. The evening meditation tape, "Canyons of Light," references 15 other dimensions that are easier to get into at night, and you'll go very high in them. It's easier to meditate at night because in the evening people shut down. They get kind of quiet. They go home, fall asleep. And the dimensions that are available—some are easier to get to at night, some in the morning. The "Enlightenment" tape is an hour long. If you are new to meditation, you might just want to meditate for half that time until you get your pace and your stamina built up, and then do the hour. The hour is great.*

*So you might sit down in the morning, put on the tape and listen to Zazen, which is the name of our music group composed of myself and three other students of mine. Zazen is a Japanese word. It means to sit in silence, to listen, to be aware of everything and nothing and what's beyond both. Zazen is also sitting meditation in Zen Buddhism.*

*If you sit, if you make your mind quiet, if you're still and you listen to the music, the music will do two things. One, it will provide kind of an auric blanket. The energy in the music is very high. I've gone to very high planes of consciousness, into samadhi, to bring a certain power into the music as a whole. When you put on the tape, the energy is so high in it that it will simply block out the thoughts and impressions of the people in this world so you will just be safe. It's as if you're sitting in a pristine environment in a beautiful power spot with no impressions. It's very easy to touch the other worlds. But, secondly, all the songs are in groups of five. In other words, there are three groups of five on the first and three groups of five on the second album. And the songs reference particular chakras.*

*A word about chakras, energy centers, the subtle body and the doorways to infinity. There are three primary meridians in the body…. The three lower chakras are the power chakras and when you start to meditate, you should meditate first on the navel center. By meditating on your navel center you'll bring up the Ki, the kundalini, from the lower centers. It will come up from the lower two centers, and it's very easy to enter the navel center and bring the power up to that spot.*

*So for the first five songs in the morning or evening tape, meditate on your navel center. Simply hold your attention—feel the area around your navel, about an inch below. If you have never done this before, if you are new to the process, simply place your fingertips of the right or left hand about an inch below your navel and press very gently.*

*Now close your eyes and feel the spot. The first few times you meditate like this, you can keep your fingers there if it helps you. It's not necessary to really visualize anything. You don't have to hold a picture in your mind. Simply feel the spot. As you become adept at meditation, you'll have no trouble feeling the spot because there will be tremendously beautiful surges of energy, of kundalini energy, around that chakra. But in the beginning, sometimes it's helpful just to put the fingers there—very gently.*

*Hold your attention on the navel area and listen to the five songs. Each of the first five songs is very different and they are designed in an ascending order. They reference different planes of light, and you move from one to another and climb up the ladder of light just by listening to them. Then when those five songs have ended, move your attention to the center of your chest.*

*The next chakra up is called the heart chakra. It's in the center of the chest. If you hold your attention there—same thing. If you want to, you can put your fingers there and apply a little pressure. Hold your attention on the center of your chest, gently press very lightly and listen to the next five songs.*

*The chest center, the heart chakra, and the chakra above it—the throat center at the base of the throat—are the centers of balance, of happiness. The best chakra, the easiest to activate, is the heart center, and it will also pick up the throat center for you. If you hold your attention there for five songs, you'll feel tremendous happiness, brightness. You might see vivid colors. You might feel sensations of lightness. But if you just listen deeply, you'll stop thought. The same thing will happen with your navel center and with the third eye.*

*After you have listened to the five songs—now you have gone through ten, you've moved up to a much higher plane of energy, climbing up the latticework of light, of dimensions—hold your attention on the third eye. Your third eye, which is between your eyebrows and slightly above, the agni chakra, is a center of knowledge. The third eye and the crown center, which is at the very top of the head, are the knowledge centers.*

*The three meridians are power; balance, which is happiness; and knowledge, or wisdom. When you bring all three together, you are complete.*

*There are five songs, of which the last five reference the higher chakras. Simply listen to them, keep your attention on the third eye. When thought comes in and out of your mind, ignore it. Simply listen to the music. Don't get frustrated if your mind is restless. There's a lot of energy in the world, and it takes patience to learn how to meditate."*
*(Rama, The Enlightenment Cycle, "Meditation")*

(Both "Enlightenment" and "Canyons of Light" can also be downloaded for free in MP3 format at https://www.ramatalks.com/meditation-

music/zazen.html, or at
https://www.imeditate.com/rama/meditation_music.html. The
"Enlightenment" album can be played for free through Soundcloud on the
Rama Meditation Society site,
https://www.ramameditationsociety.org/Enlightenment-0. It can be
purchased as a CD online at Amazon,
https://www.amazon.com/Enlightenment-Zazen-1995-01-
24/dp/B01G4CSHBQ/ref=sr_1_10?dchild=1&keywords=Zazen+%22Enlighten
ment%22&qid=1627163248&sr=8-10. "Canyons of Light" can be purchased
as a CD online at Amazon, https://www.amazon.com/Canyons-Light-
Zazen/dp/B000003IOL/ref=sr_1_1?dchild=1&keywords=Zazen+%22Canyons
+of+Light%22&qid=1627163104&sr=8-1. There is a third album they
recorded for both morning and evening meditation entitled "Samadhi." It
can be played for free through Soundcloud on the Rama Meditation Society
site, https://www.ramameditationsociety.org/free-resource/samadhi, as
well as be downloaded for free in M4A format on the Rama Meditation
Society site, https://www.ramameditationsociety.org/free-
resource/samadhi.)

The sustained concentration on the music and the chakra together is absolutely essential. But it's not an obsessive intensity. It is being alert and observant in a calm way. You're not doing this with your personality. The personality, your ego self, will try to intrude repeatedly. The way to thwart this interference is by merging with the chakra and immersing yourself completely in the music.

The yantra meditation method greatly strengthened the concentration capability of your mind. Without the ability to concentrate one-pointedly and sustain your focus on each chakra and the music, you won't be able to do this method. You'll find that you lose interest after a little while—the mind will simply wander. If that happens, just bring your mind back to the chakra and dive back into the music. Remember that you are curious, and they are so inviting and beneficial that you want to merge with them both.

You are focusing on three special access points into your higher mind. You should be staring deeply into each chakra, as if you can see a light at the end of a tunnel.

*"What's happening as you listen to each song—the first five songs for the navel center, the second five songs for the heart center and the third five*

*songs for the third eye—is you are bringing the kundalini energy up through concentration. The chakras are doorways to different dimensions, to different planes of Enlightenment. As you hold your attention on them, the kundalini energy at the base of the spine will gradually rise, first to the navel center, then to the heart center, then to the third eye.*

*The crown center is a little bit different. It's not connected to the other centers. When you open it, you go into samadhi, into very advanced states of attention. It takes many, many years of practice to be able to activate the crown center, so I wouldn't be too concerned about it at this time. Just bringing the kundalini energy eventually up to the third eye will release a tremendous amount of energy, brightness and beauty into your life. Your mind will become clear. Your life will become centered. You'll be able to use higher aspects of mind, have inner dimensional experiences, and learn to be a little bit silly and smile about even very difficult things. You'll gain knowledge and power. All kinds of wonderful things will happen just from meditating on these three chakras to the music."*
*(Rama, <u>The Enlightenment Cycle</u>, "Meditation")*

It takes willpower to do this. But combining special music with the chakra-focusing technique is an even more powerful concentration muscle-building exercise. It is more challenging to focus on two things at the same time. Over time, it will become quite natural. As the mind becomes less distracted by the physical environment, thoughts and emotions, you'll see that it has no problem doing this. It may seem hard at first, but it works! Like listening to a song that you love, concentrate on each chakra while listening to each song completely. Merge with both.

There is always a clarity and sharpness when you're really meditating. You may see or feel phenomena such as light, color or other manifestations. You may feel energy circulating, or concentrated in a part of your body, or see and feel nothing. It doesn't matter. The energy knows where it's going and what it's doing. Don't try to figure it out. Keep in mind that whatever experiences you're having are transitory and are really just surface-level manifestations of a deeper process. You may experience energy one time and nothing the next. Keeping the mind still for greater lengths of time is what's important.

There are three guiding points that also need to be understood. First, don't get fixated on feeling or seeing energy during your meditation. Also, if you feel a lot of energy, it is safe. It won't harm you. The energy is actually very healing. Just relax and let the energy move where it wants. The second point is that you are going into higher, clearer levels of your own mind. If you feel kind of hazy or dreamy or perhaps see or hear other beings, you've entered into the astral dimensions, which are full of disembodied beings and worlds of form. That is not meditation! The meditation dimensions are pure energy, nothing else—you alone in the causal dimensions of your mind. Simply open your eyes, re-focus in the physical, and then focus strongly back on the chakra and the music. Meditation always has a great clarity to it, and you should feel energized with a clearer, sharper mind. Accept no substitutes.

Thirdly, as Rama succinctly put it, meditation is a noun, not a verb. The word is actually another way to describe Enlightenment, but at first we can only perceive as much of it as our limited self will allow. So we must expend the effort to move our ego aside, which is done by becoming completely still, and then allow ourselves to be absorbed. This will be discussed more fully in Chapter 15, the third and final section on meditation.

If you do find your mind paying attention to thoughts, know that they'll be there after meditating, so just ignore them. Your human mind is constantly analyzing data, and the first step is that it is reaching out for almost any kind of stimulation. You must simply stop grasping at any thought that passes by. At those moments realize that you are what is in the way. Before beginning your meditation, put yourself on hold for the next hour. Inner peace grows through meditation.

Like with the beginning meditation technique, it is crucial not to think of other people or situations because doing so pulls so much of their attention field and energy into you, thus trashing the meditation. With this technique, Rama made clear what your options were if your mind starts to wander during the meditation:

*"It is most important during that period of time from one minute to the next not to allow your attention, your mind, to wander towards anything but four primary areas of focus. You can focus on the chakra to the exclusion of everything else. You can focus on your teacher to the exclusion of anything else, if you have an Enlightened teacher. You can focus on music, if you're listening to Enlightened music, to the exclusion of everything else, or you can focus on light to the exclusion of everything else."*

*(Rama, <u>The Enlightenment Cycle</u>, "Intermediate Meditation")*

So begin by focusing so strongly on each chakra that you cannot think during this time. It's more like a workout at first, but then the sublime energy automatically starts flowing. You feel lighter, tranquil and energized all at the same time. You've meditated. You'll know how well it went 20 or 30 minutes after it's done by how balanced you feel, and it will carry you forward the rest of the day or night.

This chakra-focusing method is a form of empowerment meditation. If you meditate twice a day, you're constantly recharging your batteries. The secret to meditation, as Rama told us, is every time you sit down to meditate, think of it as the first time you will have ever meditated. In a deeper sense this is factually true, since you are never the same person after a good meditation. By raising the kundalini up through these chakras, you loosen the glue in the causal body that defines you, and it resets a little differently. The person you went in as comes out as a more aware being.

Meditation is letting the mind enjoy stillness so that you can become the higher dimensions of light within your mind. Also, meditation is cumulative. Every time you meditate, especially using this technique, you are storing energy and a deeper kind of understanding within you which is not dissipated or forgotten. You are getting wiser, more balanced and more powerful. Every meditation is like making a deposit in a high-interest savings account. All you have to do is sit still.

*"The music from Zazen comes out of higher dimensions that are extremely pure….It ensures that you will touch worlds of light and brightness, that you'll be headed in the right direction…. so that you can just sit in your own aura and then direct your mind to infinity and move from this world to infinity, experience the ecstasy of infinity and come back, better for your journey, more conscious, happier, wiser, hopefully sillier.*

*Now that's meditation as I've come to know it, as it was taught to me by my teachers over many, many lives, and as I teach it."*
*(Rama, <u>The Enlightenment Cycle</u>, "Intermediate Meditation")*

# Chapter 11:  Power, Balance, and Wisdom

*"You're accessing all three meridians, which creates the development of a balanced being, if you rotate them…. If you just always meditate on the navel center, you get too heavy, you get too into certain energies relating to the lower three centers and you don't have enough will, you don't have enough power to deal with life and the world and the forces you have to deal with as you go through different dimensional planes and access points, in more advanced meditative states.*

*If you just meditate on the intermediate states, they're beautiful and pleasant, you develop the psychic chakras a lot, a lot of the emotional body develops—but without the other centers there's a lack of balance. The upper centers are wisdom; the central centers are feeling, emotion, identification, beauty, the perception of life as beauty and truth; the lower centers are the power centers. So we put power, wisdom, and feeling together and we have a good package in development. Otherwise, we're just developing without balance, and without balance our meditative practice will not continue to escalate.*

*Balance is the most important of all qualities. We don't want a little bit of rapid growth and then to stagnate. We want continual growth, continual development, which implies balance, always."*
*(Rama, <u>Tantric Buddhism</u>, "Focus and Meditation")*

In the preceding chapter, you learned to meditate on three important chakras to Enlightened music: the navel chakra, the heart chakra, and the third eye chakra. It is also important to realize that these dimensions are inside your mind. As he said, you're complete when you're both fully connected to all three and they're in equilibrium.

Being equally powerful, balanced, and wise is a noble goal most people don't consider in such specific terms. But imagine those three characteristics maximized in you. That's exactly what this meditation method is designed to do. All you have to do is sit still, focus, and let it happen.

To put it mildly, it's very helpful to your life today as well as to your spiritual evolution to develop your inner power, balance, and wisdom. As mentioned above, you are not reaching outside of yourself to obtain something—these are dimensions of your own mind. The reason that you are barely able to tap into them is mainly because you're directing your perception at other things instead, mostly how to fit into the human world and your emotional roller coaster ride through it. As Rama explained in multiple contexts, Buddhism is essentially about redirecting your perception—that's the essence of what is done in meditation.

In meditation you're going into your mind, which requires turning off the noise machine we call thinking. By focusing on the chakras you are venturing into largely unexplored areas of your complete mind. As explained in Chapter 3, you have three bodies, not one; the subtle physical body has doorways directly into higher levels of your mind, and a power plant at its base filled with kundalini energy to go through those doorways. That's what your true opportunity is as a sentient being.

The second thing to understand is that power, balance, and wisdom need to eventually be at the same level of development. For you to approach Enlightenment all three must be equally strong. It is natural when you start your self-discovery journey for one of them to be more developed, because as people grow up in this world they usually are more interested in one than in the other two. You need to let go of that preference.

The equality and interdependence of these three dimensions of mind are necessary in order to maintain sufficient mental equilibrium throughout the self-discovery process. Human history is full of people who over-focused on power without wisdom, or wisdom without power. The need for emotional balance, as well as having general mental equilibrium is obvious. Balance itself is a subject of surprising depth.

*"Without balance and wisdom, power becomes very destructive. It creates unhappiness and not happiness. To simply see a teacher to gain power is a mistake. You'll gain the power, but with the current mindset that you have,*

*you'll probably create more unhappiness for yourself than happiness with it....*

*So use power very carefully. Don't be afraid to have it. You have to have it to succeed. But learn balance and wisdom in addition simply to the unlocking of the kundalini, if you wish to have a happy and Enlightened life."*
*(Rama, The Enlightenment Cycle, "Power")*

Human beings often think of power as an external force that they must compete with others to obtain. Societies define it in political or financial terms, but there is also the idea of charisma. That's a simplification of the accurate perception that power is something which is within people. The difficulty in understanding it is because it's invisible. As Rama put it, power is like the wind. We feel its effects but can't see it. Many spiritual teachers have taught about developing one's internal energy. Martial arts, which was a major component of Rama's self-discovery program, certainly emphasizes this.

Your internal energy, called Ki in Japanese and Chi in Chinese, is what is harnessed and directed in martial arts. That's the same as kundalini. Martial arts is not at all about hostility or violence, it is about remaining still in the midst of a threat or in the middle of conflict. When one must engage an opponent, your physical actions come out of that stillness or emptiness. Thought slows you down and gets in the way.

As discussed in earlier chapters, one of the fundamental concepts in Buddhism is that your "normal" human mind is only a layer of a much bigger and deeper mind. The problem is that this layer is able to dominate how you see yourself and perceive the world, largely through the mechanism of thinking. You must unhook from thinking in order to directly experience the more powerful, balanced, and wiser levels of your mind. What meditation does is put you onto those levels. It is important to really appreciate this redefinition of the scale of your mind.

You already have vast reserves of power, balance, and wisdom; it's just a matter of reaching them. You know this by now, but don't stop at intellectual comprehension, which actually is staying within your ego self. Don't try to "activate" the chakras; meditation will naturally pull the kundalini energy up to them. When you merge with each chakra, you will become power, become balance, become wisdom.

*"Power in Buddhism is defined very precisely in many different ways. There is no singular word than can encompass all the different aspects of power. The general term for power, spiritual power, the power of awareness, is kundalini. Kundalini is the energy of life that creates life. Life is awareness. It is movement, it is sentient.*

*Life is the power to perceive…. Buddhism, yoga, is the study of perception, and what is most endemic to perception is power—the power to exist, to perceive, and the power to change perception.*

*… in a certain way, we are what we perceive. Or you might say, what we perceive certainly defines what we are. Now, we have to think of life in reverse. If we are perceiving other than what we are, if perception is the awareness of other, certainly, perhaps in a sense, perception can be the awareness of oneself. But if, primarily, the way we view the universe is the universe as other than what we are, perception is a mirror. In other words, we are everything that we don't perceive.*

*… Who are we? Well, we are the being that perceives. And certainly without thinking about it, a distinction is made between who we are and what we perceive. We perceive that which is other and that which is self.*

*Power is the band that we perceive things on. In radio we have AM stations, FM stations, short wave stations and others. They're frequencies; they're megahertz, kilohertz—they vibrate. Frequencies vibrate at specific rates, and within those frequencies we transmit information and receive information. Perception is made up of bands. It's a way of talking about it. And the bands of perception vary greatly. There's the human band of perception and the mammalian band of perception that would include all mammals. There is the plant, invertebrate, and so on. There's lots of different bands of perception, and simply because we are in one band of perception and aware of it doesn't mean others are not there….*

*So power, to begin with, is the thing that holds a band of perception together, and a band of perception is life for those who perceive in that band…. The ability to perceive what we call life, the ability to live, is one aspect of power. Without the power to exist, to perceive, there is no life as we know life to be. Then, specifically, within the human banding of attention, let's say on the FM frequencies, there's lots of variation. We can go from the bottom of the dial to the top of the dial....*

*Within the human frequency, well, what you see is what you get. There are different conditions—mental conditions, awareness conditions—that you see people on earth existing in. They're relatively representative. I would classify the bottom of the band as severe unhappiness, depression, alienation—things that we would consider very unpleasant. The top of the band, which would vibrate a little faster, would be happiness, contentment, peace of mind, a feeling of balance and overall wealth of spirit and ecstasy.*

*Buddhism, yoga, is concerned primarily with moving our awareness field from the beginning of the band of perception, the human band, up to the top, and eventually, of course, going from the human band to an Enlightened band, or bands, of perception—just leaving this band of perception completely. But before you do that, you have to move through the human band from wherever you happen to be to the top. You can't go beyond until you get to the top."*

*(Rama, The Enlightenment Cycle, "Power")*

Society's definition of power definitely is not this. People think of power as the human drive to conquer, to become the dominant civilization over other nations, or in strictly personal terms, to acquire what you set your sights on. These are manifestations of your ego figuring out how to assert itself within the human band of perception. The idea of transcending this perceptual band simply is not present. So the end result is to reinforce staying within that level of perception. It has more suffering than happiness, and whether you win or lose it's always a struggle. That's human life as we know and accept it.

If and when you want to go beyond the human world's limited understanding of reality, your power can open up areas of your mind not previously experienced:

*"So one aspect of Buddhism, or inner study, is the reawakening of past life knowledge, and it takes a certain type of power to do that. Past life knowledge is not necessarily a remembrance. It's not the wedding album photo scrapbook of existence. You can remember what you did last week and it doesn't necessarily change anything, the physical events. Past life*

*remembrance in Buddhism means the ability to bring a greater awareness, a greater knowledge that we had in another life into this life....*

*So one aspect of power is the power to bring our total awareness into this lifetime. A second aspect of power, of course is to go beyond that awareness, the things we've known in other lives, into new fields of awareness that we've never experienced. The very transmutative energy or power that does that is called the kundalini. The kundalini is the energy that opens up the bands of perception. It's also the energy or power that enables us to travel, mentally, from one level to another, from one plane or dimension to another, from one experience to another....*

*So Buddhism, yoga, is the study of changing who we are, modifying or perhaps totally restructuring ourselves as perceivers. Now, in a way, you really can't change who you are. Whoever you are is who you are, and that will always be. There's something in us that's eternal, and that's beyond change. The ultimate goal of Buddhism is to reach that from this side, to become conscious of that side. This side is the mortal side, the limited side, the human side. Then there's the eternal side, the timeless, divine side. We seek, in yoga, to yoke or unify our awareness field with the divine or Enlightened side, the timeless side—because when we do that there's no pain, there's no anxiety, there's no unhappiness. The eternal part of our being is perfect, free, always changing, always new and completely conscious of all things—complete aliveness, complete awareness.*

*However, in the meantime, and on the way there, Buddhism is the study of power initially. It takes a certain amount of power to even know your potential, to have a sense that you can change the way you perceive, what you perceive and that it will be very beneficial to you. It takes additional power to find out how to do that and even more power to actually do it. And of course, when you make structural changes in perception, it gives you power. It's very curious the way it all works. It's not necessarily logical....*

*The power that is most interesting is the personal power that changes or shapes consciousness, and that's kundalini."*
*(Rama, <u>The Enlightenment Cycle</u>, "Power")*

Many spiritual seekers, just like everyone else, have a hidden agenda, and that is to find the secret to gaining unlimited power. In the back of our minds lurks this very human, very inaccurate belief that that's the answer to everything. Until you recognize it as just another desire you're not going to get very far. So here's the answer about the gaining ultimate power fantasy:

*"Personal power is a feeling. It's a feeling that everybody is looking for called satisfaction. It's different than Enlightenment, but you need personal power to become Enlightened. But personal power is not the end of the process. It's another step in it. It's a tool that you use to get someplace. It's like a car; it takes you someplace. The purpose of the car is not to live in the car, it's to drive you someplace you want to go. So power is an operative force. It's a component part of the universe. You need power to listen to me, the power of awareness. You need power to walk down the street....*

*The place that you gain the most power is within your own mind. When you have the ability to stop thought, which is meditation, when you practice meditation and you become good at it, stopping thought generates power. That's why people meditate. The longer you can stop thought, the more power you gain. That's the ultimate way to gain power."*
*(Rama, <u>Zen Tapes</u>, "Personal Power")*

In his discussions about power, a pair of Native American terms are used by Rama which are analogous with traditional Hindu and Buddhist ones. These terms come from the early books of an American anthropologist, Carlos Castaneda, who studied with Yaqui (a northern Mexico Native American tribe) spiritual teachers in the 1960s and 1970s, and then went on his own path.

While some may question various aspects of his many books, Rama found Castaneda's first four books to be worthwhile:

*"A great deal has been written about personal power by a fellow named Carlos Castaneda, and I find his first four books are valuable, in this sense. After that they don't make much sense to me. But I think that based on my own experience, the first four books that he's written in his series about Don Juan and Don Genaro make a lot of sense, the principles in them. Of the experiences themselves, who knows? Fantasy? Reality? But the principles that are presented via the teaching of Don Juan and Don Genaro in those first four books, 'Tales of Power,' 'Journey to Ixtlan', 'A Separate Reality,' and 'The Teachings of Don Juan' are quite valuable for one who seeks power."*
*(Rama, <u>Zen Tapes</u>, "Personal Power")*

Those books use the metaphor of being on an island in a vast ocean, and also defining the mind as having two sections, a rational side (the island), called the "tonal," and a mystical side (the ocean), called the "nagual." This model is equivalent to what's found in Hinduism and Buddhism.

*"We deal with two things. We deal with the world of your life, what Don Juan would call the 'tonal,' and we deal with the unknown, what he would call the 'nagual,' what we'd call the 'superconscious' if we were speaking in spiritual terminology of a different type.*

*… The tonal is the sense of place. It is order and reason in a world of chaos. The world is always chaos, but we pretend that it's not because it makes us feel better. And in doing so we're able to go through it in a specific manner and form. That's the tonal.*

*Now, the nagual, as we know, as defined in these Carlos Castaneda books that we're studying, is the unknown. It cannot be talked about, it can only be witnessed. That's its definition. These are the unspeakable acts of power that occur beyond the comprehension of the mind or the tonal, and they're endless and limitless. The tonal is also endless and limitless. We like to think of it as being finite so we feel better. Don Juan speaks of the island of the tonal, something that's in the middle of an ocean, which is the nagual. It gives Carlos the sense that it's small and defined. The island of the tonal is this little thing and you can get to know your island pretty well, but that ocean is big and expansive and it goes on forever.*

*But that's not exactly true, as Carlos finds out, of course. In the sorcerer's explanation, Carlos discovers that the tonal is also infinite, as is the nagual. But for a while he needed to think that the tonal was finite…. All of you are seeking Enlightenment, seeking knowledge, power. We have different names for it. You're seeking the totality of yourselves, to experience what you are, absolutely, because it seems to you that that's what's most important in life because everything else in life is only a transitory, temporary reflection of that.*

*The tonal leads the way. You have to have a methodology, a sense of how you are going to go about doing this. Even though it's incomprehensible, still, you need to comprehend it. In the training process, then, the teacher or teachers address two sides of your being. One is the tonal and one is the nagual. Now, in the case of Carlos Castaneda, he had two teachers, Don Juan and Don Genaro. Don Juan worked with his tonal, with his logical sense. He helped him develop and strengthen his logical self so that it could withstand the encounters with the unknown, with the nagual.*

*Don Genaro, on the other hand, was what they call his benefactor. He gave him a variety of experiences in the nagual. He taught his body countless views of reality, views beyond this world. He presented absolute proof that there was something beyond.*

*In your case, you have one teacher who is two. Quite ordinarily in the study of mysticism one does have two teachers, and they address the two different aspects of your being. But in your case I address both aspects of your being. When we meet here, when we talk, answer questions, I'm addressing your tonal. I'm teaching you a way or a series of ways of dealing with the world. It's very physically oriented. We spend a great deal of time talking about careers, relationships, economics, in other words the structure, the nitty-gritty of your life and what you do with your time, because it's necessary for you to work out a way of living that's very strong and very tight and very powerful, otherwise you will not be able to deal with the unknown."*
*(Rama, <u>Insights: Talks on the Nature of Existence</u>, "Modular Mysticism: The Sorcerer's Explanation")*

This is the framework of Rama's well-defined process for bringing the student to Enlightened states of mind. Elaborating on this he stressed the need to balance the two sides rather than reject the rational side, as is found in some Hindu and Buddhist sects:

*"Your reason is not the enemy. There are teachers who tell you to destroy your reason. I am not one of them. Your reason is your friend. It defends the island of your awareness, which needs defending. But you don't want your reason to rule everything. You need it for the reasonable parts of your life and no more. Some teachers, who are not very versed in the ways of reality, have told their students that what they need to do is throw away reason, forever. If a person is capable of that, they'll go stark raving mad. They will not be able to function in the world.... So it's important, then, to address both sides of your being."*
*(Rama, <u>Insights: Talks on the Nature of Existence</u>, "Modular Mysticism: The Sorcerer's Explanation")*

The constant need for balance throughout the self-discovery process cannot be emphasized enough.

An important aspect of power that Rama taught was how to store it. Power is a basic necessity in living one's life and is something within you that you are always drawing upon. While meditation and other pursuits involving focus will release more of it, storing power is how you maintain elevated levels of awareness. In meditation, or other self-discovery experiences, the kundalini is raised and power suffuses you. Rama would take us out to the desert and these trips would always be very powerful. He included a way to store the power of those trips, which applies to any powerful experience:

*"When we go out to the desert, of course, it's pure nagual. I don't deal with reason at all there. There you witness stupendous and incredible acts of power that your reason cannot possibly deal with. The reason I suggest you keep a journal and write these experiences down is because it's a gradual and gentle way of bringing the acceptance by the tonal of alternate views of existence into itself.*

*If you just go out to the desert and you watch me send thousands of luminous lines through the sky, dissolve the mountains, disappear, grow to huge size, slip through alternate worlds and do other things that I do to you out there, not just what I do as the cosmic performer but the various states and changes that I bring you through, if you just see that in the desert, as you know and I know, it's entirely possible for you then to come back into what we would call civilization and drop it, like it never happened. You've just had an experience that should have changed you forever—your views of the world. But so strong is the command of the tonal that you can come back into the world of what you call reason, order and logic and actually explain away and push away the nagual.*

*To some extent this is necessary. You can't be floating around in the nagual at this point in your development when you're in the office working. You've got to keep the two separate. But if your tonal is so authoritarian, such a dictator that it completely blocks out the view of the nagual, then you won't progress, you won't become aware of your own luminosity. So I've devised an in-between way which I call keeping a journal... Well, obviously you're writing them down when you're at home in the world of order and structure. In doing so, you recapitulate them and of course, recapitulation is a very important aspect of storing power. Whenever you recapitulate, you store power."*

*(Rama, <u>Insights: Talks on the Nature of Existence</u>, "Modular Mysticism: The Sorcerer's Explanation")*

Self-discovery is a complex process of learning to use your internal power, the kundalini, to move your mind into higher dimensions. The simple act of meditation increases your power; the challenge then becomes how to manage your life so that it's not dissipated. That's what the systems analysis of your energy flow is for, as discussed in Chapter 6.

The challenge of how to manage your life is fundamentally about balance, about psychological equilibrium regardless of external pressures. The importance of balance cannot be overstressed. Balance is so critical yet is overlooked in the pursuit of power, even wisdom.

When balance is initially considered, the first question is what forces or states of mind are present that need balancing? Unlike weights on either side of a bar bell, the forces almost always are not equal. So being centered is all-important, not getting knocked off balance by events or interactions with people, not thrashing with conflicting emotions and thoughts within your mind.

*"Balance. Spiritual balance is the ability to be happy in spite of circumstances. Spiritual balance is the obvious answer to the obsession that sometimes accompanies religious practice, occult practice, philosophical understandings....*

*Spiritual balance is how you deal with opposition, opposition outside of yourself and opposition within yourself. Spiritual balance is tai chi. It's the center of things. It's the place where yin and yang meet, where all things come together. In the chakras, it's considered the heart chakra, anahata, the central chakra—three above and three below—which symbolizes happiness and love, psychic oneness, spiritual understanding.*

*So pure and simple, balance is happiness—happiness in spiritual practice, happiness while meditating, happiness while working, while playing, in pleasure and pain, in sickness and in health, in life and in death, in all circumstances. That's balance."*

*(Rama, <u>The Enlightenment Cycle</u>, "Balance")*

But when confronted with the reality of everyday life in this world, in society, balance can appear to be very difficult to ever attain, much less constantly reside in it.

*"How do you do that? How can you be balanced in a world like this? You've got to be kidding, right?*

*Well, the world has always been this way, at least in one form or another. I'm sure in the Middle Ages, in ancient Chinese civilization or the mystery world of Egypt, ancient Atlantis—you pick a universe, a cosmos, it doesn't matter—there's always something going on. There is always somebody on your case. Dogs have fleas; people have each other. We're born to die. Life is a continuing tragedy, tragicomedy. Everything and everyone we love suffers. We suffer. How can you be happy? Life is a horror show, isn't it? Well, sure, certainly, I mean, yeah, obviously. Anybody who doesn't see that has not grown up and known life.*

*Spiritual balance is the ability, in spite of all that, to remain happy—not to be hostile to your neighbor when they're being hostile, not to get caught up in the trivia. Spiritual balance, in other words, is the ability to climb up the mountain and be in a world of light."*
*(Rama, <u>The Enlightenment Cycle</u>, "Balance")*

There are two easy ways to become balanced any time:

*"To love is to be balanced, to extend one's self beyond just the sense of self, of what matters to me today, of what I think is going to please me, of avoiding what I think is unhappy. That's balance. That's happiness."*
*(Rama, <u>The Enlightenment Cycle</u>, "Balance")*

*"Humor is the balance of the tonal. Within the tonal you've got reason and humor. Reason is logical order and seriousness. Humor is the opposite side of the tonal and the two balance each other so that the tonal can accept and understand the journeys into the nagual in a balanced way."*
*(Rama, <u>Insights: Talks on the Nature of Existence</u>, "Modular Mysticism: The Sorcerer's Explanation")*

As a human being going through life, to advance spiritually one needs to understand that living in the world is one-half of the equation, exploring the higher levels of awareness the other:

*"... if we can walk between both, since we have two centers of our being, reason and will, and develop both those centers, which is what we are, we create a balance within the self.*

*When one side or the other predominates, there's an imbalance and there's unhappiness."*
*(Rama, <u>Insights: Talks on the Nature of Existence</u>, "Modular Mysticism: The Sorcerer's Explanation")*

So the teacher is working with the student on multiple levels. By showing the student how to keep the tonal and the nagual balanced, the student gradually learns how to take care of it themselves.

*"Don Juan says that we're all bubbles of luminosity, and he's right. The bubble has two sides—one side is the tonal, one side is the nagual. What the teacher does is sweep all of the logic and order and reason onto one side and make that side very strong... What I also do, then, is open up the bubble of your luminosity and allow the luminous being to take short excursions into the unknown. But this is done in a very buffered way.*

*It's a precise art, so that each of your excursions is balanced by the strengthening of the tonal. As we slam you with more and more devastating blows of the nagual, at the same time we strengthen and clear the tonal so that it can easily withstand them, so that there's no loss in the continuity of consciousness. Actually, the continuity of consciousness increases. You become the most sane person on earth, the most rational, the most orderly, the most capable and the most logical. At the same time, you have excursions into the unknown that would defy the imaginations of the most imaginative thinkers on earth.*

*In doing so you are prepared to one day experience the totality of yourself. The totality of yourself is not the self as you know it. The totality of yourself is nirvana. Nirvana is another word to describe it that Buddha used. Samadhi, nirvikalpa samadhi, is a term that someone else used. Satori is a term that someone else used. These are all words that point to something that is beyond the description of even the tonal and the nagual."*

*(Rama, <u>Insights: Talks on the Nature of Existence</u>, "Modular Mysticism: The Sorcerer's Explanation")*

Obsession can be a serious problem on the pathway to Enlightenment. Balance fixes that. The reason why it may seem difficult to develop balance is because the student doesn't consider it as important as gaining power. But without balance you will never make the kind of progress you so strongly desire.

One of the fundamental constructs of Buddhism is the concept of the Middle Way. This was explained through the Eightfold Path, which detailed how to approach each aspect of living by being in accord with dharma. The Buddha articulated this model and presented it as the cornerstone of his teachings, as the overall method in attaining Enlightenment. How did he teach his students about Enlightenment?

*"'Don't talk about Enlightenment,' Buddha would say. He was saying, don't talk about the nagual, but then, of course, he would talk about it. He'd talk about how to get to it, actually. The Buddha spent all of his time talking about what? The eightfold path. Well what's the eightfold path if not ordering the island of the tonal completely? But he would never speak about Enlightenment when anyone asked him because to speak about it was to relegate it to the island of the tonal. The way he taught people about Enlightenment was they sat around with him. They meditated with him. He exposed them to countless views of the nagual, which we would call Enlightenment, although even Enlightenment eventually finds a place on the island of the tonal."*
*(Rama, <u>Insights: Talks on the Nature of Existence</u>, "Modular Mysticism: The Sorcerer's Explanation")*

Another word for the Middle Way is balance:

*"To wrap all this up, then, you're engaged in a fantastic process. It's an absolute challenge. You are developing the totality of yourself, both sides. When both sides are developed, you will become the totality of yourself, something I can't even describe to you, which will happen to you one day when that's done. It's necessary for you to pay attention to both sides and not go overboard in either direction. That's what we refer to as the middle path in self-discovery.*

*The middle path means not to become too obsessed with your physical life and reason—to have a good life, live well, be reasonable and prudent, but not to go overboard and let reason rule everything, or to go too far and become obsessed with your experiences in the nagual."*

*(Rama, <u>Insights: Talks on the Nature of Existence</u>, "Modular Mysticism: The Sorcerer's Explanation")*

There is little talk of wisdom today. People are much more interested in having pleasurable experiences and being successful in the material world. In an increasingly fast-paced society, wisdom doesn't attract much interest. It probably never did of course, but at least it was included as a personal virtue worth cultivating.

If you were wiser you'd make better choices. You'd certainly factor in transience. An understanding of transience, which surely is a facet of wisdom, would enable you to have an improved perspective on life in general and yours in particular.

As Rama explained it, there are different levels of wisdom, from knowing how to sustain your personal power and mental integrity while living in the world, to perceiving the templates of the universe, ultimately culminating in being in samadhi:

*".... Love is a kind of wisdom. There's a wisdom to loving. Love is sometimes pleasurable, sometimes painful, sometimes ecstatic. But there's a wisdom, there's a knowing that comes from loving. I think it's a mistake not to love. I think some people think that spiritual practice means to divorce themselves from love and all of their emotions. I don't think so. I think one must love more deeply and without the sense of what you love being your personal possession.*

*.... There is something to this fabric of life that's beautiful, and I think if you find the world simply unpleasant, I don't think that's a sign of wisdom. I think that's a sign of a lack of wisdom.... Wisdom is the ability, I think, to realize that everyone has their own dharma, that everyone goes their own way. And your way and what works for you is not the ultimate good.... maybe you even have different ways you haven't discovered, that tomorrow you can let go of how you have to do things and who you are and how you have to be—that, to me, is wisdom—to be flexible, to be lucid."*

*(Rama, <u>The Enlightenment Cycle</u>, "Wisdom")*

Rama went well beyond these levels of wisdom to postulate that the most complete wisdom was beyond anything we can know here:

*"Real wisdom, the deepest spiritual wisdom, does not occur here — 'here' being in this body and in this mind and in this physical universe. It can't. Real wisdom is something that you have to move into the planes of the highest light to experience. And you can't bring yourself with you. You have to go to the other side. The other side is what is beyond the mind's knowing.*

*… As I said before, the other side is beyond knowing. You cannot know what you experience on the other side, here. It cannot be known. The chip size here is too limited. You can't grasp your own experience. That's the true wisdom. True wisdom is the other side of this life. Not in death, but beyond the grasp of the conscious mind. That's where real wisdom lies."*
*(Rama, The Enlightenment Cycle, "Wisdom")*

If the deep and constant happiness we are searching for simply is not available through transient physical existence, then we need to get some perspective on life on Earth. Wisdom would be altering the trajectory of your future lives so that you don't keep coming back here as basically the same person with the same karma over and over again. Meditation and the self-discovery process provide that opportunity.

# Chapter 12:  Self-effort and the Razor's Edge

*"It is not the job of the teacher—it is not their responsibility—to cause you to be Enlightened. It is your responsibility to do that."*
*(Rama, <u>The Enlightenment Cycle</u>, "Enlightenment")*

We all know that to succeed in the world requires a great deal of self-effort. We cannot rely on anyone else to master our chosen vocation. You are the one who puts in the years of study, and the many hours at your job every week. The same kind of effort is required in self-discovery, if you really want to master it.

*"Buddhism is about bringing your mind into a very clear state and from there going to a state that's more clear and so on until you become Enlightened. And that's done with a great deal of self-effort. We have to remove all the toxins, all the pollutants from our mind. The mind is originally clear. When you scrape all the barnacles off and get down to the reality of your mind, it's clear. We all have perfect minds. So it's not as if we have to go get something. It's not as if we don't have the right vehicle. But the problem is it's covered over with a lot of barnacles, with silt, with obscurations."*
*(Rama, <u>Tantric Buddhism</u>, "Buddhist Enlightenment")*

Before embarking on this journey, it is necessary to know the terrain you will be crossing: there are billions of people here who are all fixated on using power to fulfill desires, all the while ignoring transience. They do not perceive beyond each day's experiences, their personal history, and their hopes and fears about the future. Virtually everyone is afraid of death. It takes a lot of tenacity to not perceive "reality" the same way. But that is exactly what this journey entails.

*"The issue in Buddhism is perception, gaining control of the mind and directing one's attention, to raise the kundalini energy so that it flows with such volatility and force that we simply perceive life correctly. The gray aura of humanity caused by the billions and billions of individuals who live on this planet makes it very difficult just to see what is. Nothing shines because of the deadness of the human mind.*

*The aura of billions of people coats all experiences like a thick cloud of smog. Just to live on the earth is to live in that smog. If billions of people meditated, then everything would shine here. If no one were here at all but yourself, the world would shine in a way that would amaze you. But the human mind generates an auric field that covers up the naturalness, the innate divinity of life. This auric field is a field of doubt. It's a field that runs contrary to existence. Obviously it's a side of existence, for it is existence.*

*So the province of Buddhism is the stretching of perception. It's pushing the mind to its—we call it the 'natural state,' to indicate how unnatural the normal human consciousness is. You know it's kind of funny when you're first reading some of the Zen texts or the Tantric Buddhist texts, and you hear Tilopa, or one of those guys, who are saying, 'Abide in the natural state.' And you think, 'My God, what do I have to do to get to the natural state? How can he call it natural? I have to meditate for hours every day, straighten my life out, I have to do all this incredible stuff to get to what this guy calls the natural state.'*

*Everyone has sunk on this planet to such a low state of consciousness, and that has become so defined and striated in the individual mind of every single perceiver, and it's taught to every child by every mother and every father, by every political regime, by every philosophy—the total denial of what is…. It is the natural state we deviated so far from, the path of it, in this age of darkness, meaning the darkness of the human minds that are on this planet."*
*(Rama, <u>Tantric Buddhism</u>, "The Natural State")*

That's the terrain we live in. So in order literally to transcend it, certain mental traits become essential:

*"Self-discovery requires a bit of courage and a belief in a feeling. I can't define it more than that for you—except to say that there's a feeling of ecstasy, of freedom, which is available to a person depending upon how gutsy they are, how patient they are, how hopeful they are and how tough*

*they are. You have to be very, very gutsy to look the world in the face, society in the face, families, power structures and to walk away from all that. To decide that you're not going to fit in, nor are you going to try not to, but you're just going to follow the beat of a different drummer—your own. That's pretty gutsy because everyone is applying pressure for everyone else to conform. If you think about it, the constraints that humankind has set upon itself, what they've agreed upon as acceptable, is so narrow, so rigid….*

*If you seek to practice self-discovery, you've got to be pretty gutsy. You have to be willing to buck the system, to buck everyone you've known, who for some reason seems to have a vested interest in how you turn out and how you are or who you are…. I don't recommend that people leave everyone they know and leave their relatives. I don't recommend that they stay. It's a personal matter. But what must occur is you must be able to change who you are and maintain that new identity. And then change it again and again and again…."*
*(Rama, <u>Tantric Buddhism</u>, "Freedom")*

So why is self-effort so crucial in the spiritual journey? Here's a summary of some of the main points presented in the book thus far. The need for self-effort in transforming your consciousness into an awareness of higher levels of attention becomes self-evident:

1. Who you are, this human being, is only an empty shell. You pour a tremendous amount of energy and attention into sustaining a transitory fantasy, i.e. yourself. That's not good or bad, it's simply how things work for human beings on earth.

2. There are 10,000 states of mind, at least. Human beings stay in only a few dozen, all towards the lower, darker end of the spectrum. Freedom is to be able to be selective about the states of mind to be in.

3. Personal history, such as family, culture, religion and personality are only ideas that you've chosen to be attached to. The problem is that our sense of identity is overly defined by this history, which blocks the experience of higher, freer identities.

4. The only consistent truth about physical reality is that everything is transitory. Nothing is permanent. Every experience fades away and disappears. Everything in life constantly changes. Yet we act like it is more real than anything or any place else. That is a fundamental perceptual error.

5. The only thing that is not transitory is the eternal, infinite mind. It is totally real, not merely some religious belief. It is the only reality that is permanent.

6. There is more suffering here than joy. There are many dimensions and worlds above this level, where there is no suffering and joy is normal. There are also dimensions and worlds below this. In this world, it takes a lot of extra energy to experience higher states of mind.

7. Through meditation you come to experience the higher states of mind. The more your mind is still, the more it naturally rises into those higher states. You can evolve into happy levels of awareness.

Therefore, your destiny is totally in your own hands.

You can see why self-effort is such a big deal. Rama made the point on multiple occasions that the Enlightened teacher cannot magically make a student Enlightened, although of course can help immeasurably. He explained that what the Enlightened teacher does is present instruction, tasks, and challenges, all full of the purest energy and consciousness, which have the effect of sanding down the rocky aggregates of each student. The fewer and thinner the aggregates, the more light shines through the mind. But the amount sanded down is controlled by the student. Despite the teacher's transcendent capabilities, the Enlightened teacher can only do as much as the student inwardly allows. So self-effort also requires becoming much more open psychically with the teacher.

The teacher elevates you into higher levels of mind; it is you who must sustain your awareness in them. The Enlightened teacher has already done this, permanently, for themselves a long time ago. They don't need your help, you need theirs. The recognition of self-effort as crucial for Enlightenment is covered over, even denied by human societies:

*"To think that in some way—as people think both in the East and West but more so in the West—that the knowledge that brings freedom from all limitations is in some way supposed to come to you and be at your service is ridiculous.*

*It is up to you to avail yourself of that knowledge. That knowledge doesn't need you. It doesn't care. Since it's not in this world, it is completely oblivious to your suffering. The idea of a compassionate God was formulated, obviously, by someone who didn't want to do any work. If you look around you, you'll see that that's not how life is. Creatures are born and die. They go through terrible suffering and no one intervenes. Some people get angry—I guess those who don't want to do anything—and they say, 'Well, there is no God because if there was a God, God would stop all the suffering.' Nonsense. God is oblivious to suffering. God is beyond suffering. That's what makes God God, by definition.*

*That is to say, we refer to God as the part of being that is beyond suffering. Obviously everything is God, but in our definition we view the part of being that experiences the dualistic consciousness, which brings about suffering, we call humanity, squirrels, plants, astral beings, whatever it may be. But some people have a very strange idea. They think that in some way that that immortal essence, which we call God—for lack of a better word, or maybe it's the right word—should in some way come to you and assist you, should answer your prayers. Why, when it exists in perfect ecstasy beyond the dualistic consciousness? It's totally oblivious to you. It has no interest in your life or your death, it doesn't matter.*

*It exists. It is perfect. But it is up to an individual to go on a journey of self-discovery through their own self-effort and discover that, to meld their mind with that perfection and make that perfection their life."*
*(Rama, Tantric Buddhism, "Self-Effort")*

One reason that the spiritual seeker became a student of an advanced, or even Enlightened teacher is that it's obvious to them how much more advanced the teacher is than they are. In a certain way it is natural to think that since the teacher is so much more powerful and wiser than they are, that they can or even should leave it up to the teacher. Without tremendous self-effort to deeply understand purification and humility, plus the self-effort to be independent and self-reliant living in the world, you will go nowhere. Ask all the disappointed students of various spiritual teachers of the past sixty years, who barely mentioned self-effort but instead insisted on being worshipped.

The key point is that all self-discovery is the result of learning through doing, whether it is a systems analysis of your energy flow or entering higher states of awareness. Not intellectual comprehension, but actual implementation. You're fooling yourself if you think that you understand something because you thought about it. Rama took the time to carefully explain this to us:

*"The trap of words is that we believe them. The trap of words is that we say something and the thing that we say we believe—is. We say something, we say a word, and we're convinced that the meaning of that word is the reality. A word is a symbol. So the word 'infinity'—the trap of the word 'infinity'—is that when I say infinity you already know what that means, therefore you'll never know what it means because you will let it go at the understanding of the word that you currently have. See what I mean? Because you know what that word means. You have a concept all worked out. And when I say the word, you just look at the file. I could say the word now, I could say it a year from now, you'll just look at the file. The only thing that can happen is experience can change that.*

*I can say the word 'Africa.' And if you've not been there, you've got a file for Africa. So you will look at the Africa file. Jungle, seen some movies—Tarzan, elephants, South Africa, you know different ideas might come to mind. You've got a file with various data on South Africa, East Africa, North Africa, West Africa. But if you got on a plane tomorrow and you actually went to Africa and you spent several months trekking around Africa, and you came back and I said the word 'Africa' to you, you would pull out a different file.*

*The trap of words is that we're content with them. Words are the death of metaphysics. But the funny thing is we use words in the teaching of metaphysics. It's one of those weird contradictions. The trap of words is when someone says 'meditation, let's have a great meditation,' or the word 'Enlightenment,' we have already preconceived what that means. We're very certain we know what Enlightenment is. Therefore, there's no need to go any further.*

*So when I say, 'Well, God, there are countless dimensions and universes and infinities,' you go, 'Oh, right, OK, got it.' You just—real quickly we whip out all those files for those words, we look at them and go, 'Got it, got the reference point, check the map, yep, OK. Infinities, worlds, sure.' And you don't have any idea what I'm talking about. You haven't been to Africa. I mean, I'm talking about existent reality beyond your self-reflection. Beyond your self-reflection. It's not a physical place you have to go to. Beyond your self-reflection is eternity."*

*(Rama, <u>Tantric Buddhism</u>, "Metaphysics")*

Self-effort requires the correct intent, the correct trajectory of your path. Usually intent is taken for granted; we like to think that we're spiritual seekers with great purity and humility. But beware, your mind probably isn't that clean yet, and in such a desire-crazed world you're constantly walking through all kinds of unhappy, frustrated fantasies from people whose auras you're brushing up against. So reminding yourself of your intent is in fact a very practical consideration. It becomes part of your jnana yoga practice.

Another aspect of intent is being honest about your desires and hopes on a typically human, social level. It is a serious mistake to fool yourself about that. How can you become unattached to all sorts of desires, particularly hopes for social success, if you're in denial about them?

*"I think that you know whether you are a person who is interested, ultimately, if you really searched your being, in finding stillness and dissolving in the light. No one has to explain to you what that is—you know. If you don't know what that is or what I mean by that, then it will not draw you....We feel that this knowledge of Enlightenment is not something that you can convince someone that they need.... A person is either drawn to it or they're not. And if they're drawn to it, they've got to work their ass off, otherwise they don't belong there. Because that's what we get a kick out of—we get a kick out of working—really hard, all the time—to the point where we work so much that we just enter into the light because all our work is directed at bringing us into the light. Because we feel that there's nothing here on this earth that we want."*
*(Rama, Tantric Buddhism, "Buddhism")*

Traditionally, the self-discovery process is known as "being on the path." The path is all-too-often taken for granted; we're initiated by an advanced teacher who actually sets us on "the path." This is something very real; it is not merely symbolic. You know when you're on it, and when you're not. There is a basic structure to self-discovery that many traditions agree on:

*"We dream forever unless we awaken. We move from one dream to another—some beautiful, some we're the hero or the heroine, some horrible, some nonsensical, some boring. And then there's Enlightenment. To become Enlightened we have to purify the mind, we have to gradually move step by step through a series of dreams, and the dreams gradually become less tangible. And we do that by focusing our attention completely on states of mind that are pure.*

*If you want to get someplace, you have to look and see where it is you want to go. And then you keep that viewpoint. And you proceed in that direction and you get there. It's just a question of knowing where you want to go and finding the right direction and then checking once in a while to make sure that you're still on the way. If you keep traveling, you'll get there; it's really not very complicated. And the experiences that we have, we call the journey. And where the journey takes place at any given moment, we call the path."*

*(Rama, <u>Tantric Buddhism</u>, "Buddhist Enlightenment")*

A commonly used image of the path is seeing it as the edge of a razor. That enables the student to avoid taking it for granted, which is a very real challenge, particularly in this age. Just expect that you will fall off the path from time to time. Most everyone does. The important thing is to recognize and get back on it sooner rather than later. Falling off the path is because of desires, whether on your island or in the ocean. You've lost your balance. Even in the regular human world people make this mistake:

*"You have an inner bank account and there's a certain amount of power in it. If you lead a sloppy life, if you indulge in your emotions, if you're always upset and freaked out, if your stressful all of the time, if you're not happy, you're wasting power and your power level will get very low. When your power level gets low, it's dangerous; your mind doesn't function clearly, you make mistakes. And if your power level gets low enough, you'll die. You'll get in a car accident, you'll pick up a disease. That's why it's very, very important to keep your power level high, just to be a happy human being, let alone a human being who's seeking to develop their mind and enter into other dimensional planes and gain self-knowledge.*

*Someone who really wants to unfold and see what they're all about and discover themselves, has to be particularly careful about the use and abuse of power. But even your average human being just passing through another lifetime has to be careful because when your power level gets too low, you die. So it's important to keep your power level as high as possible—to survive, to be happy—let alone to truly gain control of your time, life, and mind, to become Enlightened and free and filled with knowledge."*

*(Rama, <u>Zen Tapes</u>, "Personal Power")*

When people practicing self-discovery try and use the energy from meditation and the practice in general to achieve worldly success, they learn a hard lesson. Probably every seeker does that, of course with the result that you fall off the path. It simply doesn't work that way:

*"So what yoga and the practice of Buddhism is, is the removal of the mind, of the focus of the conscious attention, from the world to infinity, to a realm of pure light. To simply increase the power of your mind through the practices that are engaged in yoga—gazing exercises, meditation, empowerments from teachers, from power places, from karma yoga, whatever it is—to simply increase the volatility and power of your mind without then using that power to move your mind to a formless realm is going to cause you much more pain than you had prior to practicing.*

*We've got somebody who's running, every chance you give him, against a wall. They just keep running into the wall. Great, let's take the guy down to the gym, make him a lot stronger. Now he can run against the wall with twice as much speed and hurt himself even more and cause himself more pain. Great accomplishment!*

*Well, that's what I observe most people are doing with yoga. That's all they're doing—they're increasing the power of their minds, but then they are going back to or they never left the world of desire and aversion. Consequently, now that they've refined and developed the power of the mind, the pain will be all the greater, the attachment will be all the greater. Desire will completely overcome them.*

*It's through the conscious removal of the focus of the mind and the body to the realm of spirit, to the realm of happiness. Now when I talk about the realm of spirit, happiness, nirvana, Enlightenment, I'm not talking about something ideal or imaginary. There are realms of light that exist that have always existed and will always exist. They're much more solid than the transient, sensorially perceived or mentally perceived reality that you're currently experiencing. They're just behind the world that you see. Oh, there are countless dimensional worlds, but they're no different than this one, really."*
(Rama, <u>Tantric Buddhism</u>, "Buddhist Yoga")

The underlying issue is truly letting go of the world. Not to fight it, not to demean it, but to comprehend that here you are, alive in this world of transience, and then not to get caught up in it. You started on the spiritual path because you want to know happiness deeply and constantly within yourself. Don't forget that. In such an overcrowded and unhappy world, just keeping that in mind takes self-effort.

Also, don't make the mistake of believing that the energy of the unknown can be manipulated for worldly success:

*"... when you can command the nagual you have a great deal of power, and people know that intuitively. They feel if they can get to the nagual, plunge themselves in it, they will become powerful, then they can get anything they want in the tonal. It's a very tricky game that the self sets up. A person, then, who directs too much of their attention to the nagual, the reason they're doing that is they're obsessed with power, not understanding that power actually, properly, does not belong to the nagual but to the tonal—the kind of power that they're interested in. What they should really do, if they want supreme power of that type, is develop the tonal to perfection. The nagual doesn't give you the kind of personal power they think. That nagual gives you the nagual. It gives you the unknown, it gives you reality. It is reality."*

*(Rama, <u>Insights: Talks on the Nature of Existence</u>, "Modular Mysticism: The Sorcerer's Explanation")*

So when you fall off the path, the underlying question is what do you really want? As Rama not so jokingly put it, Enlightenment isn't really so hard. It's just not very popular here on Earth.

The self-discovery process with a teacher is beautiful but you must be watchful and trust your intuition. While many teachers may claim to be Enlightened, only a few really are.

*"There are some teachers who you can go and see who have enough personal power to flip you into the unknown. They can push you into the second attention, and then you're on your own, and you will never reorder properly. It's a terrible experience. Some people have done it themselves by pushing their kundalini too hard, by meditating in certain ways, and they've pushed themselves too far into the unknown. But once they got there, they didn't know what to do. The reordering of the luminous fibers is a very sophisticated art. It's not something anyone should ever undertake without supervision. You can make all the changes on the island of the tonal you*

*want, you can take little excursions into the nagual, but to push yourself to the reordering process is absolutely foolish. If a person gradually pursues these arts, they will be assigned a teacher."*

*(Rama, Insights: Talks on the Nature of Existence, "Modular Mysticism: The Sorcerer's Explanation")*

In this age the journey to Enlightenment is difficult, but spiritual seekers, including students of advanced teachers, have been falling off the path for thousands of years. And then getting back on:

*"Your journey is to see how deeply you can interface your mind with infinity…. You've been properly initiated by a teacher who has put you on the path, empowered you, given you directions for meditation, and then off you go to meditate and to live your life as purely, simply, and excitingly as possible. Excitingly in the sense that your perception is that life is glowing more every day because your meditation is clarifying, and the way you lead your life and the thoughts you think are continually clarifying your perceptual body. If, on the other hand, life is glowing less, obviously you're not doing yoga properly, and you have to start over, hit the reset button and learn what yoga is. You've fallen from the path and it's time to get back on it.*

*This happens to most monks a number of times. You're not practicing yoga at all. You're not practicing real meditation. You're practicing ego or practicing laziness or practicing confusion. It happens to everybody and we don't feel bad about it. Since we don't have a self, we don't have to worry about it, we don't have to account for what we've done or not done, we simply have to get back on the path. Being on the path means we again meditate with joy, we again deal with the suffering of life and the pain of existence without perfect Enlightenment with a smile. It means we clarify our lives… we don't fill it with unnecessary clutter, with cluttering emotions, cluttering perceptions, cluttering hates, cluttering jealousies, cluttering vanities because these things simply cloud the mind and they don't afford a perfect view of existence, rather an imperfect view.*

*The perfect view of existence comes from an unclouded, uncluttered life and mind whereby the radiance of perfect attention of the mind of the universe floods us at every moment. This is Buddhism. This is being on the path."*

*(Rama, Tantric Buddhism, "The Natural State")*

# Chapter 13: The Truth About Tantric Buddhism

One of the most significant differences between Rama's teachings and those of most spiritual traditions was his constant attention on how to navigate life in today's modern world. In fact, he made the effort to stabilize one's existence in the world as the foundation for the successful growth into Enlightenment. To use living in the world as a trampoline to Enlightenment.

He taught how to live in the world and pursue Enlightenment at the same time, and specifically how to use your career to advance towards Enlightenment. Rather than living in a monastery, dealing with the modern world and being successful getting through it was integral to becoming Enlightened.

He felt that having career success, living in your own home, making your way in the world as an independent person was also more suitable for Americans. Rama always made the point that life is ultimately the greatest teacher, so trying to flee it was contradictory. Living in the world also keeps you quite aware of the reasons why you chose to pursue Enlightenment in the first place. While monasteries can facilitate meditation practice and minimize dealing with chaotic energies out in the world, they are themselves little societies with all the human hierarchies, game playing and pressure to conform found in the outside world.

Tantric Buddhism is a more esoteric form of Buddhism that differs from most monastic traditions by not rejecting worldly life. It is not that he viewed the world as something desirable to experience; often he accentuated just the opposite, as shown in multiple quotes about life on Earth in the preceding chapters. The difference in perspective is based on an understanding of sentient existence plus pragmatic energy analysis: the struggle to totally separate yourself from society not only requires a tremendous amount of energy, it doesn't actually solve the desire/aversion challenge which is the real issue.

*"The sensual experiences in life are not to be avoided. This is the philosophy of Tantric Buddhism. Nor are they particularly to be sought after. They are inevitable. They come with daily living. A cup of coffee, fasting, the way the sky looks—all of the sensual images of life are there; they can't be disputed. Most people run after them with the sense that if we can experience more, somehow we will feel better.*

*There are pathways to Enlightenment where they encourage us to control the senses, shut the senses off…. The religious hard line, in other words, that the sensual world is in some way negative and not spiritual, is from my point of view not very accurate. I can understand pathways to Enlightenment where people shun certain aspects of the sensual world because they feel that these aspects are very powerful; they're not in a position yet to control their appetites, I guess, and so people avoid sexuality, they avoid certain types of food, they avoid, they avoid, they avoid….*

*We push the sensual barrage back for a while, although we can never push it back, we're just in a different sensual barrage. The sensual world cannot be avoided. We're in it at every moment. We are part of it.*

*In Tantric Buddhism, our feeling is that the problem—there is no problem with the sensual world. There just isn't one, unless you have a tremendous attraction or aversion to it. Either one tends to postpone Enlightened mind from dawning. If you think that there's some wonderful hidden promise in the sensual world, there isn't. There's just momentary, transient sensual experience. If you think there's some terrible thing that's going to occur because you're involved in the sensual world, well, you're always involved in the sensual world at every moment. Fasting is as sensual as eating. Being celibate is as sensual as having sex. They're just different choices, different videos that you've selected to view tonight.*

*What matters is not the sensual experience. What matters is your view of it. In other words, what you're doing with your mind. In Tantric Buddhism, we just lead our lives. We don't really worry a whole lot about the sensual world one way or the other. Instead, we enter into the kingdom of Enlightened mind."*

*(Rama, Tantric Buddhism, "Tantric Buddhism")*

Tantric Buddhism is an approach to incarnation that reduces the importance of sensual experiences by quietly accepting that we're living in a physical dimension. In other words, it has decided to not overthink this thing we call life. We're in a body for a limited time, and if we're spending most of that limited time flooding our perceptual systems and thinking about the physical world around us, that doesn't leave much time for meditation and focusing within.

It's clear that while Tantric Buddhism accepts our place in this physical world full of people, the dominant focus is on inner growth, mainly through meditation. That rather than get tied up with rules about how to control oneself while out in the world, don't waste the energy to exclude it. Certainly don't dive in either. There are some popular misconceptions about tantra that use this acceptance of social interaction as the cover for actually getting more deeply involved with the sensual world:

*"Some people, of course, say they're practicing tantra. There are a lot of books on tantric sexual practice in local bookstores. These are usually pretty silly books. They are telling you how you can magnify your sexual experiences or things like that by doing certain kundalini exercises while you're having sex, and how it will keep you in a high state of attention. Now, there's nothing wrong with trying. It might work for you, and there's only one way to find out, right? But in most cases, it's just silly."*
*(Rama, Zen Tapes, "Tantric Zen")*

This is what Tantric Buddhism's approach to physical reality really is:

*"Our interest is not controlling the sensual world; our interest is placing our mind beyond it. Not focusing on it because we find that there are other kingdoms of mind. And to spend all your time worrying about what you should or shouldn't do keeps you right there, highly involved with whatever you should or shouldn't do. I mean, it's in your mind. You're thinking that you shouldn't have sex because you're celibate. So you just keep thinking about sex—instead of Enlightenment.*

*The tantric path involves taking the mind and directing it beyond the senses.... we're not particularly threatened by the senses. Our method is to enlarge the mind and let the senses do as they will....*

*We're all in the sensual world, we've all experienced it; we can do nothing but experience it every moment we have a body. There are no new revelations. It's unavoidable. And it does not bring Enlightenment…. There's a neutrality that comes with maturation in Tantric Buddhism where it just is irrelevant, it just doesn't matter. The sensual world is unimportant. What matters is Enlightenment, taking our mind and placing it in dimensions that we would be completely unaware of if we were totally immersed always in the sensual world."*
(Rama, <u>Tantric Buddhism</u>, "Tantric Buddhism")

In Buddhism, there is what's known as the long path and the short path. Long path Buddhism is the formal study of scriptures, performing rituals, prayers, and the following of numerous lifestyle rules. There is not much emphasis placed on meditating, though it is a component. Short path Buddhism minimizes all of those traditional religious observances and maximizes meditation. Both are completely grounded in the teachings of the Buddha and other Enlightened teachers prominent in the religion's history. Tantric, or esoteric Buddhism is the core of short path Buddhism.

*"The short path and long path address the same issue but in a very different way. Short path Buddhism, which is esoteric Buddhism, teaches the individual to gain control of the mind, to purify the thoughts, to have happy emotions, and to release the kundalini. The kundalini energy is very powerful and it will bring you into ecstatic states of meditative awareness. You will realize infinity, eternity, immortality, and as I said, learn to laugh. But it's fast and it's strong. It takes a relatively short period of time to have Enlightening experiences on the short path, but the short path is demanding. In other words, on the short path you meditate for several hours a day. You practice mindfulness. Your entire life becomes a vehicle, a diamond vehicle of transformation. You use your work, your school work, your play, your relationships; everything is used to advance your own awareness. Nothing is wasted. And the central point of it is meditating on the chakras and learning to release the kundalini energy, to guide it very carefully, with the aid of a teacher who is Enlightened or partially Enlightened, and to have the kundalini bring you into very pure, high states. To transform yourself, to eliminate all negative aspects of your being. Negative means limited, things that keep you in the 2% (of mind) and (instead) to experience the totality of life.*

*Long path Buddhism is, I suppose, more of a religion in a sense in that it involves more the recitation of prayers, reading the sutras. It's more mental. It's not so much a meditative practice as a philosophy, a way of looking at things. Short path Buddhism, which is esoteric Buddhism, naturally you are conversant with all the aspects of exoteric, or long path Buddhism, but you're more of an adventurer. On the long path, we get National Geographic magazine, and we read about explorers who have gone to Africa and the Arctic and the Himalayas, and we share their adventures. We, to an extent, have those adventures with them, because we identify with them, we can feel them. As we look at the pictures and read the words, our mind takes us there, we're mental travelers. And we have little adventures, maybe we read National Geographic and it inspires us to go hiking in the local woods.*

*So that's long path Buddhism. There's some meditation, there's some journeys into the inner world. But you're not working directly with an Enlightened teacher. You're mainly reading, and listening to, and talking about the experiences of others, sort of vicariously experiencing them. Esoteric Buddhism, or short path, is going and traveling, taking the photos, having the journeys. You are the National Geographic explorer, exploring the different dimensions and universes of mind. And maybe you send back reports to others, maybe you just go and explore. It's the mystical path, the hidden path, the short path. On long path Buddhism you're not necessarily meditating on the chakras, your meditation is just the stilling of the mind, but it does not involve the volatile release of the kundalini yoga.*

*Long path Buddhism is made up more of moral precepts, things to do, things not to do. It guides your life, it gives it a brightness and clarity, a moral order, a sense of duty and obligation as a part of the universe, keeping the environment clean, inwardly and outwardly. Avoid injustice, say the right thing, always do the right thing. But you're gaining those insights from others. In other words, someone says this is right, this is not right. Someone who's been Enlightened, who can see that which is true and that which is not, that which is real and that which is an illusion. So you're accepting their opinion, which is written down in the Buddhist sutras or in commentaries by Enlightened teachers, and you're taking their word for it. And if you practice what they say, you'll notice that you'll have a happy life. But the essence of practice on the short path is to experience directly what is and what is not...."*
*(Rama, standalone talk, "Buddhism")*

It doesn't disagree with anything in the long path tradition, but is for those who want to go into higher states of mind sooner. While reading about the Buddha's transcendent experiences is very inspiring, you want to experience that directly, now. Following all of the rules and observances may best be seen as a preparatory phase to get to that point.

*"There are monasteries in Japan where they teach Zen with rules, more rules than you can imagine, and you might feel comfortable with that. I don't teach that type of Zen. It is necessary to have a very liberal and simultaneously very conservative mentality to practice Tantric Zen. If your mentality is just liberal, then Tantric Zen won't work because all you'll want to do is play around and be broad-minded. If you're completely conservative, then Tantric Zen won't work for you because you'll reject all liberal attitudes and ideas and just be stuck in being conservative. Whereas, if you fluctuate between liberal and conservative, Tantric Zen will work for you.*

*In other words, Tantric Zen is not being kinky, nor is it libertinism. Nor is it being conservative and austere. It is eclectic….The emphasis in tantra is not on what you find yourself doing—it's on meditation. Tantric Zen is all about the practice of zazen meditation and the theme—or the thought—that if you meditate well, you'll be in very powerful states of mind and then it really doesn't matter much what you do. So rather than minding your p's and q's, you meditate instead. You can gain power by avoidance. You can gain power doing certain things. You can gain much more power meditating.*

*If you spend your time meditating instead of avoiding and doing, then later, as you walk through life, you don't have to avoid and you don't have to do. You can just be. Your mind will be in an elevated state whereby whatever it is you are, or what is passing before your eye, the life that you are experiencing will be experienced very differently because you'll be wandering through the ten thousand states of mind."*
*(Rama, Zen Tapes, "Tantric Zen")*

An example of this is how two people, walking in the forest together, might view it very differently. Rama told the story of the time, many years ago, when he and a girlfriend were walking in the woods, and he was noticing the human litter of food wrappers and other things along the trail. This bothered him and he began talking about people polluting the environment. However, his girlfriend pointed out that if you focus not on that, but on the larger mosaic of colors, shapes, patterns and designs combining everything that they were seeing, then it's art. She was tantric, he said.

Another key principle of Tantric Buddhism is to be open to new ideas and techniques that will add to the practice. Unlike religion, which presents a crystallized dogma and a rigid organization, Tantric Buddhism is an open-ended structure. It is very clear about the destination—reaching Enlightenment. Meditation has been proven to be the most powerful, direct way to do that. Viewed from the platform of meditation, living in the world isn't so problematical and doesn't require avoidance. But as time passes from century to century and the world changes, Tantric Buddhism is on the lookout for what features of contemporary society may be incorporated.

*"... Tantric Buddhism is structural. We're structuralists. We don't have a preordained idea of what should create Enlightenment or what shouldn't. We look to traditions and if something's in a tradition—any tradition, spiritual tradition, mystical tradition, religious tradition—if we can employ that device that someone else discovered several thousand years ago or last week and use it and it helps us stop thought, we're all for it....*

*In other words, in tantra we don't believe in commandments. We believe in the moment and the truth that is applicable for that moment—as best we can sort it out with our heart, our intuition, our knowledge, our common sense—is the proper truth. This doesn't lead to anarchy, it lends to balance— if we're doing it honestly. But everything must revolve around meditation. It's only meditation that brings us ultimately beyond the sensual world. Not because 'beyond' implies that there's anything wrong with the sensual world. But the spirit wants to be free, and the spirit experiences the senses in early incarnations, and it's enough. The sensual world is very fulfilling. There's a lot to learn through sexuality. There's a lot to learn in all expressions of the senses.*

*But then the spirit wants something more. It evolves. It wants to experience light, true knowledge, perfect oblivion, the dissolution of the self in the finite sense, in the white light of eternity...."*
*(Rama, Tantric Buddhism, "Tantric Buddhism")*

One new idea in particular that Rama found to be very good for tantric practice was computer programming. First of all, he saw that for the mind, writing a computer program is surprisingly similar to the visualization exercises taught in Tibetan monasteries. Computer programming trains the mind in much the same way. The work environment is also very conducive. As a programmer you spend most of your time alone interacting with your computer, not with a lot of people. It requires a type of constant focus and one-pointed concentration like meditation. The amount of negative energy and discordant thoughts is minimized, and when you are with people, the main focus is on the project. Lastly, given that most people aren't interested in this profession, it pays very well and job security is high. You could live almost anywhere and find a computer programming job, and with the Internet many programmers now can work from home.

So the computer programming profession solves three problems for students of Tantric Buddhism. Since Tantric Buddhism is structural, it is just looking for what works today. As discussed in Chapter 11, another addition to Tantric Buddhism that Rama incorporated were the early books of Carlos Castaneda. He found that this material presented several valuable lessons about the composition of the human mind and how we are conditioned by our families and society. It also presented several classic spiritual development concepts in a contemporary world that Rama's students already knew. Tantric Buddhism grew and changed in similar ways in Tibet, China, and Japan.

As you advance in meditation, not sitting there thinking for an hour but keeping the mind still until you reach a level where you abide in stillness, the effect of the tantric approach begins to yield great results. Often it's difficult to have a long-term perspective, especially when you're first starting out. The beauty of Tantric Buddhism is that, while it acknowledges the world we live in and accepts our existence in it, it stays focused on the awareness of the higher states of mind. In fact, it is constantly on the lookout for ways to facilitate residing in the highest mental states.

*"Tantra is spiritual, not religious. It deals with the spirit. Religion is just an applied body of doctrines that's believed or not believed by one or more individuals. Spirituality is the science of metaphysics. It is how we unlock the spirit. It's not random, it's not accidental, it's something that works very definitively. It's the chemistry of the soul. Tantra is the most sophisticated application of the chemistry of the soul.*

*So I would not be troubled particularly by the sensual world. I wouldn't be troubled particularly by anything. I would only be excited about the quest for*

*Enlightenment. And sensual experiences will come and go, always. What I would do is put your mind beyond them.*

*As you meditate each day, you will gain the mental discipline and control to place your mind in higher states of attention during any sensual experience. Then an experience is no longer sensual, is it? It becomes Enlightening."*
(Rama, <u>Tantric Buddhism</u>, "Tantric Buddhism")

nirvana
ON ROOFT
RESTAURA

# Chapter 14:  From the Path of Affirmation to the Path of Negation

*"It is through many lifetimes of shifting the aggregate of the self and refining it and transforming it that one finally reaches a point of maximum velocity whereby one can snap off the circle completely and move into a freedom that's not simply, 'Gee, now I know how to get around the circle real well, whereas before it was kind of painful and I was stuck in it and didn't really get its motion. Now I know how to get around and get to where I want to go and avoid the places I want to avoid.' But that in itself becomes another circle, which is another kind of trap. So now we know self-discovery very well, we know a system very well, and we become trapped by the system and by our knowledge of it."*
*(Rama, <u>Tantric Buddhism</u>, "The Nexus of All Pathways")*

One of the core concepts about the pathway to Enlightenment is how, through meditation and other practices, you gradually clear away the obscurations clouding your consciousness. With each meditation you get a little clearer. Chakra meditation releases the kundalini, a power that washes away the gunk in your mind. That gunk is a blend of the imprinting in your early childhood, the desires and aversions in this lifetime that keep you in such a rigid mold, and the samskaras, the behavioral patterns that have built up over your past lives to become like rocky aggregates blocking the light.

As Rama very pointedly explained, every time you incarnate it essentially is the same you, because of all of those samskaras. You've got the same deck of cards to work with, lifetime after lifetime. You may shuffle them differently each time, but it's the same deck. In other words, it's your aggregate-filled mind re-expressing those aggregates in very similar ways in every incarnation, simply because that's all you know. You will go around and around as a typical human trapped in a transient world forever, unless you do something to break out of it. Literally forever, he said.

So what most people really are as an incarnate human being is an assemblage of patterns that have been repeating themselves over many lifetimes. Those aggregates shift a little and reassemble into a self in the next incarnation. With all those samskaras there are many mini-selves competing to be in control. Depending on which samskaras hold sway at the moment, the desires associated with them become your dominant interests, and those are what you come back to pursue.

Therefore we spend most of each incarnation in reverse; we may think that we're in charge of our lives, but we're constantly being pushed and pulled by all those samskaras built up over thousands and thousands of lifetimes. Right now those samskaras are driving your personal set of desires and increasingly tangled attachments. On top of that, we're so assimilated by the society we reside in that it's hard for you to be independent even for a moment. This may sound like a harsh perspective, but it helps explain why life is difficult and painful so much of the time.

As discussed earlier, a person needs tenacity to break free. That tenacity is born out of a different kind of desire, the intense desire to stop being in the mental pain experienced living in the regular world. The immediate objective is to escape the world they were born into which they experience as a cage. Escaping usually takes the form of renunciation, of leaving family and society.

So the goal of the first stage of the pathway to Enlightenment is to be in much less pain. The solution traditionally has been entering a religious order. This is the Path of Affirmation.

*"The path of affirmation, which is the first portion of the self-discovery path, is a path in which we don't seek to understand, we seek to escape. We want to escape the pain of life, the pain of our minds, the pain of our bodies, the pain of the world. We don't really want to ask a lot of questions; we just want to know a way out—and the way out is through avoidance. We don't eat meat, we don't have sex, we don't deal with money, we don't deal with things that we know have caused us pain. The great teachers explain why these things cause us pain—attachment, desire, having a self, you know, all the different things. But—we just escape. We don't really care. You go to a*

*doctor and you hurt. You're not really interested in knowing how the medicine works, you just want it to.*

*When people seek the spiritual path—which is the path of affirmation, the exoteric path, the first path we walk on, the first part of the path—it's because they're in pain and they want to get away from the pain. So we have a series of prescriptions that we ask them to follow which causes them to regulate their lives, to separate themselves from the things that cause them pain....*

*Now, the avoidance of that which causes you pain does not produce Enlightenment. It produces avoidance. The avoidance may lessen or tranquilize the pain, but it will not produce Enlightenment. Knowledge and understanding produce Enlightenment. Religion is the avoidance of pain and suffering, I mean symbolically, in the hope for a better afterlife, meaning one less painful than the one we're in. So if I don't do this and I don't do that and I do this and I do that, my next life, be it in heaven or another incarnation, will be better than this....*

*Somewhere between the desire and the aversion we exist as a self. The self can be measured by what it avoids and what it seeks and by its sense of history—past remembrances. That makes a self....*

*What the religions offer you is—it works! Turn your attention away from the sensorial, develop the virtues, avoid injuring others, avoid hate, essentially—self-control, compassion, love, understanding—we all know what religion symbolizes. Oh, there are fanatical, crazy religions that tell you to kill people who aren't in your religion. That's not a religion. That's a political philosophy. But a real religion is something that leads us above pain. By following a number of different practices that are always the same—they may be rearranged differently in a particular religion, or given different names—but it's always the same, it's structural, it's what reduces pain, the pain that we experience in being, in our being-ness, which can't be ended by death since death is just a doorway to another condition that we experience.*

*When we follow the guidelines of religion, we find that our lives are better; we're happier. Self-control works. Patience works. Kindness works. Love works. All of these things help. When we lose them, we lose the path and our lives are miserable. When we're selfish, vindictive, angry, when we don't care more for others than we care for ourselves, life is terrible. So we*

*follow the path of affirmation and we find it's better. Life is better. It's beautiful to love. To be loved is irrelevant. But when you love someone, you experience that emotion. It's a beautiful emotion. It has its limitations, but it sure beats hate. To assist someone, to not always have to have everything, to give somebody the bigger piece of cake—when we do it, we feel better. Practice it, you'll find out."*
(Rama, Tantric Buddhism, "The Path of Negation")

While the main motivation for entering the path of affirmation is to get away from the pain of life, intertwined with that is the pursuit of the feeling when your spirit is free. You've had moments when you just felt happy and there wasn't an external event involved. That feeling also wasn't the typical transitory happiness of eating an ice cream cone. As the world keeps bruising you, your longing for that feeling gets stronger. That's also driving you onto the path of affirmation.

*"The reason that one practices self-discovery is because we're seeking a feeling. We're seeking a feeling. And when we feel that feeling, there is nothing like that feeling. It's just a feeling....*

*There's a feeling that occurs sometimes when you're standing at sunset looking out into the horizon, where you just slip away from all of this and all of that. You're at a party. You're at an office party. It's Christmas. Everybody's busy, everybody's having a good time and they're celebrating. For a moment you go out on the balcony and the sun is setting and you just look at the sky. You slip away from all the noise, all the good times, everybody looking good in their good-looking suits, all the beautiful men and women. You just go outside by yourself and you slide the glass door behind you and you just look outside, and for a moment, the noise, the excitement, the hubbub vanishes, and there's a stillness.*

*The stillness isn't the end of things, it's the beginning. It's always the beginning. You step into that stillness and you just go away. There's a feeling that comes up which cannot be expressed in words, and that feeling transports you beyond this world to other worlds, other realms, to different places inside your mind maybe. And that feeling is so perfect and so complete, it's beyond all other experiences."*
(Rama, Tantric Buddhism, "The Path of Affirmation")

You don't realize it at the time, but by entering the path of affirmation you have been victorious in beginning to switch from being controlled by your samskaras to discarding them. In tandem with this, you have created a situation in which you can more directly pursue that ineffable feeling. You've embarked on a journey to create a new person. That's why this path is also referred to as the path of creation.

Lifetime after lifetime, your interests in particular desires are the cause for rebirth. Even the desire for spiritual growth is a samskara, as are other positive ingrained patterns. The underlying issue is that there's an overfocus on physical existence. The samskaras define you as a person with a particular identity; they lay out the choice of rides you'll be taking in the upcoming incarnation. That's the direction everyone takes. The other direction is to experience more and more of your complete mind. The long-term goal of the path of affirmation contains the seeds of your redirection towards the complete mind:

*"In Buddhism what we seek to do is not necessarily just find a better ride, but we seek to find a better us. We seek to change ourselves into someone who's beautiful to be. The pure act of being who we are is beautiful, a beauty so overpowering that it becomes ecstasy. In other words, it isn't the action of doing something that produces ecstasy. The act of doing or engaging in something will only reflect who you are….*

*… states of mind engender reality. It doesn't matter what ride you get on, you are on the ride that is you.*

*What we do in Buddhism—changing rides is inevitable. That just happens, you can't avoid it in life. Life is a cyclic, changing situation. But what we seek to do is what other people don't do. We seek to change ourselves….*

*Buddhism, then, is the study of changing the self. Naturally, as the self changes, it will select different rides to go on because there are different tastes. You really don't have to worry about that part. In other words, today you like Space Mountain; tomorrow you'll like It's a Small World—various rides at Disneyland. Your tastes will automatically evolve as you do. So, if instead of putting all your attention into always trying to get a better ride but instead you put your attention into creating a better you, then whatever ride you go on is much more beautiful, much more ecstatic."*
(Rama, <u>Tantric Buddhism</u>, "The Nexus of all Pathways")

If your primary interest is to create a better you, you're doing self-discovery. There are many styles and schools, but the common goal is merging with the infinite light. There are no shortcuts around yourself, since the process is working entirely within your mind. The good news is that every time you meditate you are lifting yourself into a clearer awareness. You remove your old self one meditation at a time, and as you recognize the obscurations in your mind you can drop them, like cutting off the sandbags holding down the hot air balloon.

So the path of affirmation is the creation of a new self who is in states of mind not dominated by the world. Separating yourself from the world physically and psychologically is moving your attention away from it and towards something else. The entire process takes many lifetimes, but it took even more lifetimes to become the complex personality you were before entering the path of affirmation. Going from being an average human being, to the path of affirmation, and then to the path of negation is a protracted process.

The irony of the pathway to Enlightenment is that as real as those samskaras are, another way of looking at them is that they're the product of a very rich imagination spanning many lifetimes. You're the one, due to circumstances inherent in being incarnate, who have built a massive library of fantasies in your mind. Granted, it couldn't be helped, given living in a world with many other people all sharing the same physical space and time. But a deeper truth frees you from the shackles of these illusions:

*"All things are void. So how possibly could there be any obscurations, since everything is void, when you're void yourself? There's only the void. In the void, there's only the shining, perfect clear light of reality; there's no obscuration. To assume that wealth or sexuality or the usage of power, any of these things are not void in nature, gives them a reality that they don't actually have. They're void. In the experience of their voidness, of their vacuity, the self, the temporal self, the transient caretaker, somewhat happier self that we've evolved on the exoteric path, vanishes. It dissolves in the clear light of reality, and there's only the clear light of reality."*
*(Rama, <u>Tantric Buddhism</u>, "The Path of Negation")*

On the path of affirmation, your disciplined avoidance of the human desires that bothered you so much results in wearing down the old samskaras. They're replaced with samskaras of good karma that you've generated from serving others and studying the scriptures. You generated new, happier samskaras from helping people and immersing your mind in religious literature, and from enforcing a sizable distance between yourself and the worldly desires you fled from. But you've also developed a hostile attitude toward those worldly desires you once pursued. You're now stuck with two new types of samskaras; samskaras of good karma and of hostility to worldly desires. They are now blocking Enlightenment. That's where the path of negation comes in.

*"We are pure. That's all there is, is purity. But you don't see it that way because you're in obscure states of mind. So in the teaching of tantra, what I do is direct people to engage in specific practices, and when they do those things they negate their samskaras and the self goes away because the self that a person has on the exoteric path is propped up by their avoidances, just as the self that a person has before they reach the exoteric path, before they start religion. In other words, in the beginning the self is created by attraction; some aversion, obviously, through fears. That creates a self. That self causes pain, frustration, whatever—the absence of Enlightenment. Then in the practice of the exoteric path we gradually, as we work through it, overcome—we drop the old self. Very often on a spiritual path, they even give you a new name.*

*... You are reborn. You are reborn on the exoteric path. But now on the exoteric path you will develop history and you will develop a new self. A happier, brighter self, but it still stops Enlightenment. After many incarnations of being on the exoteric path, this self becomes as hard, as predicated and as obscure, even though not as painful, as the self you had before the religion. In other words, the good self blocks you.*

*So then, in the advanced practice, you take a person and you have them go do the things that are their opposites. But they do them in a way that they couldn't do them back at the beginning before they followed any path at all. They used to just go out and get rich but they were bound by it, you see.... They have to do that—but with purity, as part of their yoga, not as an attraction. In doing all the things that they've learned to avoid over the incarnations in religion—which has created this new, religious, better, prototype self, but which ultimately blocks Enlightenment—now they have to go do those things which they think they shouldn't do. It's just intrinsic in the multi-life memory: 'I shouldn't be rich. I shouldn't do this. I shouldn't have power' because you know it corrupts, it brings you into very painful states of mind.*

*So then the adept, the student, has to go do those things. But they're not doing them like they were all the way back, you see. Because in the doing of them, they erase the current self. In other words, what forges the self is attraction and aversion. Your aversion to the things that used to cause you pain, which has created this happier new self, block you....*

*In the beginning, wealth was causing you pain, your attachment to it, because it created a self that was ugly. Now you've created a self that's much nicer, through lives of poverty and chastity, great. But that self also blocks you. Now we have to go become wealthy again because you have to overcome your attachment to poverty that was created, and your attachment to the new, happier self. We're not going to go back to the original self that was painful; we're going to move on to no self."*
*(Rama, <u>Tantric Buddhism</u>, "The Path of Negation")*

It's not merely a matter of overcoming your negative attitudes and behaviors and becoming a very good person. In order to become Enlightened, you must let go of all of the behaviors that have aggregated over your past lives. The advanced course is based on the understanding that you must get rid of the good personality characteristics too. Unraveling of your samskaras, past life tendencies, both good and bad, is necessary simply because Enlightenment is not about being a good person instead of being a bad person. It is about erasing the self so that nothing but clear light is left. That's why it is a gradual process spanning many incarnations.

Since your life in the physical world is experienced through the senses, there's a kind of trap you are in as long as you are alive. Tantric Buddhism sees this quite clearly and breaks you out of that trap. Rather than have your ego fight the very desires that motivated you to reincarnate, in other words the ego fighting itself, you need to take a step back from that structure. Stop pouring your energy into the samskaras, stop constantly feeding and reinforcing them either through indulgence or suppression.

Whether samskaras of bad or good karma, those aggregates are the experiences in each lifetime distilled into strong behavioral tendencies. They affix to your soul. In Buddhism, the concept of a soul is different than in other religions, and that difference illuminates how it defines who you are:

"The samskaras, then, are not the things we did in an individual lifetime, but it was the way that we thought, the tendencies, the way the aggregates are formed. A human being is not made up of one self. You have many, many selves. The old motto 'Know thyself,' in my estimation, should be changed to 'Know thy selves,' because you're made up of many, many beings.

The Buddhists sometimes talk about the anatman, meaning that a person does not have a soul. In the Hindu tradition and the Christian tradition we talk about a soul, or an atman, a self, the same self that incarnates from lifetime to lifetime. Now, in most forms of Buddhism, the Buddhists don't feel that there is not a self. What they're saying is that the self is not fixed.

Buddha indicated that the self, that part of you that incarnates from lifetime to lifetime, was causal. That is to say, there was a connecting link in each lifetime. It wasn't as if there was a being that was there in one lifetime and then in the next lifetime there was no connection. In his own case, when he discussed his past lives, he was certainly implying that there was an essence that incarnated from lifetime to lifetime. But what he was trying to suggest was that most people have a concept of the soul that is almost like a personality. And what he said was, rather than that, the soul is composed of aggregates. It's like saying that there are seven or eight basic colors and we can put those colors together in varying combinations.

Perhaps there are seven musical notes and we can put those notes in varying combinations and produce different melodies. So in each lifetime the notes re-form in a slightly different pattern, but that pattern is an outgrowth of the pattern that was in a previous life. Imagine that in the first few incarnations, the aggregates, the essences that make a person—almost like the atomic structure in a nonphysical sense—are very loose. There isn't much to it. It's like an atom of hydrogen as opposed to some of the more complex atoms that have more protons, neutrons, electrons and valances. As incarnations go by, the atom gets more complex. That is, your being, the part of you that reincarnates from lifetime to lifetime, the aggregate grows thicker and denser. While this is good and it stores up knowledge and power, at the same time there's a problem with it because it means that a person becomes more fixated.

The more lives you have, the harder it is to change, yet the stronger you are. It's a kind of funny dichotomy. That's good in development. It's

*important that one become more and more fixed. But then you reach a point in higher spiritual development where what you want to do is erase everything that you've been."*
*(Rama, <u>The Lakshmi Series</u>, "Samadhi and the Superconscious States")*

The process of becoming Enlightened is the process of becoming aware that the self as you know it is just a small part of your complete mind. The term "realizing emptiness" is often used in more advanced Buddhism to point to the human band of attention's gradual release of control. This implies that who you are now is slowly being replaced by pure light which is without a sense of self. That is endemic to meditation, which is why Rama always said to just keep meditating.

The deeper truth, however, is that you are becoming aware that your mind has always been nothing but pure light which is without a sense of self. In truth, it has always been empty. Your sense of self, your personality, has been a tool. Unfortunately the tool took over your life. Self-discovery gets your life back. The perception of life in its totality is beyond the human mind's ability to grasp. Enlightenment ultimately is this complete perception of life.

While you as the ego feels threatened by this, as you progress in self-discovery your sincere desire to experience the highest light keeps increasing. For example, selfless giving is a great way to unravel samskaras. Doing it is fun because while doing it you are free from all of your constraints. It is a natural way to feel liberated from your current self.

While in this physical body, what you're doing with your mind is what you're really experiencing all the time. Therefore, if you feel so good in the higher planes that you forget about your desires, what does that imply about your life here and now? However, rather than put down life on Earth, accept and perceive that it too is a pathway to Enlightenment. The path of negation uses it in a very creative way:

*"So to go beyond karma you have to end the structure of self. Even a good self will create another good self in the next life and another one, and that good self will never be Enlightened. You'll be bound, life after life, by good karma, which is better I suppose than being bound by bad karma, which would imply more pain. That's what we mean by good and bad. So you must—if you find a tantric master, he has you go and do all the things you*

*hate to do. You won't know why you hate them, but it'll just—you don't want to do them. The things that he's having you do are things that just seem totally contrary to you, to anything spiritual. Well, of course they are because all your ideas of what is spiritual are completely based around the path of affirmation, which is where you've been for a long time and that's what caused you to get to where you are to meet the tantric master.*

*So the tantric master now will say, 'OK, good.' The things they'll tell you, you don't want to do. You don't even know why it arouses such hate, anger. It's because the self is so stuck, it's so defined. And it's got to go. Just as the other self went a long time ago before your current memory. Many lives ago you had another type of self that you had for countless lives and you eradicated it. You brought a new tenant in. This tenant is much nicer, which gives you some thought about what the other one must have been like! The other must have been a real bad dude, right? You look at this one and you can tell how impure, how uncontrolled, how filled with—you know, whatever it is that this one is."*
*(Rama, <u>Tantric Buddhism</u>, "The Path of Negation")*

The end stage of the pathway to Enlightenment is a perfect clarity in your mind. A perfect mind isn't something that you create, it is perfect when it is without any traces of self. That's realizing emptiness. That kind of mind has no samskaras. Eventually the path goes beyond all limitation. In reality the path is in our mind, but that's a difficult image to grasp at first. The path isn't another rigid structure you must conform to. It isn't another social order. It is your pursuit of a permanent inner freedom. You are moving along routes that are inside your mind.

*"The final battles are the samskaras of good karma. They prevent samadhi. But you can't just reach a mental understanding where you say, 'Oh good, I understood what you said, I've got it.' Nothing will happen; you won't go into samadhi. You have to go do these things but with complete detachment. Naturally, for a religious person, the avoidance is intensive. They just don't want to go do these things; they are so hung up on good karma and on method from so many lifetimes that there's terrific avoidance. But if they keep the avoidance, they will not become Enlightened. They will stay in whatever mental states they're in.*

*So the path of negation, tantra, has to do with silencing the self that has arisen, in a temporary sense, the wave that has arisen out of the ocean from*

*good karma. The good karma of all those past lives of religious practice has brought you to the path of negation, but you are still attached to it and not necessarily consciously. What you have to do is go and do the things that keep the self empowered, that keep it manifest. You have to go and do the things it doesn't want, which have become reflexive."*
*(Rama, <u>Tantric Buddhism</u>, "The Path of Negation")*

It can help to get a sense of your progress. There are stages on the pathway to Enlightenment. First is taking the step away from being another typecast human being in society. For some, eventually this leads to the path of affirmation. Some then go from the path of affirmation to the path of negation. A few continue beyond that:

*"So if you seek ecstasy and freedom, and again those are kind of intangible words, but—if we can get beyond them, then the only recourse is the study of the dissolution and the reformation of the self. And of course, there's something beyond that, which is—complete Enlightenment, in which we go beyond selves and reformations of selves and all that stuff. This is the process we go through just to build up speed, and if we get enough speed through either the path of negation or the path of creation, if we get up enough speed, we can flip beyond creation or negation to pure Enlightenment...."*
*(Rama, <u>Tantric Buddhism</u>, "The Nexus of all Pathways")*

# Chapter 15: Meditation, Part Three: Dissolve

*"You can't teach someone to be Enlightened. It's something you have to go and do. You can't teach someone to meditate well. It's something you have to go and do."*
*(Rama, <u>Tantric Buddhism</u>, "The Best Meditation I Ever Had")*

In Chapter 10, "Meditation: Part Two," the theme was meditation's ability to find the happiness that's already present in your mind. This was accomplished through merging with music filled with the energy of an Enlightened teacher while focusing on a sequence of chakras. This method more quickly washes away the self you came into this world with and have so doggedly remained attached to. By focusing on chakras you are letting the kundalini rise to each one. You felt better because that whole experience washed your mind and lifted you into the Enlightened teacher's aura, which has no traces of a limited self. The longer your mind stayed completely still the better you felt, because you were in the Enlightened teacher's aura longer.

Now let's take the next step: not only are you clearer with each meditation, if you really do it right you actually molt off some of the self you were at the start of the meditation. You are a new self each time. That new self sees life in more aware states of mind. Life is something far happier and beautiful than we are aware of in normal sentient mind states. We're only seeing fragments of life, and since we're in varying degrees of pain from chasing our desires and becoming more attached to them, we miss the huge scale of life. As Rama explained, ultimately Buddhism is the study of perception, of how to move into higher perceptual states.

In this third stage of meditation, the word "dissolving" comes into play. "Dissolving" is an oft-used spiritual term, but often applied in a variety of ways.

*"Dissolving is a way of speaking. You don't dissolve. It would be just as accurate to say that you become what you really are—your higher self, eternal consciousness. Then you don't even notice desire, you don't even notice attachment. If you sit there in light, who could notice? All of the ecstasies that have ever been or will ever be could present themselves in front of you, and you wouldn't even feel them, compared to the pure light of eternity. That's really the way you do it."*
*(Rama, The Lakshmi Series, "Inaccessibility and Attachment")*

So as you advance in your meditation practice, you reach a point where the earlier definitions don't cover its full scope. What's occurring is that your causal structure is gradually being transformed in completely positive ways. It's being refined, each new self letting more light through because it is more transparent. Another way of putting it is that you are becoming more and more aware of the vastness of your complete mind. These aren't just words to inspire you anymore. It is the fulfillment of your original and purest intentions for taking up meditation in the first place. It is difficult to put into words what's been happening at a deeper level all long, but Rama discussed it this way:

*"Meditation is a process of liquefying the self temporarily and then allowing the self to rebond. The ice melts and then it comes back again. But when it comes back again, it comes back in a more evolved configuration. It's less dense. It's less structured. It's more lucid.*

*Now why does it do that? It's because in between the liquefactions we're building up a level of power. In other words, why shouldn't it just come back in a structure that's about the same? Why not come back in a structure that is less ecstatic, if we can use ecstasy as a measurement? Ecstasy is a relative measurement of freedom. When we're not free, there's no ecstasy. The more free we are, the more ecstasy.*

*We're using gradients of light as an auric measurement, a quantified auric measurement of the ascension of consciousness from the relatively sensorial, material perceptions of existence to the more refined, spiritual perceptions of existence. And obviously there's a lot more ecstasy in the spirit than in the flesh. Flesh has its moments. But the spirit has a much, much higher processing rate. The body is a very low level language. Machine language. The language of the soul, of the mind, is much more evolved. There are many languages.*

*What causes that change is not simply the detonation of the self. What causes the change is that in between the restructurings of the self, one is directing oneself towards light....*

*But the magic of life, of course, is not something that can be explained. Structures can only take us to the point where they begin or end. Beyond structures is the white light. The white light is reality in a form that cannot be apprehended or understood. It can be admired, it can be feared, it can be focused upon, it can be rejected, it can be forgotten. But it's there, just as the sun is there....*

*The sun is there, whether you're aware of it or not. The white light is there. And the magic of the white light is—when we step into it, it transmutes us, it transforms us. It just does....*

*Most people don't know what to do with their minds and their lives— they're kind of stuck in their own DNA. But Buddhists have made a study over thousands and thousands of years, of how you can change the structures of the self, how you can manipulate the DNA of being. You can't change the fact that it's there—everybody has it. But you can cause it to move into new formations, into more lucid formations in which there's ecstasy...."*
*(Rama, <u>Tantric Buddhism</u>, "The Nexus of all Pathways")*

As mentioned in Chapter 10, the secret to meditation is to be a perpetual beginner. Each meditation is your first meditation. With this attitude you are more open to the fullness of the experience. Now you can see the practicality of this advice. The irony is that you have to become very advanced in meditation in order to appreciate its simplicity, and it takes a significant amount of internal power to have that insight.

This applies to other methods for spiritual growth. Applying this concept to the Tibetan Rebirth Process presented in Chapter 9, what is it really but an exceptional meditation, fully immersed in the clear light? Prolonged over several, if not many sessions, perhaps, but the same principle is operative.

You are going through what would have been a lifetime, only inside your mind. You literally are becoming a beginner, over and over again.

*"When we meditate we stop our thought. When your thought stops, the mind is perfect.... That's what is eternal. When there is no thought, no sense of self, no impressions, that's eternity.... What you feel—that reality—that's eternal, that's beyond transience. That's what we really are, of course. That is the eternal self.... That's forever.*

*When there is no self, there is Enlightenment.... The longer we can stay in the thoughtless state, the more the obscurations are washed away, because when we stop thought a tremendous amount of energy is released. That energy purifies the mind.*

*We also purify the mind through focusing on higher, brighter states of mind.... Any focus in that direction brings us in touch with the aura of Enlightenment. The aura of Enlightenment is endless light.... To become Enlightened we have to purify the mind. We do it by focusing our attention completely on things that are pure, on states of mind that are pure....*

*So if you want to become Enlightened... you have to clear up your mind completely.... We do it a little at the beginning, and then more and more, and then eventually it consumes us, literally, until there is no self, there is only light."*

*(Rama, <u>Tantric Buddhism</u>, "Transience", "Buddhist Enlightenment")*

In the third meditation method, Rama combined visual and chakra focusing but in a more challenging way. There is a long tradition in Vajrayana Buddhism and Vedanta Hinduism of the teacher giving students a meditation practice suited to their specific needs. He presented this technique to us at the end of 1997 in a weekend seminar, thus it is not present in any of the earlier recorded sets of talks. It was his parting gift to us.

It consisted of visualizing and saying three Sanskrit seed syllables, each with a different color background, each while focusing on a different chakra. This meditation combines four different kinds of focus that your mind does simultaneously:

1. The visual focus on the syllable's symbol.
2. The visual focus on the background color he associated with it.

3. An auditory focus saying (out loud or silently) the syllable.
4. A mental, internal focus on the corresponding chakra.

The innovative yantra that he created to look at for this practice is shown below:

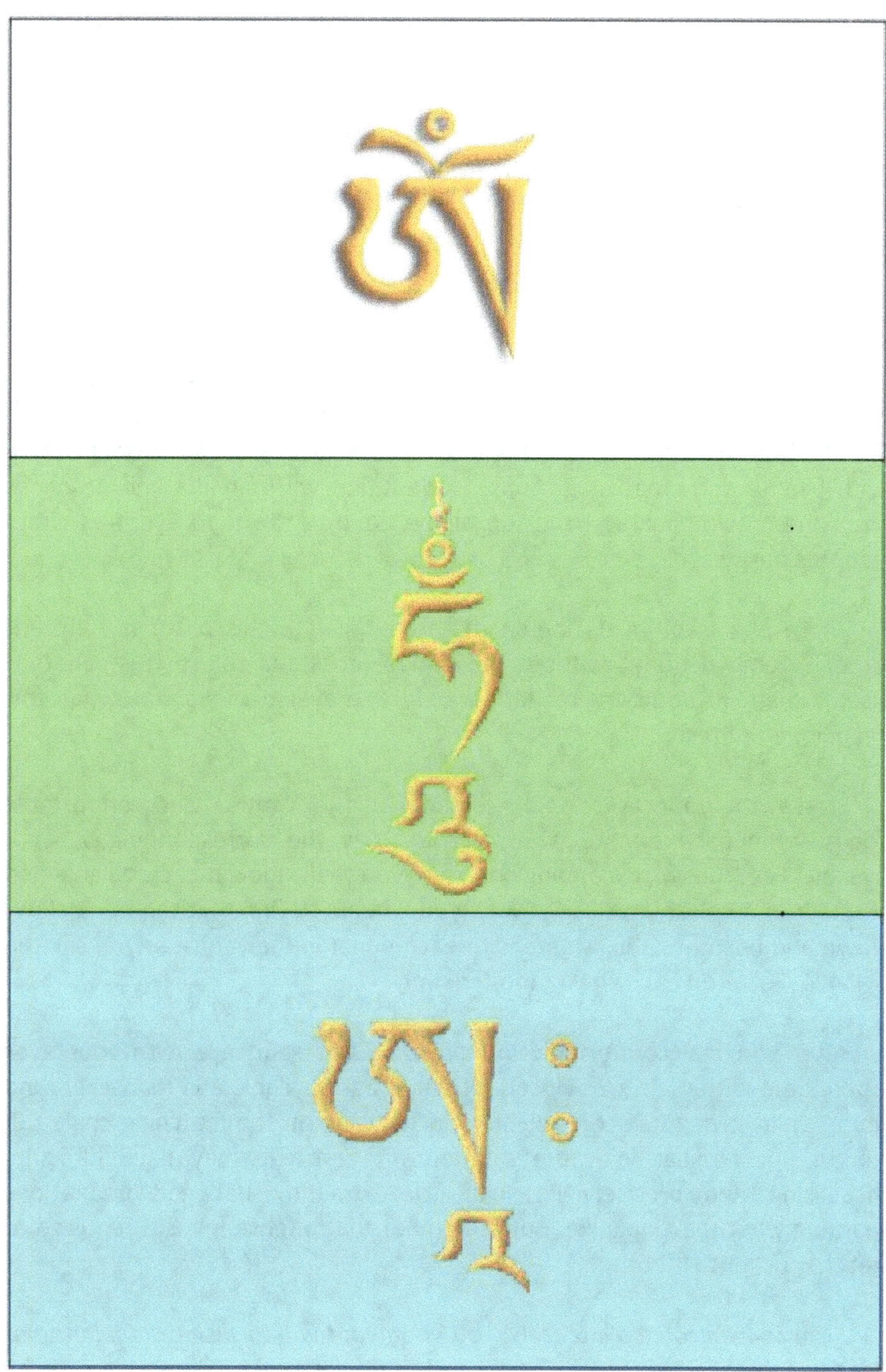

You start at the bottom and go up. The bottom one is the Sanskrit seed syllable "Ah" with a blue background, the middle one is "Hum" with a green background, and the top one is "Aum" with a white background. For "Ah," the focus is on the heart chakra. For "Hum," the focus is on the chakra at the base of the throat. For "Aum," the focus is on the third eye chakra.

Unlike many mantras, you do not elongate the saying of the syllable for many seconds, but rather say each one normally, though not too quickly.

In Vajrayana Buddhism, the seed syllable "Ah" is associated with raising the kundalini, and the color blue is associated with the heart chakra. "Hum" is associated with truth, the color green with healing, and the throat chakra with beauty and creativity. "Aum" is identified with nirvana and descends from the crown chakra at the top of the head to the third eye, and white denotes purity.

There is a traditional Tibetan mantra similar to this but in a different order, "Aum Ah Hum," without the chakra focus and colors. It is generally used as an introductory recitation before prayers. That's not what this technique utilizes.

Start with your eyes open, looking at the yantra. Get comfortable focusing on each symbol with its color. Say the corresponding Sanskrit syllable. Feel the corresponding chakra. If you really look at each syllable and its color in an alert yet relaxed way, you'll begin to find that the mind slows down and becomes still. Merge with each panel in the yantra as you say the syllable. Focus on each chakra more deeply.

After you feel comfortably immersed in this sequence with your eyes open, do it with your eyes closed. Visualize each syllable and its background color while saying its seed syllable and focusing on the matching chakra. If you're not familiar with the symbols, at first you may have difficulty visualizing them precisely. Put in a little extra time between meditations learning what they look like. But remember that intense focus is required to get the rocket to lift off:

*"You concentrate so intensely, you bring your will to such a singular point that you break through all the limited mind states. You bring in so much kundalini because your focus is so intense that you snap out of the limited*

*mental states into higher mental states, and then, of course, you experience the pure, shining void in whatever form you're capable of experiencing it as, from your sentient mind state, and that in itself is ecstasy."*
*(Rama, Tantric Buddhism, "Professional Meditation")*

At first you'll probably find it challenging to do all of these things together, but after a while it won't be a problem. It is a kind of mental gymnastics for a very specialized result. It may take several meditations, or maybe several months, but your mind will find that it is quite able to do all of the focusing elements per chakra as a unified moment. It will become natural and you will do it without thinking it through. You'll just sink deeper and deeper into the process. During each meditation session you're experiencing that the whole is greater than the sum of the parts.

There's no preset amount of time to look at the yantra and do it, or visualize with your eyes closed and do it. You're going deeper into your mind. How long that takes naturally can vary from one meditation to the next.

*"What we're really trying to do, then, with practice, is to spend more time in a complete focus. We do reach a point, however, when, while we are focusing, if we focus very completely, thought will stop. And when that happens, it's no longer necessary to focus—we can just let go. It's not as if in an hour and a half of meditation you're going to be sitting there, straining to focus on one thing the whole time. Rather what will occur is you will perhaps meditate for ten or fifteen minutes very intensely with a focus, then you'll find that your energy will rise sufficiently so that thought will stop for a while, and then you don't have focus—you can just kind of let go. And then, when you start to think again, you go back to focusing again and releasing energy."*
*(Rama, Tantric Buddhism, "Focus and Meditation")*

The key thing to do is, love each one. Yes, focus intensely, but melt into them. This is a subtle but crucial point. You're going within yourself, don't force your way in. Dissolve into your deeper self.

During this meditation you will be able to continue without needing to repeat the syllable-color-chakra sequence in order to stop thought. You can stop the repetitive steps and just let go:

*"Even just the practice of meditation which we call zazen in Zen—sitting, concentrating, doing concentration exercises to gain control of your thought*

*and learn how to focus—that creates a lot of power. Then when you move to the next stage, which is not only being able to focus thought, and say, focus on a candle flame for 15 minutes or a pretty colored rock, or one point, a chakra, or something like that—when you move to the next step, which is not just to focus, but then to stop thought completely without having to focus, you gain a tremendous amount of personal power. It comes into your life. It's like a bank account."*

*(Rama, Zen Tapes, "Personal Power")*

Meditation works when you are completely present, relaxed, and trust what you are focusing on. Completely trust each syllable-color-chakra—they are part of your own mind. They are manifestations of the ocean, of your deepest, highest self, the best things you will ever be able to trust. Let yourself be absorbed by each set. Love them. Then you will be really meditating.

At some point during the meditation you may just find yourself in a still and expansive state of mind. The paradox of meditation is that it takes action on your part to initiate it, but the goal is to be in a totally still state of mind. In a manner of speaking, meditation starts as a verb only to become a noun. In fact, that initial stage isn't really meditation, it's your self-effort to rise above your thoughts and environment. Once you've accomplished that, then you have entered the meditative state.

Meditation isn't an action. It is a stateless state of mind that is always there, outside of time and space. We make the mistake of calling those techniques which get you there, or let you touch it for a little while, "meditation."

Enlightened mind is in fact the infinite mind of the universe. The infinite mind has no qualities. It has none of our human band of attention's desires or objects in it. It is completely empty of desires and thoughts. Think of it as a vast ocean of pure energy, if that helps, though it is another step beyond that. That is what Rama meant when he spoke of the infinite mind, the understanding of which he explained in this series of steps:

*"The perception of mind in its variegated states, the perception of mind as different roses—yellow rose, red rose, black rose, primrose, various roses—variegation, coloration shifts, subtle or great changes in intonation—that is*

*mind perceiving other than mind. Mind, if it were only perceiving itself, cannot do so since there's nothing there to perceive. It's qualityless….*

*Your mind has qualities because in its apparent perception, it's involved with a differentiation process that is not yet completed and it still perceives itself as other, whereas my mind does not perceive itself as other. It doesn't perceive itself at all because it's clear light. Intrinsically they're the same. But in the act of working out perception—which we call structural being, or living, taking a body, incarnation, existence, multiplicity, duality—we perceive mind as separate and as having qualities….*

*If there is mind, and mind is qualityless, what the heck is that which we're now perceiving, which has qualities? If there is only mind, then how can there be anything out there to perceive? … We just take it for granted that the universe is complicated and we're not going to get it all in one night or one incarnation or one infinity. The universe doesn't have to be sensible and doesn't have to work out to our pleasing. It's complicated; it has variant sides. And to try and think that in one unified field theorem of mind you can get it all is ridiculous, because it's just not that way.*

*So we try and perceive it a section at a time—the section that we need, by necessity, is the section that we're in. That's karma. Karma relegates us to the reality currently extant for us because that's where we are in our perception. In other words, we're born into a world that's suitable for where our mind is at, for what we're working on. That's the assignment that we've gotten."*
*(Rama, Tantric Buddhism, "The Awareness of Meditation")*

This isn't something one quickly nods agreement with, understanding the words but not the full meaning. It takes time. You're in no rush. This is something you actually experience during meditation over many years. He waited ten years before presenting it this way. Then he connected meditation to it, and everything snapped into place:

*"We're not going to worry about the qualities that are beyond perception or that are perceivable and confusing. Our aim is to have mind in its primordial, basic, perfect, pristine state, which is meditation.*

*Meditation, in other words, is mind perceiving itself as mind, without qualities. That's perfect meditation. It's simply perfect mind. Meditation is not an action. It isn't something that you go and do. Rather, what it is, is just mind in its perfect state, without qualities, without confusion. You don't have to go and meditate. That is mind. Mind is meditation.*

*Meditation is a word that we're using to suggest something other than our normal perception, which is confusion. Confusion is the mind confusing itself and thinking that it's something at all. It can only do that through the function of ego, the sense of 'I am.' 'I am' is the confusion. 'I am' implies a quality or series of qualities, which we call self or being. That suggests that being and self are separate from qualityless mind, and this is where you get all screwed up....*

*Meditation is profound. It is mind and it is essence. So then, meditation is not a verb. It is the way mind is. That's why in Zen they call it the natural state, which means that you don't have to go and do anything to meditate. In effect, a person who is trying to meditate is doing something that's impossible since meditation is not an action. Yet at the same time, if you don't do something, you know you're not going to be meditating. That's the catch-22 of meditation....*

*It might someday lead to the awareness of meditation. Ah! There's a key phrase—the awareness of meditation, the awareness of mind....*

*So then, in order to meditate, all we have to do is stop. If we stop, it's perfect meditation because it's perfect mind. That's it. We just have to stop. Now what do we stop? Thought. Impressions, desires, aversions, states of consciousness, ideas of being, essence, substance, predicate adjectives—everything has to go. Final clearance, everything must go. Exhalation—we're going to exhale everything, all qualities, all perceptions from the mind until there's only the perfect, pristine, clear light, which does not perceive itself as other....*

*So then, if you perceive meditation as something that you don't have to do, it's easier. It's breathing out. What you have to do is simply breathe out everything in your mind. When everything is gone and there's only mind, that's meditation. See how easy that was?"*
*(Rama, <u>Tantric Buddhism</u>, "The Awareness of Meditation")*

Living in our world the idea of personal transformation is dormant. But it is a seed that grows into a mighty tree over many lifetimes. It grows most rapidly through meditation, because even though we may not be aware of what's happening, we're shifting the balance between time spent in the human band of attention and time spent in our complete mind, or just mind as Rama would call it.

The deeper your meditation, the more immersed you are in the clear light. That clear light modifies your causal body in the best possible way. That is what the process of personal transformation is at the deepest spiritual level. The glue that binds you together melts a little. When you finish meditating, the glue firms up again, but in a slightly different configuration than before. You are actually a slightly different person than the person you were before the meditation. You have dissolved the old self, and a new self is born. This is what's really happening:

*"The central nexus is the white light. Because it's a nexus that does not have an opposite point. And when we step into it, it's like taking a shower.*

*You're all dirty and grungy and you go step in the shower and you come out clean. So when you enter the white light, it does something to you. It frees you, it shifts you, it changes you. Then there will be points when one can make an ascension—one is not simply stepping into the white light, which is the equivalent of meditating each day and doing a variety of other things that give one speed in terms of energy flow….*

*All of meditation and Buddhism has to do with going into the white light. And if you go into the white light, which is a direct formation of God beyond patterns, that white light repatterns you, shifts you and transmutes you. And you don't have to know how, since God is God, and inherently God does godlike things. You don't have to hassle it, you just have to get there….*

*The light that I'm talking about, which is why we usually call it the clear light—I'm using white light because it's easier for Westerners—but we call it the clear light, and the clear light cannot have an opposite….Once you get in the clear light, you get in the shower, you'll get washed off. You get remade. You get reborn, transmuted, purified. And if that happens enough times, in enough ways, you build up enough momentum to blast off the circle completely and go into that clear light so totally that you become it."*
*(Rama, <u>Tantric Buddhism</u>, "The Nexus of All Pathways")*

# Chapter 16:  With Each Meditation You're Clearer

*"Meditation is not an action; it's not necessarily difficult. You just have to be very patient. It's something that's natural to all of us because we all are that. But it's not easy to understand. You have to work at it. Meditation is coming back to your original self, if we can use self without a sense of self. It's perfect, clear light; radiant, infinite mind of the universe, as it is, without identifying with qualities. That's something that you already are."*
*(Rama, <u>Tantric Buddhism</u>, "The Awareness of Meditation")*

You're working day after day, year after year, meditating and keeping your life tight. You may have a hidden agenda underneath all of the effort, coming from many past lives of spiritual dedication.

Rama spent the first years of our study teaching us purity and humility. This did not mean renouncing the world and taking a vow of poverty. That's just another suit of clothes. Purity means having more emptiness in our minds, letting go of more and more of our attachments to the transitory. Humility doesn't mean letting people walk all over you, it means being balanced and centered.

*"Humility—I keep coming back to it. I suppose it's the one thing that everybody forgets about. It is really the thing that liberates you. You see, humility means a lack of self-consciousness. Self-consciousness is ego. Ego is that which destroys spiritual balance…. Humility is its opposite. Humility and ego—you dance between the two in life.*

*Humility means waiting. Waiting and waiting. You're called into God's office and God has you wait. After an hour or two you begin to get impatient.*

*You read all the magazines that are there, the old, outdated Newsweek's and Time's. There's nothing left to do and you begin to get angry….*

*Humility means learning how to use your time to sit and look out the window forever, to go beyond time and to not be so concerned with you. You trap yourself in your own self-importance. You think you're important. Perhaps to yourself you are. Perhaps to a few others you are. But God will keep you waiting as long as you think you're important. Finally one day, when you give up being important, she'll show up and talk with you for awhile. Until then you have to wait. Sorry."*
*(Rama, The Lakshmi Series, "How to Achieve Spiritual Balance")*

So being impatient on the pathway to Enlightenment is inevitable if you treat the path like another transitory project. That state of mind is locking you into your ego. You're acting like your ego is going to become Enlightened. That's never going to happen. It's hard to accept that it takes thousands of incarnations even with the Tibetan Rebirth Process, and unless you're been going into samadhi a lot, you don't really know how many of those you've worked through. Since happiness is directly experienced each time you meditate, just be here now. After each meditation you're a little clearer, a little closer to the complete clarity of mind which is the hallmark of Enlightenment. A little humility goes a long way. Keep this perspective:

*"We believe that there's a jewel in the lotus with a diamond inside us. We don't mean that in a symbolic, mythologic, allegoric form. We mean directly, that there's a diamond, something that shines with infinite facets right at the very core of your mind. It is the core of your mind. But you don't perceive it as such; you don't see the glow. You don't see the infinite facets, all the realities. You don't see God in yourself, let alone God in anyone else unless they're very, very advanced in meditation, in which case they glow so brightly that if you're with such a person and you direct your attention towards them, their glow is so strong because they have become the diamond, the wisdom."*
*(Rama, Tantric Buddhism, "The Natural State")*

The antidote to impatience is humor, not in the typically human way of laughing at other people's misfortune, but laughing at yourself for forgetting what you've learned in order to get this far. That's funny.

*"There's another kind of humor. It's very bright and full and celestial and absurd. And it's the sense of humor that you have if you're a Buddhist, if you*

*practice yoga. Life itself is funny, and it's fun and bright, and even the most ridiculously on the surface unfortunate situations have possibilities, great possibilities of humor. Humor and being funny is the ability to transcend fate, and that's the essence of all Buddhist teaching. The essence of all practice is that nothing is the way it seems. If you're unhappy, if you're miserable, you're not seeing things clearly. You've become too caught up in the drama, the surface of life, and if you're only in 2% of life, which is the surface, and that's where your vested interests are, if that surface doesn't go well, then of course you'll be miserable. But most of life occurs in the other 98%. If I look at the water, if I look at the ocean, or the bay, I see the surface. The surface is 2%. There may be a hundred fathoms of water, but I'm unaware of it, of what's going on down there. I just look at the surface.*

*So most people only see the surface of life. We experience the surface of life through the senses. The surface is what we see, feel, taste, touch, and smell. And if things don't work out well on the surface we're miserable, if they work out well, well maybe we're happy.*

*Humor means to see the other 98%, in addition to the 2%. Because not only is it another 98%, but seeing that 98%, knowing it, even changes the way we perceive the 2%. Humor is the ability to see endless light, endless beauty, and endless radiance in a world like this. Or in any world, in any plane, in any dimension, any time, any place. And if you have enough energy, if you have enough brightness, then there's always something funny. We need humor the most when times are the most difficult.*

*So the essence of all Buddhism and yoga is to be happy, to be free, not just in an idyllic situation, when things are going your way, but to be able to be happy and be free when everything is horrible, when everything is falling apart, when you're in crisis. To be able to pull your attention into the other 98% of infinity, into the planes of light and into dimensions of celestial radiance and wonder, and to see that whatever's happening now is only momentary, it doesn't last, it's transient, it passes in an instant. If you are happy because the other 98% of life is happy, it's light, awareness, dimensions of mind that you've experienced each day and live in and grow into over a period of time, then you can live with the 2%. If you're sick, you can be happy. If you're healthy, you can be happy. If you're poor, if you're wealthy, whatever your karma is, you can be happy."*

*(Rama, standalone talk, "Buddhism")*

The foundation that all of our spiritual progress was built upon is the relationship between the Enlightened teacher and the student. This is a very serious issue that most students fortunate enough to get in the room forget from time to time. While it may be understandable to a certain extent that the student has a high opinion of himself or herself, since they were accepted by such an advanced teacher, it is not an attitude to stick with for more than a split second. Just putting that into perspective, i.e. if I'm pretty advanced then how incredibly more advanced the teacher must be, should vaporize such thoughts. But in this situation, once again the lack of an honest sense of humility will result in a serious perceptual error, and right attitude, as the Buddha called it, makes all the difference:

*"An Enlightened teacher teaches meditation by providing you with direct experiences, what we call empowerments. The teacher can actually transfer energy and kundalini from themselves to you. The teacher is in samadhi, a state of Enlightenment. They're very charged up with energy. They can direct that energy, which they've received through their personal meditation, to a student, to an apprentice, and lift that apprentice up, just as someone who has a lot of money can give someone else money and then they have it, they can spend it.*

*An Enlightened teacher can transfer power. That power will then lift a person up into states of awareness that they might not be able to reach on their own. In those states of awareness, if the person is mindful, they can advance their lives much more rapidly. They can learn to meditate better, they can succeed at their careers, at their schoolwork. They can just see the beauty of life.*

*Or they can use that power, if they do not listen to their teacher, in very negative ways and make mistakes. It's inevitable that that will happen to a certain extent, since none of us are perfect, or we wouldn't need to become Enlightened. All learning involves error, otherwise it's really not learning. So it's hoped, naturally, that a person will minimize the errors and a teacher explains what is necessary to avoid error. But in order to have any serious learning experience, we have to eventually go out on our own and try things. There comes a day when you solo in the plane....*

*So on the short path there's certain risks involved. The risk of ecstasy, the risk of knowledge, the risk of Enlightenment. These are the major risks. But when you do work with a teacher, an empowerment is provided and you can certainly make mistakes. You can use that power in ways that are not correct, meaning it'll put you into very low mind states and you'll be unhappy. Your teacher will explain very carefully what not to do and what to do. But if you don't listen, if you think you're smarter, you'll simply create a series of painful experiences and slow down the learning process for yourself. To an extent this is inevitable; you're going to have up days and down days in the world of Buddhism. But there are many more up than down.*

*But the most important thing if you are on the short path is to listen very carefully to your teacher and not think that you're so smart. First, ascertain that the teacher is Enlightened and if they're really transferring power to you, which will shorten your journey to Enlightenment incredibly. It's most important to try and listen to the subtleties of what they say and practice it, because otherwise you can experience a great deal of anguish and pain in empowered states of mind. They can take you down as fast as they can take you up. But if you listen it goes very well; the ecstasy is incredible."*
*(Rama, standalone talk, "Buddhism")*

Another thing many spiritual seekers trip over is the fascination with going into samadhi. We think we can overpower the challenge, as we try to do in most human situations. But as much as we might think that samadhi is the ultimate spiritual conquest, that way of looking at it prevents us from having it. That attitude also blinds us to what it really is.

*"Samadhi is another samsaric experience. Samadhi is not Enlightenment. It's a jump into a larger ocean. Enlightenment is commitment to life, in any form that life chooses. It's complete surrender to eternity, without any sense of giving up since it would have taken someone to give up; if that someone is there, there's an acceptance of that self. It's accepting, embracing existence, in every manifold aspect. That's Enlightenment. It's not a fixated state of awareness, a samadhi, an attainment. There's nothing to attain. Oh sure, there are things to attain if that's what still interests you. But those are sort of adolescent notions in self-discovery. Eventually you get down to the point where you've got to wash the dishes, you know. That's the fun in life, being behind the scenes and doing things for others, for their welfare. Being an instrument of that cause, which you can do at any evolutionary level. That is the secret teaching. And such a person is fit for Enlightenment because they've understood that the secret of life is humility.*

*In humility you disappear. You're absorbed in eternity. You can do lots of things for others and still be very egotistical. Better to be egotistical and do things for others than to do nothing at all, I suppose. But humility is folding in on yourself until you're gone. One can be humble and be active and in front of the world. It doesn't matter; it's the spirit, which no one has to know. You keep it tucked inside yourself since it doesn't need to shine. That's perpetual Enlightenment, perpetual humility."*
*(Rama, <u>Insights: Talks on the Nature of Existence</u>, "Modular Mysticism: Tibetan Yoga and the Secret Doctrine")*

What one ultimately realizes is the joy inherent in the self-discovery process itself. That's actually a wonderful, happy fact of life. You become the process, which utterly transforms the incarnation. The process is about clearing away all of the mental states and conditioning that bind you to transitory experiences. When you're doing that it's always getting better.

*"To become Enlightened is really quite simple. You have to purify the mind completely; there's no other way. It's impossible otherwise. It's only with complete purification. You have to burn away, with the fire of transmutive energy, anything that's cloudy, any states of mind that are unEnlightened. And when they're all gone, there's only Enlightenment left."*
*(Rama, <u>Tantric Buddhism</u>, "Buddhist Enlightenment")*

That's what purification actually means, not any religious or social dogma. The goal is to do what is called "perfecting your nature." That is another way of describing the same process.

*"To perfect your nature doesn't mean to have some idea of what a perfect person is and simply be that. That doesn't work. To perfect your nature means to let go of this world and place your attention fully in the plane of ecstasy, in the plane of Enlightenment. That's what perfect your nature means."*
*(Rama, <u>Tantric Buddhism</u>, "Buddhist Yoga")*

That's what's occurring during meditation. It is also occurring when you're practicing mindfulness all day long. It's an alternative lifestyle to the normal human version. Anyone can practice this, with or without a teacher. With the addition of an advanced teacher, your growth rate can be accelerated, if you have the right attitude.

So rather than wonder about crossing the Enlightenment finish line, aren't you interested in perfecting your nature? Enlightenment unfolds as you perfect your nature. Assuming that you've already figured out that Enlightenment has nothing to do with your ego and its fantasies, perfecting your nature is simply an ongoing process. There's no finish line to cross in perfecting your nature, is there?

*"It's the refinement of our nature that is perfection. It's not a thing that we go and do. You're seeking a perfect town, a perfect car, a perfect wife or husband, a perfect teacher. You're missing it. The perfection is in your apprehension, not in the thing. It's in your apprehension, in your perception of things. You want a perfect job? Create a perfect mind and whatever your job is, it will be perfect. You want a perfect life? Create a perfect mind and whatever your life is, it will be perfect. You want to see a perfect sunset? Create a perfect mind and look at the sunset, any sunset, and you'll see a perfect sunset."*
*(Rama, Tantric Buddhism, "The Best Meditation I Ever Had")*

Lastly, it is helpful not to forget what an amazing process this really is. By now, you have felt and seen light inside your mind. At first it may seem like something external, that the energy that you're experiencing is coming into you from some higher world outside of you. But by now you should be aware that what you're seeing and feeling is coming from inside of your own mind, and it is endless. If you ever doubt that, remember this:

*"Meditate and realize that when you meditate, no matter how high you go, no matter how deeply you perceive, that you're only touching the bare surface of infinity. Just hold in mind the fact that beyond your perception is ecstasy. Not far beyond. Just with the stoppage of thought there's ecstasy—power, understanding, in limitless amounts. And no matter how far you go, you can never experience all of it. And if you dissolve the self completely, it doesn't end. The self is just a filter that prevents us from seeing completely. It has its place. Sometimes we need that filter, but sometimes we don't.*

*So I would simply say—meditate. Sit and meditate as deeply as you can. But when you meditate, don't get so caught up in doing it that it's kind of like the vitamin pill you take every day. You take it just because you assume it's doing a good thing, and maybe you didn't take it for a week and you noticed your energy was low, so you went back to it. That's not meditation. Meditation is about ecstasy. It's about the understanding of truth. It's about changing ourselves and making ourselves God-like. Our mind melds with the mind of infinity and we become infinity. And we become perfect by virtue of the fact that the universe is perfect in its nonphysical aspect. It's perfect in its physical aspect, but it's transient, it changes. But the light itself is perfect.*

*So I would just say meditate on the light and merge with it. And always remember that you're only touching the surface of infinity. That it goes on forever, and that you have before you limitless ecstasy....*

*... Infinity is endless. None of us can compromise it or understand it. But we can swim in it. It's like the ocean. You can go swim in that ocean. That ocean is big. It connects to other oceans and it changes all the time.... And it's deep! The mountains under the ocean are higher than the Himalayas. But we don't even see them. There are many worlds there.*

*So when we meditate, we're going swimming in the ocean—the ocean of bliss, the ocean of ecstasy, the ocean of transmutation and personal refinement. Just remember that it's big and that every part of it is perfect and it's fulfilling beyond imagination. And if you do that, I think that you'll find that you will be more likely to touch more of it, just with that simple understanding."*

*(Rama, <u>Tantric Buddhism</u>, "Professional Meditation")*

# Chapter 17: Innocence and Happiness

*"Eventually the natural state becomes so natural that it really doesn't require effort. We abide in it perpetually. But it's only by modifying the mind and one's perception of life continually for a number of years before that occurs, with a grand sense of brightness, enthusiasm, and humor. But life should be continually brighter. We are seeking an innocence that escapes humanity. We are continually seeking our own innocence. We want to recapture it for eternity. It's in there, but we lose touch with it.*

*We come to the path because we know it's there, we feel it there, we remember it being there, whether as children or in another life. We seek our own innocence. We have to continue to seek out our own innocence in a world that doesn't care for innocence, which doesn't even acknowledge the divinity of existence. In a world of beings basically gone mad in a sense with their societies and their structures and their technologies, but who are completely oblivious to the religious experience of every given moment."*
*(Rama, <u>Tantric Buddhism</u>, "The Natural State")*

He also reminded us that it helps to keep in mind that you're only a visitor here; the Earth is like a motel you've stopped at for a little while. Seeing human civilization this way is both funny and accurate. You've got to fill the time doing something, so either it's chasing desires or traveling on the pathway to Enlightenment. Which path gives you freedom?

*"Meditation is a process in which we are seeking to liquefy the self by raising the kundalini energy. When that happens, we experience an ecstasy. That ecstasy is the freedom of moving beyond a self that is much too structured. It's like you've chained somebody and they've been sitting in shackles. Suddenly you take the chains off and there's just an innate ecstasy*

*to getting up and moving and being able to just get around and not being chained to a particular place.*

*No one likes being a slave, and the ultimate slavery is being a slave to yourself. Being stuck in who you are is the ultimate slavery. In other words, what causes pain in life is being specifically who you are. The less definitive, the less you are who you are, the more ecstasy there is. The pain in life is caused by being someone.*

*Now, being nebulous is not particularly ecstatic. It's a condition of light— hard to explain in words, obviously—it's a condition of light that creates ecstasy. It's being up in the world of light, looking into the lake, watching the shifting aggregate formations of existence perfectly moving without a sense of direction, constantly forming new patterns. That sense of freedom, when the mind stops and folds into itself, when thought stops, when the perception of self as separate from the rest of life ceases—at that point reality is apparent."*
*(Rama, <u>Tantric Buddhism</u>, "The Nexus of All Pathways")*

That sense of freedom has innocence at its heart. That's what you feel after a good meditation, and utilizing mindfulness keeps it alive:

*"To be innocent is the essence of all practice. Not to be stupid; innocence does not necessarily mean a lack of knowledge. It means a lack of self-consciousness. It's the consciousness of self that inhibits us from freely experiencing life. Buddhism deals with that by teaching us not to focus or think of the past. We eliminate the past from our mind. Part of the practice of mindfulness is to constantly bring your mind into the moment."*
*(Rama, standalone talk, "Buddhism")*

The more we are completely present the more our mind remains innocent. That doesn't mean being taken advantage of, in fact the more present we are in the moment, the more clearly we perceive it. If you're experiencing innocence more and more, it's quite likely that you've been doing self-discovery for many lifetimes.

*"And at a certain point in its evolution, after certain incarnational experiences have been worked out—where we've had pleasure and pain, loss and gain, fame and fortune, sexuality, the lack of it—we progress to a point where we practice occultism, self-discovery. We go through thousands of*

*lifetimes where we learn to meditate. We study, grow, develop, learn the katas of Enlightenment, practice them until they're perfect, gain complete control of the mind so that we can let the mind roam, without control, in complete innocence. In innocence there can be only innocence. Purity is innocence, the innocence of lack of self. Desire is innocent unless it's connected with self. It's just an impulse....*

*There is nothing else but innocence, if there's not a priori motivation of an ego. Life itself is perfect innocence. It's only when we're in lower gradated states of mind that we perceive duality and things to be different."*
*(Rama, Tantric Buddhism, "Tantric Buddhism")*

There is a common association of innocence with being a child. The reasons behind the truth of this show how it results from a certain kind of behavior:

*"Wisdom is the ability to let go. Children are wise in a funny kind of way. Perhaps their interests aren't as vested; they haven't developed as many vested interests of self.... There's a wisdom, a lack of self-consciousness, that is innocence. I think innocence is the greatest wisdom."*
*(Rama, The Enlightenment Cycle, "Wisdom")*

People who study theology, or become experts at a particular spiritual practice, can become so engrossed in the subject that they become it. As Rama once said, it's not that they've mastered the subject, it's that the subject has mastered them. There's a partial innocence in that. For someone interested in Enlightenment, don't stop at that point. Look beyond that body of spiritual knowledge and see yourself as part of life with the humility and humor which that entails. Be aware of the innocent state of mind and let it carry you forward.

*"Profundity is not enough. Happiness is essential. If we have too many rituals, and too many robes, and too much incense, and too many ceremonies, we can get caught up in that and we think that solemnity is the religious experience. It's an aspect of it at times. But you are the religious experience, your life, your moments. The religious experience, the spiritual, metaphysical experience of existence, which is Buddhism incarnate, is something that is perceived in a new way at every moment, by every sentient creature. Life is light, and whether it's a sparrow, whether it's a virus, whether it's a celestial being, whether it's the person next door, or yourself,*

*we're all experiencing Enlightenment. The only issue is how much of it are we experiencing?*

*In other words, everything is Enlightenment. Most beings are only experiencing 2%. When you meditate you may experience another 20 or 30%, or sometimes for short periods of time, 100% of the radiance, the infinite light of the cosmos. But without mindfulness it's transient, it's short. In other words, mindfulness, the practice, keeps us in the light all the time.*

*But the thing that I find absent, the true sign and hallmark of Enlightenment, in addition to power, balance, wisdom, is laughter. Silliness, a sense of innocence. Not being stuck in the practice itself, not taking everything too seriously. Doing what has to be done, winning what has to be won, learning how to both win and lose with grace and dignity. Working hard at everything, harder all the time, but being happy, seeing a brightness to life, watching the glow of existence. Taking difficult and trying circumstances and making them into challenges that make you happy. Laughter.*

*These three things combined are Buddhism."*
*(Rama, standalone talk, "Buddhism")*

Happiness is simply having more light in the mind. The more light that is in the mind, or rather our increased awareness of the light that already fills our mind, is happiness. In order to increase the constant awareness of light, we must refine the causal body. The less dense the causal body, the more light shines through. Gradually, with each meditation, we loosen the glue that binds the causal body. The heat of the kundalini that's released during a strong meditation melts the causal body a little, and then the deeper mind, the infinite mind, reforms it into something freer and more evolved. That new "self" is inherently happier than the preceding one.

Don't forget that happiness is not dependent upon external events, but is the result of inner balance. As Rama described it:

*"Meditation is the journey to happiness. As you meditate and as you enter into the planes of light, you'll become happy, immediately happy. That happiness will enable you to compact your life, transform yourself, and open yourself to those planes—not just when you're meditating but eventually all of the time, so that you're in a perpetual state of meditation....*

*So while you are at work, typing at the keyboard or doing whatever it is you do, or at school or playing or doing some sports, athletics, when you are in a very difficult situation where everybody is pounding on you because they're not too happy, or you are just doing something bright and beautiful—at those times while you are physically engaged in your activities, your mind can be wandering through the planes of light forever, having constantly new and greater experiences that cause you happiness....*

*Real happiness comes from the experience of meditation and from getting to the point where you like life. You can enjoy it, but you don't center your happiness on what happens here. Meditation is a direct and vivid encounter with immortality. It's not a ritual. It's not based upon wishful thinking. It's something that you go and do. It's like swimming. You jump in the water and there you are. You're swimming. It's an actual, very visceral experience. But the experience of meditation, the experience of the planes of light, which I would define as the experience of meditation, changes you. That is to say, it causes all the blockages, the meanness, the unhappiness, the self-destructive tendencies, to pass. When you take a shower, all the dirt is washed off. When you go into the planes of light, all the incorrect ideas, the incorrect ways of seeing and understanding life that you pick up along the way, on the journey, are washed away.*

*So if you go into the planes of light in the morning and in the evening in your meditation, then you wash everything away that you've picked up. But you also gain ground, in a sense, because as you go into the planes of light, more light comes back with you each time you meditate. You get better at meditation. Each morning when you meditate, you can experience a deeper ecstasy. Each evening when you meditate you can experience a more profound reality. You can have a better understanding of life.*

*In other words, the planes of light certainly give you power, the power to rise above circumstance, the power to rise above your desires and your aversions to happiness....*

*The way we gain wisdom in meditation is not by having someone explain something to us. All the teacher does is explain how to get to the planes of light, how to go deeper into them, how to avoid the things that keep you out of them.... But real wisdom is gained personally in meditation.... in the planes of light.*

*So meditation is the short path to happiness. It is the way to become completely happy. It streamlines the process. It takes you beyond the desire-aversion operating system that offers very limited happiness and a great deal of frustration. As you practice meditation— it's no good to talk about it but you need to do it—if you can bring an earnestness to your meditation, if you can really try, in other words, you will find that happiness is something that will run through your life constantly.*

*At first, when you begin the practice of meditation, of course, your happiness will be limited because you can't get that deeply into the planes of light. But through the practice, you'll gain a little bit of happiness, and that will inspire you to meditate more...."*
*(Rama, The Enlightenment Cycle, "Personal Happiness")*

He even recommended two simple meditation techniques to shift you into happy states of mind. You have to have some innocence, though, in order to do them. Most of all, you have to slow down, and as the saying goes, stop and smell the roses:

*"I'd like to suggest two simple exercises that I think will greatly improve your happiness. One is passive zazen and one is active zazen. Let's do the active one first.*

*... you're concentrating, focusing on something, a visualization, focusing on a candle flame, trying to stop your thoughts and all the different things that are involved with the practice of meditation so you can move beyond the level of mind you're in now into other states of mind, which is why you meditate—sort of ungluing the glue that binds you to a particular perceptual mode, a way of seeing life or the world which is an illusory one.*

*Sit there and smile. This is a very simple practice, but it works. Sit there with your eyes closed or open, as you're sitting in meditation, and stop meditating for a minute. Stop trying to meditate; that's good to do. But just smile. Let your smile get bigger and bigger. Oh, you're* unhappy, you're miserable, nothing is working out in life, doesn't matter. Smile anyway. Practice smiling for five minutes. And feel grateful. Feel grateful for the fact that you're alive, that you can sit and feel grateful. Feel grateful just to be, to be happy. Sound simple? Sound facile? So is a warm puppy. So is life. Hey, if you know so much, try it. Sit and smile, for five minutes a day. At some point during your zazen practice, your meditation practice each day, take five minutes and smile—for five minutes, continuously.

You will find that as you do that—and of course while you're smiling, it's not just a physical smile, but you're focusing on the feeling of the smile, of happiness—you have become much happier, that the whole world around you will glow. You're invoking a certain state of mind, which you've experienced. You've experienced happiness at one time or another in your life. You don't need to focus on the moments, just on the essence of happiness because, you see, what you focus on, you become.

We become what we focus on. This is how the mind works. If you're just focusing on unhappy things all day long, unhappy states of mind, then you will become unhappy. But if you spend time focusing on happy states of mind, hopeful states of mind, then it will grow in you. We aren't anything in particular. There is no self. There are only ideas and states of mind. You can generate whatever state of mind or ideas you would like, and that's what you'll live in, my friend, that's the quality of your life—what's inside your mind. Most people don't generate it, they just experience whatever happens to be lying around. But in Zen, you're going to begin to gain control of what you experience, not necessarily externally, but internally—your reaction to things.

So to start with, I'd like you to practice smiling for five minutes a day... while you're sitting in meditation, which is a very powerful time. Everything you do in meditation is amplified. If you meditate for five minutes, totally, with your complete mind focused on happiness, that's like focusing on happiness for several hours as you're walking around. Everything is so intensified. And that happiness will carry over into the rest of your life.

*Then the passive form, when you're not formally meditating and sitting, is just to see beauty—beauty is happiness—and as you walk through your day, to look at things, to feel things, to touch things… whether it's through your senses or through your mind. To unhook from your thoughts and all the busy things you're doing and all the things you're feeling and all the emotions that are shooting through you, and just to start to look at life. This is mindfulness.*

*In the particular form of mindfulness I would like you to practice… I'd like you to just look at beauty. Not just physical beauty, or the beauty of things you see with your eyes, but beauty—beautiful feelings, beautiful awareness. Remember, again, there is no such thing as reality. Reality is what you make it. And in Zen, you're learning how to make new realities, to build things inside your mind. So you need to start to focus on beauty more all day long, and just realize how incredibly beautiful your life is….*

*Even when you're in a painful situation, look at it, and if you look deeply enough and you don't get freaked out by it, you'll see that there's a beauty in everything. You'll see there's a beauty in you. The beauty you see is just your own mind. There is no external anything. There's only the mind and the mind is endless reality. Endless perfection.*

*So if you'd like to be happy for now and forever, do these two things."*
(Rama, <u>Zen Tapes</u>, "Happiness")

# Chapter 18:  Dharma and Samadhi

Throughout this book, an underlying theme has been that there are methods and techniques that definitely bring one into advanced levels of attention. This is one of the cornerstones of Tantric Buddhism. You could summarize all of its methods as ways to cut off the sandbags holding us down. Those sandbags are our attachments to desires and aversions, our personal history, and our samskaras. Be free of them and we regain innocence. But what is taken for granted is being in accord with our dharma.

We know that the world is not supportive of the pathway to Enlightenment. The relationship you establish with the world through seeing, inaccessibility, balance and wisdom enables you to stay on the path.

There is a dharma for the universe, for this world, but also for each individual, and they're not necessarily identical. It is assumed that you were in tune with your individual dharma when you were inspired to begin the study. Like the systems analysis of your energy flow, you need to periodically review how in tune you are with it. If there's a poor match you will not enter into the highest states of awareness, the samadhis. You have to be in accord with your deeper nature to progress that far.

*"There is something that we call dharma. Truth. The idea is that there is a universal movement or motion that is correct. When desire is in concord with dharma, then desire does not create pain. When desire runs contrary to dharma, then desire creates pain.*

*Let me give you an example. You have many different sides to your being. And each of those sides seeks happiness in different ways. Now, if we go to your absolute self, your highest aspect, we find nothing but light. Your real being is timeless and endless light. It has no beginning, it has no ending. It's*

*static and ecstatic consciousness, beyond description. When you are absorbed in that light, meaning when your attention is fully focused on your own infiniteness, then you feel no suffering, no pain, no desire, no frustration. Everything is perfect perfection. This is the stateless state that all human beings, and all beings, sentient and non-sentient, seek…. And it exists right here and now. You simply have to become aware of it."*
*(Rama, The Lakshmi Series, "Inaccessibility and Attachment")*

Before you become in tune with your individual dharma, you have to want to. That's not always the case, even though you'd assume that a spiritual seeker serious about Enlightenment automatically would. Those samskaras discussed in Chapter 14, as well as your imprinting and acculturation in this life, can disturb your deepest quest. You still have desires and aversions. You must look into all of that, in strictly personal terms:

*"Stopping thought isn't simply a disciplined practice. Stopping thought also involves shifting our values…. In order to lessen our thoughts and therefore to increase the flow of kundalini that will alter our perception and give us a larger view or vision of life itself, and freedom and happiness in the face of any circumstances, it's necessary to clarify the purpose of our being. This is to come to understand dharma.*

*Dharma is a Sanskrit word. It simply means that which is right, that which is correct, that which is the divine law. It is necessary first, in the practice of kundalini yoga, to determine what the dharma is. There is a dharma for yourself, for someone else, for a family, for a nation, for a planet, for a universe. There are collective dharmas and individual dharmas.*

*Your dharma is what kind of work you should be doing, what kind of people you should associate with, whether you should be practicing meditation or not. If so, what type? Whether you should have a teacher or not. If so, what type? How you should see the world, how much you should give selflessly, how much of your money you should donate to spiritual activities, how much of your time you should spend by yourself and alone in a reclusive mode, how much of your time you should just have a tremendous amount of fun and just be frivolous and silly, whether you should be reverential and follow the path of the heart. Dharma encompasses all things, and it's specific to the individual.*

*So the first task is to discover that dharma, and this is done through introspection, by continually questioning yourself and asking yourself, 'What is the right thing for me to do? Not simply the thing I want. Not simply avoiding the thing I don't want. What is right? Because not to follow dharma leads to disaster. Life will be unhappy.*

*Following dharma puts you in a proper field of attention. And in a proper field of attention, regardless of what your outer circumstances are, happiness will flow. To not follow the dharma, either intentionally or through lack of awareness, creates a very low level of attention, and in this low level of attention, we make all kinds of mistakes and we're unhappy, no matter what good fortune apparently befalls us.*

*You will be unhappy if you do not follow the dharma. Happiness does not come from external objects. It comes from peace of mind.... Naturally, to follow dharma, we have to first find out what it is. So ask yourself continually, in every situation and also in the larger context of life, 'What is the right thing for me to do?'*

*And you have to struggle with it. You have to fight with it to find out. The answer will not come easily. You will be swayed by your desires, by your conditioning, the things that you've been taught to do or to avoid. You will be swayed by those around you who have ideas about what you should do, what is proper, what is improper. All of these thoughts and feelings will affect you. But if you're determined, if you won't give in, if you're joyous, if you truly want to celebrate life, then you will persist in discovering dharma. No matter what apparent obstacles appear before you, you'll laugh your way through them, or you'll work your way through them, or you'll glide through them. Whatever is necessary, you will do."*

*(Rama, <u>On the Road With Rama</u>, "Kundalini Yoga")*

Rama makes it very clear that consciously trying to be in accord with your dharma is a constant challenge, and if you're not, not only will your meditation practice stall but your mind will be stuck in lower levels of attention. He rarely discussed this, leaving it up to us. Presumably we had to be in sync with it in order to seek out such a spiritual teacher in the first place and dive into the study. But after a while you can meander, you can become distracted. You can lose touch with your dharma. Here's where his emphasis on self-effort directly applies. And his prescription is to constantly consider it, to always find it before embarking on anything. He described the core methodology as clearly as he could, and the importance of this issue. The ultimate solution becomes even simpler:

*"The answer then, is love. Love is the bridge that joins all of the worlds together. Love permits us to see who and what we are. The only thing that will truly inspire us to find the dharma, to find the wonderful path that leads us to awareness, is love. Only love will give us that strength. Love is something that comes to us in life. Quietly, it overwhelms us. It is something that you cultivate. You make it happen.*

*... The technicalities of the movement of the kundalini are easy to master. Dharma is much more complex, and if the kundalini is flowing through you at a very rapid rate when you practice kundalini yoga, if you are not in harmony with the dharma, then you will have great problems with the study....*

*So from my point of view, kundalini yoga then depends upon a sense of dharma, a sense of that which is right. That which is right is different for each one of us in each situation. There isn't a moral code that I or anyone else can lay down that will tell you what your dharma is. But there is a simple way to know when you are following it.*

*When you are following dharma, you'll be happy, at peace, still inside. There will be a sense of purpose in your life. Your life will go well. Difficulties will not seem unconquerable. When you're not following dharma, then you will not be at peace. You will not be happy. The simplest things will seem to be endless obstacles.*

*It is not what we do; it's who we are. And who we are varies according to our awareness. When you're more aware, you're someone else than when you're less aware....*

*It has been my experience as a teacher over the years and incarnations, let alone as a student, that what really counts are not techniques. What really counts is spirit—love. What really counts is a sense of propriety and dedication. These are the qualities that manifest in self-realization....*

*So my recommendation is—if you seek to practice kundalini yoga—to meditate, of course, and you can meditate on the different chakras and feel what that's like. But what will really release the kundalini is something much simpler and more effective, in addition to meditation techniques, breathing*

*techniques, and so on. And that is by creating stillness in your life. This stillness will come about through deep caring and introspection. It will come about slowly and then quickly. It builds in momentum."*
*(Rama, <u>On the Road With Rama</u>, "Kundalini Yoga")*

That momentum is what carries you into samadhi. Samadhi is the process which dissolves the finite self into the clear light, or in other words, when your mind takes a huge leap in its recognition that in reality it already is the clear light.

The entire self-discovery process is built atop this truth; every step is the stripping away of what's blocking this recognition. The problem has been that our ego and the world which supports it won't accept such an amazing fact of life. Samadhi is the last stage of our awareness of this truth, though full recognition and acceptance will still span many incarnations. You can be a saint for a long time. If we understand that sentient existence is dependent upon perception, then through self-discovery we are moving from perceiving with our senses, which is looking outward, to looking inward, exploring the mind of the perceiver.

That's what you do every time you meditate, and when you're practicing mindfulness. Even the human band of attention is vast, and it takes virtually every spiritual seeker a very long time—many, many incarnations—to reach a thorough perception of it, much less transcend it.

*"What we're seeking to do is internalize perception. Perception is very much involved with the senses and the mental processes and the emotional processes. That's what 100 percent of our perception is usually engaged in. But what we're going to do is gradually remove our perception from the sense world—seeing, tasting, touching, all those sorts of things. We're going to remove our awareness from our thoughts, the thinking, cognitive process. We're going to remove our awareness from feeling emotions and we're going to take all of our awareness and take it someplace else—into luminous realms, into inner light, into the very thing that we are that perceives."*
*(Rama, <u>Tantric Buddhism</u>, "Focus and Meditation")*

Samadhi is commonly viewed as the end point of spiritual practice, crossing the finish line. While of course it represents a significant milestone in self-discovery, it should be seen as the start of something, not the finish. Rama pointed out that Swami Brahmananda, one of Sri Ramakrishna's most advanced disciples, said that true meditation begins with samadhi. All of the work you've done so far has actually been preparation to become completely aware of meditation as a comprehensive state of mind rather than as something that you do, as explained at the end of Chapter 15.

*"It's as if all your past is written on the blackboard, and if we could erase it, your past would no longer exist. So what we're going to do is erase what's written on the blackboard. The way you do that—the only way you do that—is in samadhi. When you go into samadhi, either salvikalpa or nirvikalpa, what happens is you erase, you loosen, the aggregates. You simplify them. The way that you're able to go into salvikalpa samadhi is through spiritual refinement. After many years of meditative practice and many lifetimes of meditative practice, you gradually loosen the ties that hold you."*
*(Rama, The Lakshmi Series, "Samadhi and the Superconscious States")*

Applying the Six Worlds model, we may physically be in the desire plane right now, but our minds are free to roam through all of them. While the next level up is heavenly and without suffering, it is something we experience in our astral, or subtle physical body. Experiencing that plane is not samadhi. The level above that, the unmanifest, is where the first type of samadhi occurs, and to take it a step further, nirvana is in its own unique category. If this may seem like a fairy tale, that's only a manifestation of the human band of attention, the ego self's inability to grasp.

*"There's the world of the physical. There's the astral, the dimensions, the dimensional planes that you can tour; it's in your astral body. There are the planes of light, which are referred to as the causal, and which you experience in your causal body. Those are the meditative planes and dimensions, the planes of light, but that's still something that you can reference. Even the planes of light, while the experience in the higher planes of light is certainly a kind of samadhi, salvikalpa samadhi, nirvikalpa samadhi is to go to the other side, to experience the other side....*

*Nirvana is the other side, the source of all things, where all the aggregates come from, where the templates of infinity are.... Wisdom is getting there. Wisdom is nirvana, and it's something that can't be known here. I know it seems incongruous, but it's only incongruous from this perspective, from the perspective of the dialectical consciousness of division, of time and space."*
*(Rama, The Enlightenment Cycle, "Wisdom")*

If you've been meditating, especially with the techniques presented in this book, you've been moving beyond that now for a while. It is also important not to tie this to any ideas of success or failure. That way of looking at it is totally mistaken. The only bad meditation is the one you skip. Rama pointed out that you've spent thousands of lifetimes building up those samskaras, and it can take thousands to dissolve them, even though studying with an Enlightened teacher can greatly accelerate their dissolution.

As the title of Chapter 16 put it, with each meditation you're clearer. That is the only thing that's important, regardless of how you might evaluate your progress. Each time you go into salvikalpa samadhi, it is the deepest kind of meditation.

The characteristics of the unmanifest dimension, the level immediately below nirvana, give you an idea of the difference between our ego self or human band of attention, and what we call God, eternity, or the infinite mind. In Buddhism, however, our complete mind is in reality the infinite mind. The human band of attention is a layer of it while being a perceiver.

*"The world of the unmanifest is the undifferentiated reality. That is a world in which there is no form whatsoever. It's the world of samadhi. It's a world where there is no dimension, but yet it has a specific existence as something that's not manifest to the senses. When we say manifest, we mean apparent to the senses. Reality exists beyond the senses, obviously. Otherwise there would be no life. But the sense worlds cannot penetrate... the unmanifest."*
*(Rama, Tantric Buddhism, "Six Worlds")*

So the experience of the unmanifest plane is called salvikalpa samadhi. Rama went on to describe it, and the overall structure of the samadhis in these terms:

*"... Pantajali and some others have said that there are a number of different samadhis, and there's no exact agreement on how many there are because there's no way to describe them. Where one begins and another ends is very difficult. Some say there are three, some say there are four, some say there are five.*

*I have a very simple system for explaining the samadhis. I feel that there are two samadhis, only two. One is salvikalpa samadhi, the other is nirvikalpa samadhi. Salvikalpa samadhi would include all of the lesser samadhis because I don't think they're really all that different. Nirvikalpa samadhi, however, is qualitatively different....*

*Now, salvikalpa samadhi means the following. When you enter into salvikalpa samadhi, any of the lesser samadhis, not that they're very lesser, you merge with eternity, you become God. In most advanced states of meditation, a person meditates on God or truth, light, joy, nirvana, the Buddha, the Christ, whatever it may be. As they meditate, they have experiences, but there's always the sense of being the enjoyer: 'I'm enjoying eternity. I am experiencing the ecstasy of existence. It's all-pervasive and there's an awful lot of it. There's a reservoir. It's filled with wonderful, clear, pure water, and I'm sitting here drinking it. Some days I drink more, some days I drink less.' That's meditation. Advanced meditation is drinking a lot of this pure water, which is more than most people do, who don't drink at all or don't even know that there's pure water to drink or run away from it or shoot those who drink it and oppress them.*

*Salvikalpa samadhi means not simply sitting around drinking lots and lots and lots of this water, which has a purifying effect on one's life and one's being and gives you strength and clarity; that is advanced meditation and it occurs after many, many years and lifetimes of practice. Salvikalpa samadhi, in other words, doesn't just mean having a really high meditation where the room fills with light and everything is bright and shiny and you feel one with the dharma and the flow. That's not salvikalpa samadhi, that's a high meditation.*

*Salvikalpa samadhi means that you lose your individual awareness as a person. You no longer have a name, an address; you're no longer in this world at all. There's no sense of the earth, time, space, past history, future possibilities. All of that goes away. All of that is completely erased. You dissolve, but in your dissolution you become something. You become God. You become eternity. There is a sense—not in the human sense, not in the way of thinking, 'I'm God' or 'I'm eternity,' if you're thinking these thoughts you're not in salvikalpa samadhi—that you are the all-pervasive existence, that existence has an awareness which cannot be described in words. That is salvikalpa samadhi.*

*In other words, you are no longer drinking the water. You jumped in the water and dissolved in it, and now you have the sense—not as you did as a*

*human being, not through thought or understanding—that there is an awareness that permeates all of eternity, and that is what you are. Thou art that. That thou art. That sense of timeless perfection, which you are, again, not from a human point of view—that's salvikalpa samadhi."*
*(Rama, The Lakshmi Series, "Samadhi and the Superconscious States")*

The impact of just one timeless moment in salvikalpa samadhi, also known as satori, is difficult to describe, since literally there are no junctions with ordinary consciousness. But its impact on your life can be put into words:

*"The realization of satori, the day-to-day Enlightenment, the nine-to-five Enlightenment, changes one forever—to experience satori for what in linear time we would call a few minutes. You will never see life the same way, let alone self. A permanent change is made in one's structural awareness. More circuits of the mind come on. Forever. "*
*(Rama, Tantric Buddhism, "The Natural State")*

The characteristics of the Unmanifest plane are consistent with the generally accepted definition of God. Repeated immersions in it is what creates a saint. As wonderful as that is, it too is a multi-incarnation process. The entry into nirvana, nirvikalpa samadhi, is Enlightenment. Nirvana can be thought of as the source of God. That concept is challenging, especially for Westerners, since something beyond God is not included in any branch of the Abrahamic religions which most Westerners were raised in. Rama explained this larger perspective, which is a fundamental part of Buddhism, as follows:

*"Tantric Buddhism is the study of Enlightenment. Enlightenment is part of everything. And so our minds have to be very, very big to encompass all things. To see the Tao in a grape, the act of sexuality, meditation, work, play, taking a shower, brushing your teeth, being sick and hurting. Watching someone we love suffer and die and go back into the void. Watching ourselves grow, become strong, become weak, live, love, die, suffer. This is all just sensual. These are sensual experiences. You're just seeing it. You're tasting it, you're touching it, you're smelling it, you're hearing it. It has nothing to do with reality. It's just a film you're watching, that you're so engaged in that you forgot that you were watching a film and it all seems real. Enlightened mind is beyond the realm of the senses.*

*We live in a sensual world, and at the same time we live beyond it in billions of dimensions that are non-physical, which we experience when we stop thought. The dimensions go on forever in all directions, some higher, some lower, some neither. No words can apply. They're inhabited by beings, some by nothingness. Universes collide and conjoin inside us. And beyond all of that—not beyond in a spatial sense—is nirvana, the final, absolute resting place of the soul.*

*It's where all transient experience of the phenomenal world ceases. In nirvana there is no such thing, there is only nirvana, perfection. No pain, no suffering, not even ecstasy. The ecstasy is finite, ultimately. Even spiritual ecstasy is finite. In nirvana, there's just perfection. No words."*
(Rama, <u>Tantric Buddhism</u>, "Tantric Buddhism")

No one "attains" Enlightenment, rather Enlightenment absorbs you. The apparent difficulty is because our ego self makes it seem impossible, because it knows that its control over our life will cease. That game deceives us, since in nirvana we finally become the totality of ourselves.

*"If you're meditating and you sense that you are in ecstasy, that's not really samadhi. If you sense ecstasy, that's not really samadhi. Samadhi is beyond those things. Samadhi means that you have become the light, for a time, and there is no sense of an experiencer. There is no sense that, while I'm sitting here and even though I'm not thinking, I'm having an experience— I'm experiencing ecstasy, I'm experiencing wisdom, knowledge or something profound. Real samadhi is off the game board, friends...."*
(Rama, <u>The Enlightenment Cycle</u>, "Wisdom")

Salvikalpa and nirvikalpa samadhi are qualitatively different. In the following description, Rama explained what happens in nirvikalpa samadhi, the entrance into nirvana, this way:

*"Nirvana's not like anything you've ever known or experienced because it can't be known or experienced. I can't say the end product of self-discovery is nirvana because that would imply that there was a beginning and an ending, and there isn't really. In other words, is there life after nirvana? No. Nor is there death.*

*Upon being absorbed in nirvana, there will be no memory of anything else. Not because you'll forget, not even because you'll go away.... Imagine that you can see a certain amount of light through the retina of your eye, and let's say that light is ecstasy. Let's say that there's a beautiful, wondrous light, more wonderful than anything. To see that light is to experience ecstasy, joy, beyond comprehension....*

*But the kind of ecstasy that we experience in this world or in the subtle physical worlds, the astral worlds, in any worlds, is limited. If you could imagine going into the sun, or perhaps a sun a thousand billion times brighter than the sun we see, and if you could go right into it, and if that light was ecstasy, unfathomable, endless—there would be so much of it that you would forget after a while that you were even seeing it; you would be so dazzled by its splendor that all the pain of life would go away. That ecstasy would not be a narcotic ecstasy in the sense that it's simply a forgetting, but rather your awareness would merge with that endless vortex of light, which is existence itself."*

*(Rama, Insights: Talks on the Nature of Existence, "Modular Mysticism: Tibetan Yoga and the Secret Doctrine")*

In addition, there is a stage associated with nirvikalpa samadhi called sahaja samadhi. This is when, after going into nirvikalpa samadhi many times, rather than return to a remnant of your human consciousness, you remain in samadhi but are also able to deal with the world. Rama called it "perpetual wakefulness."

This is how the original mind works. The scale is what seems intimating, but that's really only to the ego self. It's not intimidating if we understand that there's a kind of magic that we are a part of. It is magical that this huge mind of the universe is also what our individual minds are. Rather than look at it from our human band of attention, we try to see it as the Buddha did, as reality.

*"You're waking up from the amnesia of birth, the forgetting of life, and you're remembering. And remembering is a flood. Suddenly you remember billions of lifetimes. Suddenly you remember the perfect, immaculate nature of the clear light of mind. That's what meditation is. It's not a state, it's not a condition, it's not an ecstasy, it's not peace. Those are things you go through as you eliminate qualities from mind. It's the identification. You experience ecstasy, peace, perfection, bliss, naturally, pain, and all those—frustrations, desires. Everything goes away. All the things that are negative go away and then all the things that are positive go away until there is just clear light....*

*But if God does not have qualities, if God is beyond all consideration of the mind—God's really big, you see, and your mind can't quite—God does not have qualities. That's the clear light. But that's what we are.*

*That's the message of all Enlightened beings to all unEnlightened beings, that we are God. We are the clear light and you really don't have much to worry about. You just don't know that right now. Someone who is Enlightened has shifted their perception so that the clear light is aware of itself as such, without qualities. Yet it acts and exists and takes form. And that's what you already are, but you just forget that.*

*Meditation is a remembering. And each time we meditate, we are remembering that simple thing.... So meditation is melting into the light but what I'm suggesting is, the confusion is—you think that you are the person that is melting into the light... Whereas truly, you are the light that is being melted into, but you don't know that now, and I do. I don't mean know as a phrase meaning 'I accept that idea, I believe in it.' I mean it as an actual, visceral experience. You know it. Not just as a thought that, 'Yes, I agree with the concept' or 'No, I don't.' But knowing implies reality in Buddhism."*
*(Rama, Tantric Buddhism, "The Awareness of Meditation")*

Every time you meditate, if you really reach a level of no thought, you experience some of that huge mind. So in Buddhism, Tantric Buddhism in particular, the idea that that huge mind actually is your mind is why so often you hear statements to the effect that you don't really exist. The point is that you are something far more vast than your ego self, however difficult it is to perceive in this plane of power and desire.

*"We could take all the pleasures that have ever been and will ever be in all of the universes that have ever been, are now or will ever be, and add them up into one experience. And if you were absorbed in nirvana, it would not be noticed. There's no way to calculate the pure and perfect stillness of absorption in nirvana. All the existences, all the creations, the manifold lives, the beings, the pageant of infinity, which always is, is unnoticeable in nirvana because its silence, its essential nothingness, is so complete, and so perfect and so pure that there is no relation point. You know, holding a candle to the sun."*
*(Rama, Tantric Buddhism, "The Path of Affirmation")*

The good news is that you can know this. You can be fully conscious of this. It just takes a lot of swimming in the ocean to finally become it.

*"So Enlightenment simply means that you've gotten above the body-mind complex. You've refined the self, dissolved it in the white light of eternity and gone through all the gradient shifts. I mean it's technical. But it doesn't end there. In other words, we have this view that Enlightenment is, once you're Enlightened, that's sort of it. That's the end of the show. You just kind of hang out in this quiescent state. You don't know that the quiescent state changes and moves all the time. It's never the same. If you become the quiescent state, which is what Enlightenment means, it means that you're never the same. You move and shift as the quiescent state, in a body or out of it. And since the quiescent state is perpetual and endless ecstasy, therefore you are endless. You're not finite, you're infinite…. Enlightenment can be refined, which may seem like a strange concept, but who cares about concepts? The reality of the issue is there's no end to it. Since infinity is by its very nature infinite, then Enlightenment by its very nature is infinite and thus can be experienced in infinite ways, by itself or without itself.*

*So the most beautiful day hasn't dawned, the most beautiful lifetime has not been experienced. The most beautiful meditation has not been had, even by the Enlightened. I guess that's the good news—it doesn't end. Enlightenment is not an end. Nor is it a beginning. It's just—there's no separation between the quiescent perfect state and anything else, inside your mind. Everything's inside your mind. Enlightenment isn't out there; it's just inside your mind. But it's not an intellectual understanding. It's not a knowledge that can be taught.*

*… You can explain, 'Well, do this, focus on this, dissolve the ego this way—there's a lot of technical material that you learn as you advance. A lot of it very technical, as you go in and out of the different samadhis, as you learn to dissolve the self in a variety of ways—things that we don't teach to people unless they're very far along—it wouldn't make any sense, it wouldn't be understood—the motions of infinity. You have to learn the motions of infinity with your mind. Your mind becomes a perfect mirror to the motions of infinity."*

*(Rama, <u>Tantric Buddhism</u>, "The Best Meditation I Ever Had")*

# Chapter 19:  The Enlightenment Cycle

The preceding chapter presented information that may make Enlightenment both irresistibly attractive and overwhelming at the same time. One can't help but wonder how any human being can get there. You have to have tenacity and you have to be inspired. You have to be an intrepid explorer. So it is very helpful to keep this in mind:

*"You can do it. I did it. If I can attain liberation, anyone can attain liberation. That should give you great hope. It's not that difficult. If you really love light and you really want that and you simply give everything that you have and everything that you are for what you believe, it's quite simple. If you don't do that, then how can it possibly happen? If you give 60 percent of your attention to self-discovery and to overcoming your attachments and suffusing yourself with light, then it will happen in 60 percent, and 40 percent it won't be. If you find a path and follow it and devote 100 percent of your attention to it, then you will become the path itself—in time. It just takes time to become timeless. And it's kind of fun. There's no rush to get there. Going there is a beautiful experience also."*
(Rama, *The Lakshmi Series*, "Inaccessibility and Attachment")

"Going there" is what he called the Enlightenment cycle. The Enlightenment cycle was the overarching concept behind what and how he taught.

*"So in the Enlightenment cycle, attention is paid to bringing back the awareness field, the total you, from other lives. This does not simply mean the memory of experience past—that may or may not be helpful—but rather to draw on the internal power and intelligence, the knowledge, the wisdom that you've amassed in other lifetimes. And if you amassed any siddha*

*powers, to bring them back also because they can be quite useful on the journey to Enlightenment.*

*To do this, meditation is the key that unlocks or opens the door. Meditation will bring back the powers and awareness of the past. Even more immediately, it will expand your consciousness today to places you've never been, to experiences you've never had.*

*Meditation is the pathway to Enlightenment."*
*(Rama, The Enlightenment Cycle, "Enlightenment")*

The Enlightenment cycle is a lifestyle in which daily meditation is the core, and every day you are both refining your mind and clearing away the energies picked up in the world. Its cornerstone is the teacher, who is dynamically supporting and empowering your self-effort. The objective is to increase the constancy and brightness of the inner light in your life. A key caveat is that the Enlightened teacher can only do as much as the student inwardly lets them. Even though you may not be fully aware of it, it is the light—the actual reality of the original mind—that you're gradually realizing is omnipresent in your mind. Given the typical life as a human being here on Earth, the opportunity to learn about and experience it is something to be thankful for.

*"If you sit down and meditate in the morning, you will be filled with happiness, and that happiness will last you all day. Then, in the evening, you'll meditate again and you'll wash away any of the debris you picked up during the day—wrong views, that sort of thing—that can lead to unhappiness. You'll be filled and flooded with a different kind of happiness, the happiness of the evening. Then you'll be happy all night. Meditate in the morning and wash away anything you picked up in the dream plane. It's a cycle, the Enlightenment cycle. It's based on meditation.*

*The role of the teacher is to make sure that the practice is pure, that is to say, that the methods are taught properly. By giving proper empowerments and by guiding the student, you make sure that they really are going into the planes of light and they're not fooling themselves. Because the astral and the astral dimensions are not places of great happiness necessarily. As I said, they're just like journeying to another country....*

*Then the rest is up to the light. As you go into the light, it will cause you to become happier and happier. Each day, you will gain a deeper happiness, a more subtle or perhaps a more profound happiness, and that happiness will free you from the desire-aversion cycle or syndrome.*

*It sounds pretty good, doesn't it? It's better than it sounds. And it's such a simple thing that people miss it. It's worth your while to sit, to practice meditation—if happiness is one of the important things in your life."*
*(Rama, The Enlightenment Cycle, "Personal Happiness")*

At its root, Tantric Buddhism is based on the idea of your growing awareness of inner light, which is another word for the complete or original mind. Gradually you become more aligned with it—that's recognizing your dharma and following it. If you don't stop, then eventually you become the inner light completely. You become self-effulgent, like Krishna.

The term "surrender" is bandied about in spiritual circles and usually has a wide range of cloudy definitions, but alignment with your dharma is all it means. The presence of the Enlightened teacher is always aligning you with dharma; it is your responsibility to recognize it and not fight it. Since dharma is dynamic, the teacher is mirroring what really is a dynamic force, not something static:

*"Sometimes people say it is a revalidation of the experiences of past buddhas. Buddhism, the essence of yoga, is that there's not one person who's achieved Enlightenment and that's all there will ever be. But people from time to time become fully Enlightened…. But in my opinion, it's not really just a revalidation, because while you will obviously go through the successions, the different states of mind that someone else did on their way to Enlightenment, Enlightenment is unique at the same time for each of us, and it actually changes. The universe is not static; nirvana is not a final state at all.*

*When we get beyond the mind, when we get beyond dimensionality, nothing can possibly be final, so to try and impose limitations on nirvana and say that it is always the same, that it was the same for the first Buddha as it is for you when you attain to Buddhahood, when you become Enlightened, that's not necessarily true. It's beyond quantification. Real Enlightenment has nothing to do with any of this. It has nothing to do with this plane, this world, these words, or anything.*

*What an Enlightened teacher can do is point a direction, they can say, 'Well, try down there, go down the block and turn left and keep going and you'll probably run into nirvana. On the way you'll have lots of experiences and here's some guidelines, things that will save you time, that will save you pain. When you encounter this, try this move. If that doesn't work, try this.'*

*That's what really all teaching is. Teaching is simply the avoidance of drudgery and pain. We learned something, we codified it, so a person doesn't have to go through the initial discovery of those things, but can just learn those things more quickly and move on to another stage of knowledge we teach them.*

*Buddhism is the experience of Enlightenment. It's the experience of eternality and infinity. It's the experience of infinite consciousness and awareness. It's learned with a teacher on the esoteric path, it's learned from a book on the long path. The way a teacher teaches Buddhism is not simply by example. If you have an Enlightened teacher, if you act like they do, dress like they do, walk like they do, talk like they do, that doesn't mean that you'll become Enlightened.*

*It's their mind that is light. After many incarnations of meditation and practice, they've merged their mind with the clear light of reality. It's something I really can't explain in words."*
*(Rama, standalone talk, "Buddhism")*

We could say that Enlightenment ultimately is becoming completely aware of, and thus dissolving into, eternity and infinity. We almost become numb to such words, not seeing their precision, which only demonstrates the limitations of our human band of attention. Rama described his own evolution this way:

*"Yes, I say that I am Enlightened. What does that mean? It means I live in a condition of light. After many years of meditating, practicing, I've reached a point that can't be described or discussed—but one is always in a condition of light. There is really no primary self anymore. It comes back in every life without me seeking it. One has to refine it, but it just comes back unsought. I live in a condition of light inside my mind. Nice. But that condition of light can be refined."*
*(Rama, Tantric Buddhism, "The Best Meditation I Ever Had")*

So the process of self-discovery culminates in Enlightenment, if you don't stop. It takes many lifetimes. You'll keep incarnating anyway, here and elsewhere, so is there something better to do with an incarnation? The experience of being with an Enlightened teacher isn't an immediate rush into it. It is far more subtle than that.

As you learn, you change, and actually begin to understand more. So the "you" who learned a spiritual lesson earlier is not the same person as the "you" you are now. Ideally spiritual growth is a process of spiraling upward, but it has its twists and turns for everyone. The teacher is very aware of that and it must be quite funny to watch.

As has already been pointed out, since the basic problem for human beings is that there is not enough light in the human mind, people are acting out their confusion most of the time. For those who want to fix this problem, the pathway to Enlightenment's combination of methods with faith develops an attitude we all can understand:

*"I've been teaching yoga and Buddhism for a while—many, many, many lifetimes. I've had lots of students, disciples. A long time ago, many lives ago, I had great teachers, radical, radically wonderful teachers who brought me through the Enlightenment cycle like I'm bringing some people through the Enlightenment cycle in this and other lives. And the thing that I've noticed, that I learned from my own teachers a long time ago in another universe, the thing that I've observed in the successful students that I've had over the lifetimes is a quality which I think you can develop. I think it's something that's in each of us and it's a quality of gentleness but strength, silliness but maturity, optimism but a sense that it's not going to be easy, if not impossibly difficult, but we're going to get it done anyway, a kind of quiet fortitude that is renewed by a person's love of light."*
*(Rama, <u>The Enlightenment Cycle</u>, "Balance")*

One of the most central realizations someone has on the pathway to Enlightenment is the incomprehensible depth and breadth of eternity. The term "humility" is commonplace in religion; it is a virtue we are all told is important, and we nod and agree, though not really understanding or adopting it. But when you have a glimpse of the immensity of what's called the infinite mind, you become humble. You are struck with the recognition that you can never know it with your finite mind. Humility shouldn't be something you need to be trained in. But in the thrill of working on becoming Enlightened, you can miss the simple point that it really is beyond the human band of attention's ability to grasp:

*"In other words, it is the mind that weaves the dream of life that convinces us that what we see is what is apparent and what is real, and that there's nothing outside of our perception. But I can assure you, as a practitioner of Buddhism, that there are ten thousand states of mind, at least, give or take a few billion, which can be seen and experienced and known, and each one goes on forever, and in each one you're something else forever.*

*So metaphysics is a process where we go on journeys. We travel. We're mental travelers. We travel step-by-step. Not too far too fast. Step by step we travel into other dimensions of mind and gradually we gain new orders, new understandings of what life is and what we are. We have an awakening where we see that we are, oh gosh, I couldn't tell you; there are no words for it. If I give you words, you'll be satisfied with those words, and you'll think, 'Oh well, I understand that now, I don't have to go do that, I understand, I can appreciate intellectually what he said.'*

*You have no idea what I'm talking about…. Metaphysics is a process whereby we awaken, step by step, to larger understandings of existence. And those larger understandings of existence change our self-reflection. This is the key. They change our self-reflection. And that self-reflection is important because the self-reflection is sanity….*

*If you change your self-reflection, you change. You become someone else, and reality changes since reality is only your self-reflection."*
*(Rama, <u>Tantric Buddhism</u>, "Metaphysics")*

We can readily see how true humility would generate a sense of compassion towards others. Compassion must be understood beyond its commonplace connotations. As explained in Chapter 12, a "compassionate God" is an inaccurate belief because it reverses the fact that we must merge our minds with the infinite rather than the other way around. It becomes an excuse to be lazy. For someone who thinks they're serious about the pathway to Enlightenment, self-effort is crucial, yet all too often some individuals coast through an incarnation living in a monastery rather than taking maximum advantage of its relative peace and quiet. As Rama put it, you mistakenly think that since you're on the train, it will carry you to Enlightenment and you don't have to meditate deeply or learn selfless giving.

But he also discussed compassion as an important trait to be developed, and how Enlightened beings come here to help us. In this way one could say that God, or the unmanifest plane, was being compassionate to humanity:

*"Compassion allows us to accept everything. That's why there's always a tear in the eye of the Buddha that no one sees, for the pain and suffering of others. Without a requisite knowledge of that pain and suffering, you're mortal. You only become immortal when you feel the suffering of others and are one with it, as you feel the joy of others and are one with it, yet step beyond both into immortality itself and dissolve in eternity. Yet that tear remains even after Enlightenment, even though it's invisible. It's only visible to those who know. And there's no way to will that, it will come when it will, through the grace of God.*

*Therefore to be so absurd or knowledgeable or even, as a teacher, autocratic to assume anything at almost any time seems to me to forget that there's a tear in the eye of the Buddha…. what matters is the welfare of others.*

*It's only with that complete commitment and simplicity and humility and humor that is engendered by taking on the impossible task of selfless giving and doing it anyway, perfectly, without any sense of self, that the real progress begins to occur. That's the preparation for the higher Enlightenment. 'Tis a noble endeavor.*

*All the rest is just the fun of the process. The craziness, the idiosyncrasies of the Enlightenment process, the development of the relationship with the teacher, being in a spiritual community, going off on your own, mystical visions, developing powers—all these things are irrelevant, don't you understand? Enlightenment, in other words, is not the point. That's only the point for those who don't understand yet…. But in the secret teachings, it has nothing to do with that. The secret teaching was the bodhisattva ideal—to live for others, for the welfare of all beings. That's Enlightenment. Not some flashy state of luminosity. That's just another samsaric experience."*

*(Rama, <u>Insights: Talks on the Nature of Existence</u>, "Modular Mysticism: Tibetan Yoga and the Secret Doctrine")*

There were two things mentioned in the Introduction about Rama being an Enlightened teacher that should be elaborated upon: seeing golden light around him when he meditated with us, and how, after each seminar, you would feel so "refreshed, clear and empowered." He explained the golden light around a teacher who is Enlightened in structural terms as follows:

*"When they meditate they glow. If your subtle physical vision is developed at all, when you watch someone who is Enlightened meditate, you'll notice that they're suffused, they're surrounded by a golden glow. People who are partially Enlightened may give off different auric emanations; you might see red, or blue, or green, or magenta, or different lights. When a person who is fully Enlightened meditates, you will observe perhaps those colors, but you will see a bright, shiny gold. It's a very diffuse gradient of light. This is the light of the crown chakra.*

*Enlightenment means that a person has established, has benchmarked, their awareness in the crown center, the top center, the thousand petalled lotus of light which is at the top of the head in a way of speaking.... You might not be able to see them if you are new to meditation, but when you sit with an Enlightened teacher and you watch them with your eyes open, you can actually see the light around them and its colorations. So you will notice this beautiful diffuse gold glow of light around an Enlightened teacher, and that's the hallmark of Enlightenment."*
*(Rama, standalone talk, "Buddhism")*

The reason that his students felt cleansed and recharged after a seminar was because he pulled the negative energies and thoughts which had accumulated since the previous seminar, and some of the negative samskaras out of us each night of the seminar. The way that is done is by the teacher pulling all of that gunk, from several hundred students, into his body. That in itself is ample reason for students of an Enlightened teacher at a minimum to do everything they are taught about mindfulness, exercise, and managing your energy.

Rama said that while he felt wonderful from meditating strongly enough to lift and hold all of us up each night, he also became extremely toxic. He had to go to natural environments and exercise, meditate and in other ways wash all of his students' toxicity out of him. But still, over time, it takes a serious toll. He said that was the reason why some spiritual teachers die at a relatively young age.

It is also worth noting that he pointed out that spiritual seekers needed to be very careful about who they studied with. This is because there are teachers claiming to be Enlightened who aren't, and working with them under their false pretenses can be harmful, not to mention disappointing. You have to trust your inner judgement on this, but beware. For the first years that Rama taught, he repeatedly told his students that he was not Enlightened, and continued to use the spiritual name Atmananda ("one who has realized the bliss of the self") that his teacher had given him. He also said that he was being pulled into nirvikalpa samadhi many times a day, without any effort on his part, which actually is how it works.

There is a long-term perspective about the teacher's role on the pathway to Enlightenment that you rarely hear. Here is how he framed the entire process:

*"What the teacher does is gradually—over a period of time, really over a period of years—enable the being to change their self-reflection by compacting their life, strengthening it, getting all the junk out of it, learning to be happy, free, and strong, and then gradually, again I use the word 'gradually,' stepping into other dimensional realities—very specific ones, where for a while we will stand and gaze with awe and wonder at the universe.*

*It's like looking at the sun. You can glance up at it, but if you look too long, you'll go blind, even though it gives us light and we couldn't see without it, it's one of those funny contradictions. Look at the thing that allows you to see and you'll go blind. That's how infinity is. You can't look at it for too long or you dissolve. The bands of your attention break. But if you look at it in specific ways, as you become stronger and stronger by changing your life a little at a time, you're able to step in and out between the realities of mind and you can become something or someone much more conscious.*

*It is possible, in other words, to become someone else. This is what all metaphysics teaches us. Otherwise, why get involved? Metaphysics is not religion. Religion is the complaint department, where you go and complain and someone says to you, 'That's too bad.' That's religion.... All our complaints and all our hopes are based upon who we are. But if we can change who we are—not just to being another human being or in another crappy situation, and we're just exchanging one crappy situation for another—but if we can change who we are as a perceiver, if we can go beyond the human level to the divine, if we can have a mind like God's, you see, that's worth doing. God's mind is endless. It reflects all realities. It is all realities—and beyond them.*

*So Enlightenment means having a mind like God's. It means your mind is God's mind. It doesn't mean you are God, that's rather an objectification of the file word 'God' where you just become the president of the company as opposed to somebody who works on the line stacking boxes—you become the CEO. You're God. You can tell people what to do. You make more money, live in a bigger house. That's the file word God.*

*The mind of God is reality without limitations—perception not limited to its own field. That's what we call Enlightenment. And to have that mind, to be the perfect mind of the universe, that's the only thing really worth doing because all other self-reflections trap us and cause us pain. In other words, self-reflection is painful because it's a condition of limitation and any condition of limitation vis-à-vis the experience of endless freedom is painful."*
*(Rama, <u>Tantric Buddhism</u>, "Metaphysics")*

One of Enlightenment's features is that it is the complete liberation from rebirth, but that's optional. After Enlightenment, if you choose to have another incarnation, you are not bound by karma. The Enlightened state reawakens automatically, as Rama pointed out. You are a jivanmukta, a being who is liberated while alive. As he stated several times, Enlightenment is the complete awareness of life without mental modifications. Really consider that for a moment. Your limited mind totally out of the way, not filtering your perception and awareness whatsoever. What the pathway to Enlightenment does is answer the question Rama posed to us, what is it like to have a mind like God's?

*"So a teacher is not someone who you have to have. That is to say, you don't need them perpetually. You need them to show you how to get through the doorway, but once you get through the doorway, you're on your own. Then you have to grow and experience Enlightenment. Then you come back— if you want to go through a higher doorway—and so on and so on. They show you how to refine yourself until you're able to enter into nirvana on*

*your own. Then no more teacher. Guess what? Only Enlightenment everywhere."*
    *(Rama, <u>The Enlightenment Cycle</u>, "Enlightenment")*

Rama always stressed that Life was the ultimate teacher. Recognizing and then actually becoming this enormous thing is Enlightenment. Enlightenment is the complete awareness of Life without mental modifications.

# Chapter 20:  The Free Source Material

This book is a detailed overview of what Rama taught us. It consolidates over 120 recorded talks into a single volume that assembles highlights into the main topics he focused on. These topics combine to create his model of the mind and how to navigate life in this world. However, with so much material it can't help but be incomplete. Hopefully this book will encourage you to explore the recorded talks themselves.

*"One day I will not be with you. We will not be together. If I've done a good job, that won't mean a thing because you will have learned how to do this yourself. As you sat at all these countless meditations, went on desert trips, went to Disneyland, whatever we did while we were together, I was teaching you how to rearrange and arrange your luminous cluster of fibers. Also, I was teaching you how to strengthen your tonal to deal with that. So when our time has ended together, if I've done a good job and if you've paid some attention, you will be prepared to continue your journey into the unknown. True, it will not be at the same rate because I'm not lifting you up. But you will be far enough along to continue at a proper rate."*
*(Rama, <u>Insights: Talks on the Nature of Existence</u>, "Modular Mysticism: The Sorcerer's Explanation")*

He always told us not to over-focus on him as a physical body, that he was not really in physical reality as we think of it. Instead, he often said we could feel his mind through listening to his voice and all of its subtle inflections. The important thing was to follow his mind, and in doing so we could experience the dimensions he was in as he was explaining and describing their characteristics to us. So the many talks that he recorded are a unique opportunity to directly experience an Enlightened teacher and the higher dimensions he was showing us.

Every time an Enlightened teacher appears, they refresh the Dharma and describe it in terms that the society they reside in can understand. They present the infinite mind in part through helping solve the problems facing the people in that society. Rama's many lectures and instructional recordings definitely are not your typical "New Age" pep talks, nor are they austerely "spiritual." In fact, Rama defines what might seem to be a new set of spiritual issues that people today identify with much more readily, though one comes to realize that these issues have been around for a long time.

For example, in addition to classic discussions of desire and attachment, Rama talks about "Storing Power" and "Seeing." Instead of relying on the hierarchical framework of spiritual aspiration, he talks about "How to Make Friends with God." Certain hot-button issues, both in contemporary social and classic spiritual circles, are taken on directly. Sexuality (it's not a big deal) is given its own talk, and a constant argument among those who practice Zen--how long does it take to become Enlightened?--is tackled in "Instant Enlightenment."

Most of all, he said that the change which would result in the largest positive development of humanity would be having more women who were Enlightened. He said that advanced spiritual study had been denied to women by all religions for thousands of years. Changing that was the key for the future of humanity. His talks on this subject, such as "Why Don't More Women Attain Enlightenment" in the *Insights* set, and "Women, Men, and Self-Realization" in the *Lakshmi Series*, in addition to all of the career success and psychic development work he did with the women students, are historic achievements in the history of spiritual teaching.

The overall impact of these talks is an exhilarating and refreshing master class on how to become Enlightened while living in today's high-pressure urban world. His explanations of subtle spiritual concepts as well as the psychological issues we all confront always convey deep understanding. He can also be very funny, which helps immensely in putting yourself in perspective in what can become an ego-centric obsession.

He insisted that each student had to personally validate all of this information and the structure behind it, never blindly accept it. That personal validation was how actual spiritual growth occurred. That's why he called it self-discovery.

*"Each aspect of the teaching must be individually validated for it to be meaningful, real, and for it to lend a power to your life." (Rama, <u>Zen Tapes</u>, "Reincarnation")*

The many instructional recordings were grouped into distinct sets that he recorded in the following chronological sequence:

<u>The Lakshmi Series</u>

First there was the *Lakshmi Series*, in 1982-3, a set of 30 talks which presented a large amount of foundational information and training. He devotes a talk to each of the traditional Four Yogas (Love, Selfless Giving, Discrimination, and Mysticism and Power), and such "standard" topics for spiritual students as "Purity" and "Humility" (which have nothing to do with sex or being meek), "Pleasure, Pain and the Senses," "Dharma and Karma," and "Zen, Taoism and Buddhism." But even more time is spent teaching about the nature and composition of our minds and how to work on ourselves, in such talks as "The Caretaker Personality," "The Tibetan Rebirth Process," "Living and Working in the World," "How to Achieve Spiritual Balance" and "The Subtle Physical Body." Of special importance, he explains the unique capabilities of women to attain Enlightenment and how male-dominated societies have blocked them for thousands of years.

<u>Insights: Talks on the Nature of Existence</u>

Later in 1983 he recorded a set called *Insights: Talks on the Nature of Existence*, a set of 13 talks in which he gave deeper discussions of some of the themes in the *Lakshmi Series*. The talk "How to Make Friends with God," is the only time he addressed this directly. "Why Don't More Women Attain Enlightenment?" is the most complete explanation of this core issue in a single talk. In "Instant Enlightenment," Rama discusses what he did in this incarnation to regain his Enlightenment from past lives (anything but "instant"). There's a group of talks about different aspects of what he termed "modular mysticism," and talks about Tibetan Yoga and Love. The "Sorcerer's Explanation" talk is unique in its directness explaining how advanced teaching works.

<u>3 Workshops</u>

In 1985 he held public talks, and recorded a 3-evening workshop in Los Angeles with 7 recordings, *A Workshop with Rama*, a 6-talk set, *Psychic Development with Rama*, and a 3-talk set, *Rama Live in LA*. The *Psychic Development* set was recorded at the end of 1985 in Boston, and contains some of the most in-depth instruction and extended discussion of the subject, which he taught as something essential to growing into Enlightenment. The "Selfless Giving" and "Dharma" talks of that set also have some of the funniest moments in all the recorded talks. The "Dharma" talk also has a brief section, starting at about the 31:00 minute mark, when Rama has you focus on your Third Eye as he transmits a block of high attention to you. He makes clear that this will work regardless of how many years in the future you listen to it, whether he is in the body or not on Earth. In the "Caretaker Personality" talk, he walks you through an extensive list-building exercise to assess each component of your current personality and outline replacements for it.

## On the Road with Rama

Also in 1985, he recorded his impressions at seven power spots around the country and released the set as *On the Road with Rama*. The objective is, as you listen to each talk, keep you mind so still that you can actually feel each power spot, which included locations along the Continental Divide, and at Walden Pond, Lake Tahoe and Hawaii. So in reality, these were specialized psychic development training talks for us where we had to "see" each place.

## Buddhism

There is one standalone talk, "Buddhism," that is not included in any set which is unique. It is one of the most comprehensive on this subject that he ever recorded, with numerous references to contemporary American life as well as personal stories.

## Zen Tapes

In 1986, he went into depth about Zen and its applications to our lives today, giving us an 18-tape set, the *Zen Tapes*. Here he uses that wonderful, off-beat Zen humor, which constantly reveals the shaky architecture of socially-accepted beliefs about "reality" in order to begin taking us out into the ocean of our true mind. He directly applies classic Old Zen to such modern topics as career success, sport and athletics, overcoming stress, and how to be a successful student, as well as delving deeper into reincarnation, happiness, and meditation.

## Tantric Buddhism

From the end of 1989 through mid-1990 he recorded portions of our seminars. The result was *Tantric Buddhism*, a set of 27 talks. Clearly these are at a new level that he felt we could now comprehend. Such talks as "The Best Meditation I Ever Had," "The Nexus of All Pathways," "The Path of Negation," "Buddhist Yoga," and "Light" open new doorways of understanding. His talks on Thoreau in "A Clean Room" and on Krishna in "The Bhagavad Gita" reveal states of mind essential for spiritual progress. The "Tenacity" talk has the most forthright statement about what it takes to become Enlightened, and what it really is, that I am aware of. In "Buddhist Yoga," Rama points out the pitfall of using spiritual practice not to move the mind to happier levels but to try and succeed in the world. The "Six Worlds" discussion that begins this book is taken from the second talk by the same name in the *Tantric Buddhism* set. The "Enlightenment" talk is one of the very highest moments in all of the recordings.

## The Enlightenment Cycle

In 1994 he presented a set of 10 talks called *The Enlightenment Cycle*, which was the last set he made. They represent a distillation of everything he taught us, compacting large amounts of material into succinct and lucid explanations. It takes many hearings to begin to appreciate their depth. A pair of additional talks, on "Intermediate Meditation" and an overview of the entire "Enlightenment Cycle" were also included. If there's one talk to listen to in order to best understand exactly how to meditate properly, it's the "Intermediate Meditation" talk.

They are all available, as well as a collection of videos and music albums, as free downloads at the Rama Meditation Society website, https://www.ramameditationsociety.org/resource-library/ . A YouTube channel has also been setup that has all of the free tape sets, at https://www.youtube.com/user/zenaghori. The YouTube channel for watching the collection of Rama's videos is at https://www.youtube.com/channel/UCurfLkdyFo0ug9KSIU0o5DA. If you'd like to know more about the Lenz Foundation for American Buddhism, which

has given out over $7 million in grants through 2021, visit
https://www.fredericklenzfoundation.org/.

All of the material presented in this book can be found in these talk sets (with the exception of the final meditation method that came later), but of course they contain vastly more. Since each set was carefully designed by Rama, it helps to listen to the talks in a set in the order in which they were recorded. Of course you may be intrigued by the title of a particular talk and want to listen to it now. No question you'll benefit from it, and learn many things that you wanted to find out. However, by listening to an entire set in the order it was organized will be the most educational. Each talk builds on the prior ones; the knowledge is cumulative. The idea of "gestalt" applies— that the whole is greater than the sum of its parts.

It should also be pointed out that starting with the first set, The *Lakshmi Series*, and then proceeding to the next set in chronological order, likewise is cumulative. The later sets reference material presented in the earlier sets. In particular, everything in the *Tantric Buddhism* set assumes a thorough understanding of concepts and techniques presented in the *Lakshmi Series*, and especially in the *Zen Tapes* and *Insights* sets. The *Zen Tapes* and *Insights* sets explore more deeply information introduced in the *Lakshmi Series*.

Some specifics explained in earlier talks were modified by him in a later set. For example, meditation techniques in the later talks are different than in the earlier talks, but the core concepts and key points remained the same. This is because the talks were only intended for his students, and as we developed he'd explain things at a larger scale or give us a more advanced technique. Since it is Rama talking directly to his students on every one, many of which were recorded live at our seminars, you can be in the room with us. While there is a great deal of information, you cannot miss his ever-present happiness and insight, as well as appreciate his focus on explaining even the most difficult concepts very clearly. Most of all, enjoy his sense of humor.

Hearing a person's voice can reveal many levels and in Rama's case, actually move your mind into new dimensions. Even beyond that, as he told us many times, he was teaching us telepathically more than verbally. You may sense that, although please don't strain or fantasize about it too much. Don't worry about your conscious mind comprehending what he's saying. Just be still and pay complete attention. Really listen. Let your aura absorb it.

There's a wonderful moment in the "Wisdom" talk in *The Enlightenment Cycle* where, as he talks about moving through the higher dimensions to Nirvana, his mind is actually doing it:

*"Existence is infinite. There are countless universes and creations taking place simultaneously, all times present and past. The far-flung universes exist forever, and all manner of beings and creations are there. Everything that can be and everything that can't be exist somewhere. It's beyond the mind's ability to grasp. Certainly, nirvana means seeing and knowing that vastness. But beyond the far-flung infinities there's something else. Beyond the planes of light there's something else—that isn't a broad-based knowing, that isn't the sense of a person perceiving what knowledge is, what wisdom is. That's nirvana. It's a word that's used to describe the other side.*

*Somewhere there's an essence. It's not a physical somewhere. But there's an essence for all of this. There, there is nothing but light, but not even in a temporal, spatial sense. It just is. And there, there is no time, no space, no self. Existence just is perfect. There's no sense of this world, of time and space. That's nirvana. It's the center of things.*

*Then there are the outer bandings of attention. In other words, the universe is a mind, and at the center of its mind is nirvana—center not so much in a spatial sense—that's nirvana. Nirvana is the pure and perfect suchness or thatness of being. Then, outside of nirvana, the planes begin— the subtlest planes that vibrate the fastest, the planes of light, all the way down through the astral realms through the physical and so on."*
(Rama, *The Enlightenment Cycle*, "Wisdom")

Reading it is inspiring and you may feel what he's saying very deeply, but listening to him is transporting.

# Appendix:  List of Talks in Each Set

Lakshmi Series:
1.  Introductory and Intermediate Meditation
2.  Purity
3.  Humility
4.  The Yoga of Love
5.  The Yoga of Selfless Giving
6.  The Yoga of Discrimination
7.  The Yoga of Mysticism and Power
8.  Spiritual Absorption
9.  Nirvana
10. Death and Reincarnation
11. Samadhi and the Superconscious States
12. The Caretaker Personality
13. The Tibetan Rebirth Process
14. Living and Working in the World
15. Pleasure, Pain and the Senses
16. How to Achieve Spiritual Balance
17. The Subtle Physical Body
18. Women, Men and Self-Realization
19. Inaccessibility and Attachment
20. Spiritual Experiences, Dreams and Visions
21. Zen, Taoism and Buddhism
22. The Occult Body, Auras and Chakras
23. Spiritual Teachers and the Enlightenment Process
24. Advanced Meditation
25. Dreaming
26. Gods, Goddesses and Carrier Beings
27. Dharma and Karma
28. Tantra and the Left-Handed Path

On the Road with Rama:
1. Neutral Density – Continental Divide, Colorado
2. Unity – The Big Island of Hawaii
3. Magic – Lake Tahoe, Nevada
4. Electronic Tribe – Nantucket, Massachusetts
5. Kundalini Yoga – Haleakala, Maui
6. Power – Continental Divide, Colorado
7. Transcendentalism – Walden Pond, Massachusetts

Standalone talk: "Buddhism"

Zen Tapes:
1. Personal Power
2. Career Success
3. Happiness
4. Overcoming Stress
5. Enlightenment
6. Reincarnation
7. Karma
8. Psychic Development
9. Zazen: Concentration and Meditation
10. Tantric Zen
11. Developing Willpower
12. Managing and Increasing Your Energy
13. Overcoming Fears
14. Rapid Mental Development
15. Advanced Meditation Practices
16. The Zen of Sports and Athletics
17. How to Be a Successful Student
18. Winning

Tantric Buddhism:
1. Tantric Buddhism
2. Six Worlds
3. The Mature Monk
4. The Natural State
5. Freedom
6. Enlightenment
7. Self-Effort
8. Possibilities

# Endnotes

1.    "This May Be the First Planet Found Orbiting 3 Stars at Once," by Jonathan O'Callaghan, <u>New York Times</u>, Science Section, September 28, 2021.

It's called a circumtriple planet, and evidence that one exists suggests that planet formation is less unusual than once believed.

GW Ori is a star system 1,300 light years from Earth in the constellation of Orion. It is surrounded by a huge disk of dust and gas, a common feature of young star systems that are forming planets. But fascinatingly, it is a system with not one star, but three.

As if that were not intriguing enough, GW Ori's disk is split in two, almost like Saturn's rings if they had a massive gap in between. And to make it even more bizarre, the outer ring is tilted at about 38 degrees.

Scientists have been trying to explain what is going on there. Some hypothesized that the gap in the disk could be the result of one or more planets forming in the system. If so, this would be the first known planet that orbits three stars at once, also known as a circumtriple planet.

Now the GW Ori system has been modeled in greater detail, and researchers say a planet — a gassy world as massive as Jupiter — is the best explanation for the gap in the dust cloud. Although the planet itself cannot be seen, astronomers may be witnessing it carve out its orbit in its first million years of its existence.

A paper on the finding was published in September in the Monthly Notices of the Royal Astronomical Society. The scientists say it disproves an alternative explanation — that the gravitational torque of the stars cleared the space in the disk. Their paper suggests there is not enough turbulence in the disk, known as its viscosity, for this explanation to suffice.

The finding also highlights how much more there is to learn about the unexpected ways in which planets can form.

Anyone who has watched George Lucas' original "Star Wars" is familiar with planets that can have two stars rising and falling in its skies. Luke Skywalker's dusty home of Tatooine was in such a binary star system. But a planet orbiting three stars would be more unusual.

If a familiar life form could dwell on a gas giant like the one that would be orbiting GW Ori, it would not actually be able to see the three stars in its skies. Rather, they would see only a pair as the two innermost stars orbit so close as to appear like a single point of light. Yet as the planet rotated, its stars would rise and fall in fascinating sunrises and sunsets unlike any other known world.

"'Star Wars' missed a trick," said Rebecca Nealon from the University of Warwick in England, a co-author on the paper.

Scientists have been on the lookout for a planet orbiting three stars, and found potential evidence in another system, GG Tau A, located about 450 light years from Earth. But the researchers say the gap in GW Ori's gas and dust ring makes it a more convincing example.

"It may be the first evidence of a circumtriple planet carving a gap in real time," said Jeremy Smallwood from the University of Nevada, Las Vegas, lead author of the new paper.

William Welsh, an astronomer at San Diego State University, said the researchers "make a good case. If this turns out to be a planet, it would be fascinating."

Alison Young from the University of Leicester in England who has argued that GW Ori's stars caused the gap in the system's disk, rather than a planet, notes that observations from the ALMA telescope and Very Large Telescope in Chile in the coming months could end the debate.

"We'll be able to look for direct evidence of a planet in the disk," Dr. Young said.

If the planet hypothesis is confirmed, the system would reinforce the idea that planet formation is common. Several worlds, known as circumbinary planets, are already known to orbit two stars at once. But circumtriple planets have been harder to come by — despite estimates that at least a tenth of all stars cluster in systems of three or more. Yet their possible existence suggests that planets spring up in all sorts of places, even here in this most bizarre of systems.

"Three stars is not enough to kill planet formation," Dr. Nealon said.

That suggests that exoplanets are likely to arise in more and more unusual locations. "What we've learned is any time planets can form, they do," said Sean Raymond, an astronomer from the University of Bordeaux in France who was not involved in the paper.

Perhaps even a world orbiting four, or five, or six stars at once?

"I don't see why not," he said.


2.  "Answers: Discussions with Western Buddhists," <u>Snow Lion Summer 2001 Newsletter & Catalog Supplement</u>, Volume 16, Number 3, pg. 13.

This article presented excerpts from <u>Answers: Discussions with Western Buddhists</u>, by H.H. the Fourteenth Dalai Lama, edited by Jose Cabezon:

"Q: *Can you explain how Tantric meditation achieves the Enlightened state so much more quickly than vipasyana, i.e. insight meditation?*

HIS HOLINESS: In Tantric meditation, particularly in the practice of Anuttarayoga Tantra, while one is realizing emptiness, the ultimate truth, one controls thought through the use of certain techniques.

In the Sutrayana, the non-Tantric form of the Mahayana, there is no mention of these unique techniques involving the yogic practices of controlled breathing and meditation using the inner channels and chakras, etc. The

Sutrayana just describes how to analyze the object, i.e. how to come to gain insight into the nature of the object through reasoning, etc.

The Anuttarayoga Tantra, however, teaches, in addition to this, certain techniques which use the channels, subtle winds, etc. to help one to control one's thoughts more effectively. These methods help one to more quickly gain control over the scattered mind and to achieve more effectively a level of consciousness which is at once subtle and powerful. This is the basis of the system.

The wisdom that realizes emptiness, that has gained insight into the nature of reality, is of varying kinds, depending upon the level of subtlety of the consciousness perceiving the emptiness.

In general, there are rough levels of consciousness, more subtle levels, and then the innermost subtle level of consciousness. It is the uncommon characteristic of Tantric practice that through it one can evoke this most subtle consciousness at will and put it to use in a most effective way.

For example, when emptiness is realized by this subtlest level of mind, it is more powerful, having a much greater effect on the personality.

In order to activate or make use of the more subtle levels of consciousness, it is necessary to block the rougher levels—the rougher or grosser levels must cease.

It is through specifically Tantric practices, such as the meditations on the chakras and the channels (*nadis*), that one can control and temporarily abandon the rougher levels of consciousness. When these become suppressed, the subtler levels of consciousness become active. And it is through the use of the subtlest level of consciousness that the most powerful spiritual realizations can come about.

Hence, it is through the Tantric practice involving the most subtle consciousness that the goal of Enlightenment can most quickly be realized."

# About the author

Lawrence Borok was a student of Rama-Dr. Frederick Lenz from 1982 to 1998. During the 1990's he led Rama's medical software company, which successfully developed two healthcare systems and brought them to market. He continued with the business until retiring in 2015. From 2000-2015 he taught meditation through adult education programs at high schools and community colleges. He has been a Buddhist practitioner for over 50 years.

Lawrence Borok has a BA in Individual Field Studies from UCLA, an MA in Architecture from UCLA, and a Certificate in Business Data Processing from UC Berkeley. Other notable experiences include serving as a workshop leader for Buckminster Fuller's World Game, as the director of the UCLA Experimental College, and as a Thought Leader for Predictive Modeling News.